NORTON PARKER CHIPMAN

NORTON PARKER CHIPMAN

*A Biography of the Andersonville
War Crimes Prosecutor*

JEFFERY A. HOGGE

McFarland & Company, Inc., Publishers
Jefferson, North Carolina, and London

LIBRARY OF CONGRESS CATALOGUING-IN-PUBLICATION DATA

Hogge, Jeffery A., 1961–
    Norton Parker Chipman : a biography of the Andersonville war
crimes prosecutor / Jeffery A. Hogge.
        p.   cm.
    Includes bibliographical references and index.

    ISBN 978-0-7864-3449-7
    softcover : 50# alkaline paper

    1. Chipman, N. P. (Norton Parker), 1836–1924.   2. Legislators —
United States — Biography.   3. United States. Congress. House —
Biography.   4. Lawyers — United States — Biography.   5. United
States. Army — Officers — Biography.   6. Andersonville Prison.
7. United States — History — Civil War, 1861–1865 — Biography.
8. Washington (D.C.) — Politics and government — To 1878.
9. Judges — California — Biography.   10. California — History —
1850–1950 — Biography.   I. Title.
E664.C43H64   2008
328.73092 — dc22   2008018690
[B]

British Library cataloguing data are available

On the cover: *Chipman at Gettysburg* (painting by Terry Flanigan);
Rebel prison at Andersonville and surrounding fortifications
(Library of Congress)

Manufactured in the United States of America

McFarland & Company, Inc., Publishers
  Box 611, Jefferson, North Carolina 28640
    www.mcfarlandpub.com

In memory of Robert K. Puglia (1929–2005),
who served as presiding justice of the California Court of Appeal,
Third Appellate District — Chipman's court — for 24 years

amount of time transcribing records from the Chipman collection at the California State Library, and Sarah also provided valuable editorial and photographic assistance.

When I told my dear wife, Kimberly, that I intended to write a biography of Chipman, she gave me her complete support, knowing that an undertaking like this would take away from family time. Under her influence, my family allowed me the time and the resources to research and write, which for me is a pleasant pastime. By her example, our children, all six of them, have learned to be supportive, not only of me but also of each other in their many pursuits. Boredom and isolation are not options in such an energetic household. I gratefully acknowledge the love and support of each family member and aspire to ever reciprocate. Everlasting joy, with God's grace, is our objective.

Acknowledgments

In 2006, the University of Cincinnati College of Law, Chipman's alma mater, and the school's chapter of the Federalist Society, honored Chipman with a program, display, and portrait. Vasilios Spyridakis and Jonathan Bennie, students at the school, worked tirelessly to make the event a success. The display was created with the help of Dennis McKenna, chief executive officer of e.Republic, and his talented graphic artists.

The portrait *Chipman at Gettysburg*, featured on the cover, was painted by Terry Flanigan. Mr. Flanigan is a prominent California attorney and lobbyist. He served as the appointments secretary to governors Pete Wilson and George Deukmejian, and he is an accomplished artist.

Over the course of three years, many people and organizations have assisted me with the research necessary to compose this biography. A few of the most outstanding advisors and helpers were Gary Kurutz, curator of Special Collections at the California State Library, and the staff of the California History Room of the California State Library in Sacramento. Linda Wallihan, librarian of the Court of Appeal, is the keeper of the flame when it comes to court history, and she willingly shares her knowledge and the court's collection. Frank J. Williams, chief justice of the Rhode Island Supreme Court and chairman of the Lincoln Forum, shared invaluable insights with me concerning the Civil War period and made numerous suggestions to enhance the biography factually and literarily. Roger Billings, professor of law at the Salmon P. Chase College of Law, collaborated on the Cincinnati commemoration and reviewed the manuscript. And Janice R. Brown, an associate justice of the Court of Appeal during Justice Robert K. Puglia's tenure as presiding justice, reinforced my resolve to preserve Chipman's history by committing it to print.

Mindy Hogge, Hilary Hogge, and Sarah Clift spent a considerable

Contents

Preface

My first exposure to the name Norton Parker Chipman came after I was hired as an attorney at Chipman's old court, the California Court of Appeal, Third Appellate District, in 1990. The court's presiding justice, Robert K. Puglia, who hired me, had a keen awareness of Chipman's legacy and an appreciation for Chipman's devotion to the court. Both Chipman and Puglia were natives of Ohio who served in the military and eventually became presiding justices at the Court of Appeal. They are the two longest-serving presiding justices in the history of the court.

Justice Puglia discovered that Chipman had bequeathed a Civil War painting to the court, but it had been loaned and forgotten. He found the Emanuel Leutze painting *Fort Sumter After the Bombardment*, in a Charleston, South Carolina, museum in 1987. When Justice Puglia brought it home to California in 1995, I attended the courtroom ceremony and observed Justice Puglia's obvious pleasure in returning this piece of history to the court. In this and many other ways, Justice Puglia was an inspiration.

As the centennial of the Court of Appeal was celebrated in 2005, Associate Justice George W. Nicholson of the Court of Appeal suggested that I do some research on Chipman and prepare an article about him. My preliminary research revealed some of the aspects of his life with which we were familiar, such as his involvement in the Civil War, his presence at Gettysburg when Abraham Lincoln gave his famous address, and Chipman's service in the House of Representatives as a delegate representing the District of Columbia. A more extensive search into materials as yet unscrutinized revealed a richer and more complex history of the man.

When Justice Puglia, who had since retired from the bench, heard of my research and the additional information I had uncovered, he encouraged me to undertake a more comprehensive project. "Chipman deserves a book," he said. Sadly for the court family and many others, Justice Puglia passed away

3

in 2005. His enthusiasm for the project, as well as Justice Nicholson's encouragement and mentoring, prompted me to continue what turned out to be a three-year project to chronicle Chipman's life.

Before Chipman passed away in 1924, he gave his papers to his daughter to donate to the California State Library. She did so, and the collection has remained there, virtually untouched for more than 80 years. This rich collection was my main researching focus. Along with the plentiful resources of the Library of Congress and the National Archives and the immense existing scholarship on the Civil War era, the Chipman Collection allowed me to piece together his life and add the context to better understand him. Published historical accounts have included some of Chipman's accomplishments and contributions, but this work is the first to recount his life, providing the details that allow the reader to understand his role in history and his character.

Although I am employed on the legal staff of the Court of Appeal, this project — research and writing — was undertaken as a personal project and on my own time. Any errors are my own, as are the views stated.

Prologue (1906)

Sacramento celebrated great presidents on George Washington's birthday in 1906.

The state senate began its session with a prayer by the chaplain in which he remembered the first president at length. A recitation of Washington's farewell address followed.

Around the city, private organizations joined in the spirit of the senate's Washington commemoration. The Young Men's Institute memorialized both Washington and his most prominent successor, Abraham Lincoln, with a party at Serra Hall, while the First Baptist Church sponsored a patriotic program with a Spanish-style dinner. The Improved Order of Red Men and the Degree of Pocahontas threw a ball at Turner Hall, and the Companions of the Forest, a national women's organization, held a social dance at Pythian Castle.[1]

A group of young men calling themselves the Cherry Tree Club gathered at Sacramento's Golden Eagle Theater. The name of the club referred to Washington's mythical chopping down of the cherry tree and identified the annual birthday of Washington as their appointed meeting date. Their announcement of the program in 1906, the second annual, ran in the *Sacramento Bee*, the McClatchy family's newspaper, and was printed next to the advertisement for Sacramento Electric, Gas and Railway Company's "Perpetual Sunlight under the light of a Gas Arc," evidence of Sacramento's modern conveniences.[2]

The Cherry Tree Club's honoree in 1905 had been George Washington. This year they would honor Abraham Lincoln, nearly 41 years after his death, with an address by one much older than the young men of the club. The elderly guest's formerly long beard was now fashionably shorter than it had been when he served as the District of Columbia's delegate to Congress more than 30 years earlier. His graying hairline had receded noticeably. And his pace as he walked to the theater from his judicial chambers in the state Capitol was slower than when he walked each day into the nation's Capitol in 1865 to prosecute for war crimes the commander of the South's most notorious prisoner of war camp.

In an era in which good oration was admired and sought after, the Cherry Tree Club had invited a man who had delivered speeches of interest and renown, nationally and in California. The septuagenarian not only lived through the Civil War years, but also fought in that war and was wounded as a young Union officer while leading a charge at Fort Donelson in Tennessee. What interested the club members even more was that this Civil War veteran knew Abraham Lincoln personally, sat on the platform with him at the dedication of the Gettysburg cemetery, and transported the president's dispatches to his field commanders. The honored veteran, General Norton Parker Chipman, presiding justice of the Third Appellate District of the California Court of Appeal, went straight to his task of impressing on the audience an appreciation for Abraham Lincoln.[3]

"As I am informed, the Cherry Tree Club meets once each year to commemorate the birthday of the Father of his Country. Your club is composed almost entirely of young men, most of whom were born since the close of the Civil War, and few, if any, of you were old enough at that time to have any personal recollection of the events that marked the most tragic period in the history of the Republic. I am asked to portray the character of the man who was not only the most central figure in that Titanic struggle, but whose memory is, and will ever be, enshrined in the hearts of all liberty-loving people throughout the habitable globe."[4]

The young men of the Cherry Tree Club could scarcely fathom the depth of Chipman's dedication to his country, forged in the furnace of national strife and affliction. They may have viewed the old general as something of an anachronism, left over from an age of sacrifice and suffering unparalleled in the history of the United States, an age that had become only a chapter in the history books studied by this newer generation. While the club invited Chipman because of his association with the revered president who saved the Union, it is doubtful they understood the great contributions Chipman himself made on the battlefield, in Washington, D.C., and in California. They may have known him only as the lawyer who had, just one year before, accepted Governor George Pardee's appointment as the first presiding justice of the newly created state appellate court in Sacramento — the appointment that brought him to reside in the capital city.

Characteristic of Chipman's many writings and speeches, this address included very few details of his own life and accomplishments. But Chipman did not disappoint the young businessmen and professionals in their desire to connect with the legendary president, to shake the hand that shook the hand of Honest Abe, the Illinois Rail-Splitter, the Great Emancipator. The Cherry Tree speech provided a glimpse of Lincoln and his times through the eyes of a contemporary. Today, the 1906 speech casts Chipman in the dual role of historian and subject. We can see Lincoln's day through Chipman's eyes and learn something about Chipman from the way he recounts Lincoln's day. And we can understand the era in which Chipman lived by studying his life, which touched so many incidents and issues of national importance.

"May I ask you then," Chipman proposed to the young men, "to give me your attention while I shall endeavor to place before you Lincoln the man and Lincoln the President as he appeared to me." Chipman's praise was unrestrained: "In devotion to his country; in breadth of statesmanship; in exalted character; in blameless private life, the name of Abraham Lincoln will grow brighter with the ages — the synonym of true greatness — the harbinger of that period to which we all look, of peace on earth, good will to man."[5]

When Chipman finished his long speech, the men gave him three cheers, then continued the celebration into the early hours of the morning, enjoying orations, both prepared and spontaneous, and drinking toasts to the greatness of Lincoln and their fortune in hosting the man who knew the great president.[6]

1
Unrestrainable Manifestations (1834–1859)

From his Ohio beginnings through his maturation in Iowa, Chipman lived on the frontier. Though his family preferred the wide open spaces of the West to the crowded cities of the East, the Chipmans were refined and educated people. They were patriots, tracing their roots to colonial times, through the American Revolution, and into the United States of the nineteenth century. They were also politically active, participating in local politics and keeping a close eye on national contests and issues.

Chipman continued this tradition. He was educated in highly regarded schools and earned his law degree. Coming of age in the era featuring the rise of the Republican Party and the growing popularity of the party's leading light, Abraham Lincoln, Chipman found that the new party's positions matched his own passions and priorities. Lincoln gave voice, with reason and persuasiveness, to what Chipman had come to believe. He developed an early and abiding commitment to Lincoln.

Beginnings

Chipman's parents, Norman and Sarah Chipman, were both born in the newly admitted state of Vermont. Norman "drifted" to Ohio when he was 18 years old, or so said his obituary. Sarah also relocated to Ohio, and Norman and Sarah married in 1821 in St. Albans, Licking County. The schoolhouse was used for services because no church building had as yet been erected. The electors named the township St. Albans after the town in Vermont because one of their number, a native of St. Albans, Vermont, furnished four gallons of whiskey to the other 17 electors present. Norman and Sarah had three children in the next seven years. All three died in 1829.[1]

After this sad period, Norman and Sarah moved to Milford Center in the Union Township of Union County, so named because it was created from the "union" of parts of several other counties. Norman ran a general mercantile business at Milford Center and, for a time, was the proprietor of the old American Hotel in nearby Marysville. Between 1830 and 1840, the population of Union County more than doubled from 3,192 to 8,422, as settlers such as the Chipmans moved west. Norman served as Union Township treasurer and, later, as township clerk.[2]

Norton Parker Chipman, with blond hair and blue eyes, was the third of six children born to Norman and Sarah in Milford Center and Marysville — four girls and two boys, after the three children died in St. Albans. Born on March 7, 1834, in Milford Center, he was the only son who survived to adulthood. His middle name was his mother's maiden name.[3]

Centrally located in Union Township on the south bank of Big Darby Creek, Milford Center was a post town, without the modern amenities Chipman enjoyed more than 70 years later in Sacramento. Though it was only five miles from eventually larger and more prominent Marysville, Milford Center grew into a self-sufficient town around a grist mill and a saw mill. In 1837, when Chipman was a toddler, the town included 30 homes, 3 stores, a tavern, and several mechanics' shops. The townspeople attended either the Presbyterian or Methodist Church. And a town physician watched over their physical well-being.[4]

While Chipman's family never engaged in agricultural pursuits, farms and ranches were all around them. Located on the Darby Plains, these lands enjoyed deep, rich soil. The more valuable land was in the rolling hills because the flat areas were too wet for cultivation. The native grasses of the township grew so tall it is said a horse rider could grab a handful on each side and tie it together over the horse's back. In town, where the Chipmans lived, Milford Center was composed of one main street, called Water Street, and five cross streets. As gravel roads did not arrive in Union County until 1876, the streets of Chipman's youth were dirt, and much of the time mud, a more primitive provision for transportation than the fine roads and sidewalks he would see in Washington, D.C., after the Civil War.[5]

Early Union Township residents believed in the value of education as most of them came from New England, the land of schools and colleges. Before the arrival of the Chipmans, the township created six school districts, each of which ran a public school. In these public schools, Chipman received his early education.[6]

Although his family lived in Milford Center until he was 14 years old and, later, he returned to Ohio to attend law school, Chipman did not consider Ohio his home state because the urge to move west again overcame Norman and Sarah in 1848 when they moved 500 miles west to Illinois and lived briefly in Nauvoo, which had been left virtually vacant by the western migration of the Mormons. Again moving west in 1849, the Chipmans moved across the Mississippi River to Iowa, which was to be the home state of Norman and Sarah for the rest of their lives. Chipman's identification of Iowa as his home state after he was grown and had gone on to other pursuits in Washington, D.C., and later California can be attributed to his close fellowship with the Iowa regiment of volunteers with which he served in the Civil War.[7]

Admitted to the Union on December 28, 1846, as the 29th state, Iowa was a free state under the Missouri Compromise to equalize the balance between free states and slave states when Florida was admitted as a slave state. The Chipman family resided in various Iowa cities — Keosauqua, Mount Pleasant, and Washington, all in southeastern Iowa, near Illinois, home of Abraham Lincoln, and Missouri, site of much of Chipman's later military service.

Iowa, in the middle 1840s, was on the frontier of America. Its inhabitants were distinctly American — those not born in Iowa were born in other states, mainly Ohio, as was Chipman, or New York. Only a few foreigners settled in the state. Neighboring states had a foreign-born percentage as high as 34 percent (Wisconsin) by the end of the decade, while in Iowa only 11 percent of the 1850 inhabitants were foreign-born. Geography was an important factor in this demographic. Immigrants tended to collect close to the ports through which they arrived in the United States or along the waterways or railroad lines leading from those port areas. Iowa was relatively isolated in this regard. Though the state was bounded by the Mississippi and Missouri Rivers, no natural or railroad route provided convenient travel to the interior.[8]

The southern portion of Iowa was picturesque. An 1846 observer described a veritable Garden of Eden,

> abounding with grassy lawns and verdant vales, interspersed with groves and meandering rivulets.... The soil of the prairies of Iowa, and particularly the alluvial bottoms, is extremely rich and fertile. It is a black vegetable mould, sometimes intermixed with a sandy loam, easily cultivated, and stands a drought remarkably well.... All the grains, fruits and plants, of the temperate regions of the earth, grow luxuriantly in Iowa.[9]

Not all was pleasantly bucolic and friendly in southeastern Iowa as the Chipman family searched for a permanent home in the area. Missouri and Iowa were in the midst of a dispute over the location of the border — a dispute known as the Honey War. When Missouri became a state in 1820, its constitution identified the northern border, ambiguously, as the "rapids of the river Des Moines." According to who interpreted it, this could refer to a point in the Des Moines River, 13 miles into present-day Iowa, or rapids in the Mississippi River, known to rivermen and Indians as the "Des Moines Rapids." The area in dispute was forested and rich in honey trees — trees with honey bee hives. As honey was a valued commodity in that era as a replacement for sugar, it caused a stir among the locals in the late 1830s when a Missourian cut down three of the honey trees. Locals tried to arrest him, but he escaped into Missouri. About the same time, an Iowa sheriff arrested a Missouri sheriff for attempting to collect taxes in the disputed area. Missouri and Iowa, the latter still a territory, both raised militias and prepared for battle. As the militias marched, cooler heads on both sides set about finding a peaceful solution. When their leaders agreed that a peaceful settlement could be reached, the militias disbanded and went home.[10]

In 1846, when Iowa was admitted to the Union, and in the late 1840s, when the Chipmans moved into the disputed area near Keosacqua, the disagreement still simmered. Legend has it that one woman naively hoped the disputed area would not be given to Missouri because the climate of that state was not good for crops. The two states finally submitted the intractable problem to the United States Supreme Court. The court decided the dispute in Iowa's favor in 1849, ordering the installation of more than two hundred miles of iron posts to mark the border. The decision settled the issue, but the rancor between the states on the border issue portended the discord between the states on the issue of slavery before and during the Civil War.[11]

The Chipman family finally settled north of the disputed area, in Washington, the seat of Washington County, about 30 miles northeast of Mount Pleasant. The 1846 observer described the county as "well supplied with timber, ... high and rolling, climate salubrious, the soil exceedingly rich and productive." Washington boasted stores, hotels, schools, and churches. Norman owned and managed the Iowa House on the town square, earning a comfortable living boarding gold seekers on their way through Iowa to California. Entrepreneurial in an agricultural economy, Norman was never a farmer but found his niche on the frontier by offering the necessary products and services even a frontier town needed.[12]

Norman was of high social status for a small town. He was a charter member of the Washington lodge of the Freemasons, a fraternal organization emphasizing morality, justice, patriotism, and the necessity of brotherly love. He was elected Worshipful Master, the lodge's leader, each year until he later left Washington, after Chipman was grown and gone. He also held the position of junior grand warden of the Iowa Grand Lodge, the state organization. His son associated with Masonic lodges throughout his life, in Iowa, the District of Columbia, and California.[13]

Norton Parker Chipman attended the Mount Pleasant High School and Female Seminary, also known as Howe's Academy after its chief incorporator Samuel L. Howe. Earlier in his professional career, Howe, in Ohio, instructed the future general, William Sherman, and his brother, the future senator, John Sherman. Howe brought to the academy firmly held opinions concerning the manner of teaching youth. He emphasized individual responsibility for mastering the subject matter with sufficient clarity to be able to teach it to the other students. "Every student, in every science," maintained Howe, "is trained individually and in concert to do his own work, give his reasons for so doing, and exhibit before the class how, in the best possible manner, he would impart his acquisitions to others. He is taught, and made to observe the teaching, that the moment he begins to talk or to write on the blackboard he becomes a teacher of others. If he cannot perform his duty *well*, he must step aside and let another, who can at least do it better, take his place. Whatever he knows at all, he is compelled to know well...." The discipline described here by Chipman's schoolmaster reflects well Chipman's later mastering of the activities in which he engaged and the dedication he exhibited to every meaningful aspect of his life's work. Howe expressed a hope that his students would excel in life: "If in [life after school], [the student] use this wisely, which a correct education ought surely to teach him to do, he will fulfill his destiny."[14]

Aside from his educational philosophy, Howe brought to the institution a firm abolitionist creed, which was the minority position in Mount Pleasant. Formerly affiliated with the Whig Party, he joined the newly formed, antislavery Liberty Party. Pro-slavery mobs persecuted him and destroyed property, even threatening to take his life. Howe held to his principles and eventually saw their hard-fought vindication. Chipman later referred to Howe as the "old abolition warhorse." When Chipman was a teenager and deeply impressed by the abolitionists, he was convinced of the morality of Howe's position and alarmed when Howe was attacked for his beliefs.[15]

Preaching his abolitionist philosophy in Washington, Chipman's hometown, Howe was physically threatened by some who disagreed. He persisted in his oratory, which further inflamed the unsympathetic crowd. Finally, someone hurled eggs, striking Howe, much to the pleasure of the Iowans. Fifteen years later, after Lincoln issued the preliminary Emancipation Proclamation, Chipman spoke from the same stand where Howe was egged and noted that Howe's rhetoric had been much more moderate than the president's proclamation. "All honor to those old heroes who fought slavery for truth's sake," pronounced Chipman in his later speech. "The wild fanaticisms and visions of that old man (God bless him he was my teacher once) were prophecies of today's jubilee."[16]

Chipman's father, who had served as a general in the state militia, was also an unabashed abolitionist, as seen in an incident which took place at his inn. A party heading for the California gold fields stopped at the inn, accompanied by a black driver. Norman provided breakfast to the party and made a point of seating the driver at the head of the table. One of the other boarders, astonished, dropped his knife and fork and said, "General, is that the order of the day?" "Yes," replied the older Chipman. "Well, I'll leave then," threatened the boarder. Norman allowed, "That's your privilege." Then, laughing, he added, that the driver "has got to eat whether the rest of you get anything or not."[17]

Law and Politics

In the mid–1850s, political disputes over slavery began breaking down the two-party system in the nation and the various states. The specific question of whether the ban on slavery in the North should be repealed ignited passionate differences. The main parties, the Whigs and Democrats, each developed geographical schisms, with northern party members opposing slavery, though not necessarily in a united fashion, and southern party members intent on preserving and even extending the rights of slave owners. This schism led to dissension in the Democratic Party and the gradual collapse of the Whig Party. Several parties vied to fill the void created by the disintegration of the Whig Party in the North. The Republican Party sprang from the eventual coalescing of some of these newer parties, along with some disaffected northern Democrats. Though Abraham Lincoln, who had served in Congress and in the Illinois legislature as a Whig, clung for some time to the doomed party, he eventually recognized his affiliation with the Republican Party.

By 1856, the Republican Party nominated its own candidate for president. The party nominated John C. Frémont, the "Pathfinder," to run against the Democratic candidate, James Buchanan. Frémont explored much of the territory between the Rocky Mountains and the Pacific Ocean and served as a military governor of California and one of California's first U.S. senators. Chipman campaigned for Frémont and, during that campaign, gave his first political speech. Frémont lost to Buchanan, but the Republican Party continued to grow in strength, building to its dominance in the Union during the Civil War.

Chipman enrolled in Washington College, a Presbyterian school in his hometown, and studied law. The school blew down in a storm in 1862, but Chipman had, by then, left the institution to complete his legal studies at Cincinnati Law School, graduating in 1859.[18]

While Chipman studied to become a lawyer, the United States Supreme Court decided the *Dred Scott* case in 1857. The decision made a lasting and negative impression on Chipman and offered him an early opportunity to study the question that would have an intense effect on his life — the slavery question.

Dred Scott was born into slavery in Virginia. He later lived in Illinois, a free state, and the northern territory of the Louisiana Purchase, in what is now Minnesota, where his owner was in the military. Slavery was illegal in the territories under the laws of the United States. After Scott was taken to Missouri, a slave state, he attempted to buy freedom for himself and his family. When the owner refused to sell, Scott sued for his freedom. He claimed that, because he had resided where slavery was outlawed, he was free. The lower court sided with Scott, but the Missouri Supreme Court reversed and declared that Scott remained a slave despite his sojourn in areas were slavery was illegal. The case found its way to the United States Supreme Court, which was controlled by a Southern majority led by Chief Justice Roger Taney.[19]

Although he could have taken other less-controversial routes, Taney determined to issue a sweeping opinion that would protect the institution of slavery. He first held that Scott did not have so much as a right to sue because he was not a citizen, even if he was free. When the Constitution was adopted, reasoned the opinion, those of Scott's race where not considered members of the community and therefore did not obtain the rights and privileges, including the right to sue in federal courts, accorded to citizens of the United States. Even if a state chose to allow a foreigner to obtain equal footing with citizens of the state, that did not accord the foreigner any rights under the federal constitution. Having decided Scott had no standing to sue and that the suit could be dismissed on that ground without more, Taney needlessly continued on to the question of whether Scott's residence in Illinois and the northern territory of the Louisiana Purchase freed him. To uphold the rights of slave owners, the opinion concluded that slaves were the property of their owners. Every citizen had a right to take anything the Constitution recognized as property into free states without losing the ownership of the property. Any act of Congress that took away a slave owner's property was an unconstitutional taking. Congress never had the right to interfere with property rights; therefore, even the Missouri Compromise, which had settled for a time the slavery question, was unconstitutional.[20]

Taney's decision, and the language he used in the decision, offended Chipman, who recalled that blacks

> had for more than a century before been regarded as beings of an inferior order, and altogether unfit to associate with the white race, either in social or political relations; and so far inferior, that they had no rights which the white man

was bound to respect; and that the negro might justly and lawfully be reduced to slavery for his benefit. He was bought and sold, and treated as an ordinary article of merchandise and traffic, whenever a profit could be made by it. This opinion was at that time fixed and universal in the civilized portion of the white race. It was regarded as an axiom in morals as well as in politics, which no one thought of disputing, or supposed to be open to dispute; and men in every grade and position in society daily and habitually acted upon it in their private pursuits, as well as in matters of public concern, without doubting for a moment the correctness of this opinion.[21]

The moral dimension of the *Dred Scott* decision, the declaration that American slaves were "justly" reduced to slavery, to be "treated as an ordinary article of merchandise," further polarized the North and South. Instead of deciding the slavery question once and for all, the decision raised the dispute to a new level, paving the way not just for political debates but also for resolution of the issue by extra-political means. Coming, as it did, in the middle of Chipman's legal education, the *Dred Scott* decision and its immorality influenced his view of the courts and instilled in him the necessity for virtue in judicial decision making.

Chipman's interest in the *Dred Scott* decision was not a passing fancy. Southeast Iowa found itself in the center of the debate over the morality of slavery. Located just north of Missouri, a slave state, it was an area to which slaves escaped. The natural geographic tendency toward interest in the slave was enhanced by stories and rumors that circulated among Missouri slaves of the Underground Railroad. These circumstances forced southeastern Iowans to decide where they stood on the issue of slavery. As a result, public opinion, even if generally in agreement that slavery should not exist in Iowa, was divided between those who sympathized with the rights of slaveholders in the South and others who opposed slavery regardless of the effect on citizens of other states. It was difficult to remain neutral on the question in a region where escaping slaves were actually present.

This was no theoretical debate without observable, real world consequences. And with the issuance of the *Dred Scott* decision, no one could deny there were constitutional problems involved in the debate. Those who supported the South's right to maintain the institution of slavery could argue that the Constitution allowed slavery and that, as decided by the Supreme Court in the *Dred Scott* case, the ownership of slaves was a matter of property rights, which the Constitution protects. Their argument continued that abolitionists sought to impose their morality over the requirements of the Constitution. Indeed, it was an assertion the abolitionists could not directly deny. The authority for the abolitionists' argument was a higher law, with support from the Declaration of Independence. They believed that obedience to the fugitive slave laws was a violation of the laws of God. As neither view clearly prevailed in southeast Iowa, some refused to assist in returning slaves to their owners, while others actively assisted slaves to make good their escape.[22]

There is evidence that slavery as practiced in neighboring Missouri was more humane than in the Deep South. Children of masters and slaves were more likely to play together in Missouri. Slaves in Missouri were given more opportunities to work land and use the proceeds from their work at their own discretion. Slaves and masters in Missouri may have attended the same worship services, even if they sat in separate, designated areas. This apparently kinder, gentler slavery, though equally abhorrent to abolitionists, may have influenced some Iowans to refrain from interfering with what was asserted to be the constitutional rights of slave owners. Still, slave owners in Missouri understood that, if their slaves went missing, they probably had escaped to Iowa. There were numerous people willing to help them, such as the Quakers who facilitated the Underground Railroad through Iowa.[23]

About the time Chipman was finishing his legal studies, Abraham Lincoln and Stephen A. Douglas were debating the question of slavery. Chipman shared with the men of the Cherry Tree Club his impression of Lincoln in the period prior to the Lincoln-Douglas debates, though the view is in retrospect as there is no evidence Chipman knew who Lincoln was until Lincoln burst upon the national consciousness:

> There was nothing in this period to mark him as distinguished above a thousand other plodding lawyers by whom he was surrounded. He had been in the Legislature, had been in Congress, and while we now, looking back, may see in him then some of those characteristics that distinguished him in after life, they were not so pronounced as to lead his most intimate friends to predict for him a career in any sense conspicuous. [¶] And yet in all those years his sturdy common sense; his matchless honesty and probity of character; his sympathy with the people and his vigorous mental capacity, were gradually preparing him for his great work, and as gradually centering public confidence upon him as the type of American leadership in the great anti-slavery struggle then developing.[24]

Candidates for a United States Senate seat from Illinois in 1858, Lincoln and Douglas — Douglas the more famous at the time — held seven debates. For the people of the North, what to do about slavery had become the superlative political issue. Neither man was an outright abolitionist, as yet; however, the positions of Democrat Douglas and Republican Lincoln were at odds, reflecting the division in Illinois voters. And Lincoln's position on slavery was much closer to Chipman's anti-slavery background and education. Douglas advocated popular sovereignty — each state and territory would decide the slave question for itself. Lincoln, understanding the inexorable judicial expansion of a court's own creative doctrines, countered that the *Dred Scott* case would logically lead to the next case in which the Supreme Court would turn every state into a slave state by federalizing the property rights of the slave owners. Slavery, as an institution, was morally wrong and eventually must yield to the statement of rights in the Declaration of Independence, argued Lincoln. It could not be allowed to spread. Yet the states were locked in a bitter standoff. "A house divided against itself cannot stand," he declared. The emotions ran high inside and outside of Illinois. Popular newspapers ran frequent reports of the debates.

Always keenly aware of the politics of the day, Chipman paid close attention to the Illinois debates. The publicity surrounding the debates made Lincoln a national public figure. If Chipman was not already a Lincoln supporter, the debates crystallized his opinion, at least as between Lincoln and his senatorial and future presidential opponent, Douglas. At the time, the state legislature elected the state's United States senators. Although Republicans in the Illinois state legislative races received more popular votes in 1858, Democrats retained enough seats in the Illinois legislature to give Douglas the victory over Lincoln.

In the last half of 1859, after Chipman completed his legal studies and returned to Iowa, Lincoln made a tour of Iowa, Ohio, Indiana, Wisconsin, and Kansas, making speeches along the way, speeches that were well-received. Chipman may have attended one or more of these gatherings, but, regardless of his physical presence at the speeches, he certainly would have been informed of their content and the warm reception. A speech Lincoln gave in September 1859, at the Wisconsin State Fair, in Milwaukee, would eventually be more influential in Chipman's life than Lincoln's numerous speeches and debates on the issue of slavery. At the Wisconsin fair, Lincoln's subject was agriculture. His reputation in Wisconsin, borne of his humble rearing and life on the western edge of civilization, was as the champion of farmers. As president, he signed legislation creating the Department of Agriculture and appointed a farmer as the first Commissioner of Agriculture. With these accomplishments, he transformed American farming.

In his speech, he addressed the purpose of the fair, to aid in improving agriculture. "Agricultural fairs are becoming an institution of the country," started Lincoln. "They are useful in more ways than one. They bring us together, and thereby make us better acquainted and better friends than we otherwise would be." Continuing on the theme of the importance of fairs, Lincoln counseled: "Constituted as man is, he has positive need of occasional recreation, and whatever can give him this associated with virtue and advantage, and free from vice and disadvantage, is a positive good. Such recreation our fairs afford. They are a present pleasure, to be followed by no pain as a consequence: they are a present pleasure, making the future more pleasant." Lincoln transitioned to a theme extolling the "mutual exchange of agricultural discovery, information, and knowledge; so that, at the end, all may know everything which may have been known to but one or to but few, at the beginning; to bring together especially all which is supposed to be not generally known because of recent discovery or invention."[25]

"The successful application of *steam power* to farm-work is a *desideratum*— especially a Steam Plow," advocated Lincoln, who shared with the farmers at the Wisconsin State Fair his theory of how technology could improve agriculture, but only if properly applied. But his focus then changed to theories of labor, a particularly timely discussion considering the South's tradition of slavery and large plantations in contrast with the North's small farms and self-employed farmers. According to Lincoln, "[t]he prudent, penniless beginner in the world, labors for wages awhile, saves a surplus with which to buy tools or land, for himself; then labors on his own account another while, and at length hires another new beginner to help him. This, say its advocates, is *free* labor — the just and generous, and prosperous system, which opens the way for all — gives hope to all, and energy, and progress, and improvement of condition to all." He contrasted this system of free labor with the "mud-sill theory" by which "it is assumed that labor and education are incompatible; and any practical combination of them impossible." Arguing a preference for free labor and the necessity of education under that theory, Lincoln imparted his most famous insight from the Wisconsin State Fair speech: "Every blade of grass is a study; and to produce two, where there was but one, is both a profit and a pleasure."[26]

Chipman later owned the collected speeches of several of the presidents, and he wore thin the pages of the speeches of Abraham Lincoln. The addresses on slavery presented a view consistent with Chipman's beliefs. But after the Civil War, emancipation, and Chipman's move to California, those speeches were little more than historically interesting. The Wisconsin State Fair speech, however, played an influential role in Chipman's life. He spent twenty years promoting fairs, speaking at fairs, studying agriculture, advocating technological applications to agriculture, and promoting California agriculture to the other states and to the world. Lincoln's inspiration on fairs and agricultural, particularly from his Wisconsin State Fair, defined a major part of Chipman's career.[27]

About the time Chipman graduated from law school and returned to Iowa to start his career, Norman retired from business. With sufficient resources to sustain himself without his prior proprietorships, Norman was listed in the 1860 census of Washington County as a 63-year-old "gentleman." Twenty-six-year-old Chipman lived at home while nursing along his fledgling law practice. His sisters, Celia and Helen, 22 and 20 years old, respectively, both taught school. They also lived in the household with their parents.

As was Chipman, Iowa was turning strongly Republican. The gubernatorial election of 1859 featured abolitionist, Republican Samuel J. Kirkwood against aristocratic, Democrat Augustus C. Dodge, the former ambassador to Spain who pledged to enforce the laws of the land, including the *Dred Scott* decision. The two candidates held a series of debates, the last of which was in Chipman's hometown. Kirkwood arrived in town on a hayrack drawn by a team of oxen. Dodge rode in the best carriage the Democrats could find, drawn by four white horses. The overwhelmingly Republican crowd cheered for Kirkwood. The statewide election was close but favored Kirkwood, and pleased Chipman.[28]

Young Lawyer and Lincoln Republican

As a young member of the bar, Chipman's attention turned to presidential politics and possible southern secession. On February 27, 1860, Lincoln, an unannounced presidential aspirant, addressed a packed house at Cooper Union in New York City. Building his argument against slavery in a lawyerly, logical, temperate way, Lincoln exposed the flaws in Douglas's popular sovereignty arguments and the Supreme Court's property rights analysis. He concluded with the admonition: "Let us have faith that right makes right, and in that faith, let us, to the end, dare to do our duty as we understand it." Commonly regarded as the speech that launched Lincoln to the Republican nomination, the Cooper Union address titillated the young lawyer in Iowa. Whether it was because of the famous Lincoln-Douglas debates in 1858, or perhaps Lincoln's swing through Iowa in 1859, or Lincoln's February 1860 speech at Cooper Union, Chipman was a Lincoln Republican by the time of the Republican Convention assembled in Chicago in May 1860. Twenty-six-year-old Chipman made the 250-mile trip from his hometown.[29]

The Republican Party built a convention center, called the "Wigwam," to accommodate the throng, more than 10,000, that would attend. William H. Seward of New York was the clear frontrunner for the nomination. Other candidates, including Illinois's favorite son, Lincoln, would surely garner fewer votes on the first ballot. But, as long as no one received a majority of the votes, additional ballots would be taken.

Lincoln, who, like other candidates of the day, did not attend the convention, believed that, after the first ballot, he would pick up the votes of weaker candidates. His delegation, led by Judge David Davis, took over the entire third floor of the finest hotel in Chicago. Leonard Swett, Lincoln's close lawyer friend and associate in the Illinois courts, would go to work on the delegation from Maine, the state where Swett grew up. By political maneuvering, and some hometown antics such as isolating the New York delegation in the seating assignments and printing duplicate tickets to fill the Wigwam with people sympathetic to Lincoln, Lincoln's delegation obtained the potential votes, at least in later balloting, to win the nomination.

On the day of the presidential balloting, Seward's delegation, one thousand strong, marched through the streets of Chicago with a brass band. But when they arrived at the Wigwam it was already full, including numerous Lincoln supporters with duplicate tickets. On the first ballot, Seward led, as predicted, but not by enough to win the nomination. On the second and third ballots, Lincoln gradually gained votes until he stood only one and a half votes from the 233 needed for nomination. A delegate from Ohio rose and changed four votes from Salmon P. Chase to Lincoln, clinching the nomination. The resulting cheer was so deafening and prolonged that it drowned out the sound of the cannons firing outside the Wigwam.

Present in the Wigwam when the vote officially gave Lincoln the nomination, though not a member of Iowa's official delegation, Chipman described the selection of Lincoln as "both logical as well as a natural expression of [the Republicans'] wisdom and foresight." In hyperbole typical of his endearment to Lincoln and the Lincoln legacy, Chipman described the scene of the nominating vote, with allusions to the later inauguration and administration:

> I was a spectator of that splendid and inspiring scene, when it seemed as if the pent-up protests and accumulated remonstrances of long years against Southern aggression and arrogance broke forth in unrestrained and unrestrainable manifestations, and rang out in one great burst of defiance — at once a clarion note prophetic of war, and the death knell of human slavery in America. It was a scene of wild rejoicing, and unfaltering consecration to an exalted purpose. The Annunciation of the Nation's Savior was proclaimed at that hour. The Solid South repudiated the Messiah, but the Loyal North made him President and crowned him with immortality.[30]

Lincoln and Douglas replayed their rivalry, now as presidential nominees of the two major parties, campaigning through Iowa. The parties organized bands and glee clubs, trained marching squadrons, and conducted rallies, processions, picnics, and barbecues. On Election Day 1860, Iowa came out in force for Lincoln, giving him its four electoral votes on his way to his easy victory over Douglas and the other parties' presidential candidates.

2

For the Preservation of the Union (1860–1862)

Chipman's early life experiences and his character combined to create in him the model Unionist during the American Civil War. Over the years preceding the war, Chipman developed a deep and abiding respect for and trust in Lincoln. As a young lawyer, Chipman saw the same flaws as Lincoln exposed in the institution of slavery and in the official actions of the United States government toward slavery. Also as a lawyer and as a member of a family that believed in the greatness of the American form of government, Chipman agreed with Lincoln that states did not have the right to withdraw unilaterally from national unity. Educated and not yet married, Chipman was not only in doctrinal agreement with Lincoln but he was also available for the service the Union would need from so many. He was tall, fit, healthy, and capable. He volunteered for service in 1861, with no military experience, and received his honorable discharge just four years later as a brevet brigadier general of volunteers.

Lincoln's First Inaugural

Because Lincoln's inauguration did not occur until March 1861, four months after the November 1860 election, the South had time to prepare for what it perceived to be an unfriendly administration. Chipman's view of that period between the election and inauguration was decidedly critical of the South: "The interval between his election and inauguration was an interval of war-like preparations by the South; of larceny of the munitions of war, and rape of the fortresses of the Union." Several southern state legislatures acted before Lincoln's inauguration, passing ordinances of secession, beginning in South Carolina in December 1860. In February 1861, these southern legislatures adopted a constitution and inaugurated Jefferson Davis as the president of the Confederate States of America.[1]

Even as the United States slipped toward confrontation or disintegration, the Chipman family faced a tragedy of its own. Chipman's mother, Sarah Parker Chipman, passed away on February 18, 1861, in Washington, Iowa. Chipman never wrote much about his mother, but he gained, at an early age, a deep respect for the influence of women in his life. After his mother passed away, Chipman related his feelings toward women in general in a speech he gave in his hometown: "I believe woman is naturally more constant, more heroic, more devoted in her likes, more earnest and patient, more patriotic because there is more love in her nature than man's." Except for his relationship with his father and with his only son, who died in infancy, Chipman's family relationships were all with females. The only two siblings that he knew were sisters. He married before the end of the war — a marriage that lasted more than 50 years. And he adopted two daughters, both of whom cared for him in his old age.[2]

When Lincoln was inaugurated in Washington, D.C. on March 4, 1861, Chipman was practicing law in Washington, Iowa. Having disagreed with Chief Justice Taney's decision in the *Dred Scott* case, the young lawyer noted the irony of the inauguration, during which Taney, the dogmatic defender of slavery, administered the oath of office to Lincoln, the president who stood against slavery and would eventually oversee the resolution of the slavery question.[3]

In his inaugural address, Lincoln sought to placate those who perceived his ascendancy as a sign the federal government was turning against them. He disclaimed any intention to tamper with slave owner's rights in slave states. He even went so far as to pledge, citing the Constitution, that slaves who *escaped* from slave states into free states would be returned to their owners. However, Lincoln attacked the *Dred Scott* decision:

> Again, in any law upon this subject, ought not all the safeguards of liberty known in civilized and humane jurisprudence to be introduced, so that a free man be not, in any case, surrendered as a slave? And might it not be well, at the same time, to provide by law for the enforcement of that clause in the Constitution which guarranties that "The citizens of each State shall be entitled to all privileges and immunities of citizens in the several States?"[4]

If a slave owner *voluntarily took* a slave into a free state, as opposed to a slave escaping into a free state, and that state's laws provided freedom for the slave and citizenship in that state, other states could not deny him the privilege of freedom — a logical reading of the Constitution, yet in conflict with the *Dred Scott* decision, which proclaimed the supremacy of the property rights of slave owners over the privileges and immunities of the slave who had become a state citizen. Lincoln maintained that, while the courts must adjudicate disputes between parties, the sovereign people, not the Supreme Court, must decide broad policy issues: "[I]f the policy of the Government, upon vital questions affecting the whole people, is to be irrevocably fixed by decisions of the Supreme Court, the instant they are made, in ordinary litigation ... the people will have ceased to be their own rulers...."

This jab at the Supreme Court, never mentioning the *Dred Scott* decision by name, may have gone unnoticed by some because Lincoln dealt more directly with the right of states to secede from the Union. He provided his theory of preservation: "I hold, that in contemplation of universal law, and of the Constitution, the Union of these States is perpetual. Perpetuity is implied, if not expressed, in the fundamental law of all national governments. It is safe to assert that no government proper, ever had a provision in its organic law for its own termination." He declared that "no State ... can lawfully get out of the Union." He would protect the Union from rebellion. "In doing this," he announced, "there needs be no bloodshed or violence; and there shall be none, unless it is forced upon the national authority."

Having notified the South of his intention not to allow peaceful secession, Lincoln assured southerners he would not be the first aggressor: "In *your* hands, my dissatisfied fellow countrymen, and not in *mine*, is the momentous issue of civil war. The government will not assail *you*. You can have no conflict, without being yourselves the aggressors."

Commenting on the inaugural address, Chipman observed: "Lincoln's plea for peace, designed to placate the South, had little effect upon her people, but it turned upon the rebel leaders the responsibility of beginning hostilities."[5]

Lincoln could scarcely bear to end his address and allow the inevitable to happen. He concluded with what Chipman characterized as "one of the most remarkable perorations ever uttered by man." Lincoln lamented:

> I am loth to close. We are not enemies, but friends. We must not be enemies. Though passion may have strained, it must not break our bonds of affection. The mystic chords of memory, stre[t]ching from every battlefield and patriot grave, to every living heart and hearthstone, all over this broad land, will yet swell the chorus of the Union, when again touched, as surely they will be, by the better angels of our nature.

Chipman assessed the address and its effect:

> Alas! As an appeal with a promise of immediate fulfillment it fell on many unresponsive ears. As prophecy it now reads to us as a vision of light from on high, though its realization came after long years and long after the close of the most sanguinary strife in modern history.[6]

Both before and after the inauguration, the southern states plotted and acted where they had the clear upper hand. They took over Union forts and government property in the South, the larceny and rape referred to by Chipman. Within a week after the inauguration, the Confederate Congress passed a bill to organize an army and soon thereafter sent commissioners to Washington to negotiate a treaty. Lincoln gave them no audience but sent them a copy of his inaugural address.

Lincoln consolidated his power by appointing his rivals for the Republican presidential nomination to cabinet positions: U.S. Senator William H. Seward of New York as secretary of state, Governor Salmon P. Chase of Ohio as secretary of treasury, U.S. Senator Simon Cameron of Pennsylvania as secretary of war, and former congressman Edward Bates of Missouri as attorney general. Chipman gave further insight:

> With characteristic magnanimity and against the advice of many friends he called to his Cabinet four men — Seward, Chase, Bates and Cameron — who had been candidates for the Presidency when Lincoln was chosen. He refused to believe at such a time that men worthy to serve as his advisers would be unfaithful in their trust and seek self-aggrandizement. He said to his friends: "Let us forget ourselves and join hands, like brothers, to save the Republic. If we succeed there will be glory enough for all."[7]

Second Iowa Infantry

True to his word, Lincoln required the South to take the first shot. The hostilities over the issue of secession began in earnest on April 12, 1861, when Confederate troops fired on Fort Sumter in South Carolina. Three days after the attack, President Lincoln issued a proclamation asking for support from the state militias. He requested 75,000 volunteers. Waiting for actual aggression rather than acting on simple resolutions of secession turned out to be a boon for Lincoln's status and the popularity of the war to put down the rebellion. Throughout the North, citizens gathered in war meetings, expressing patriotic sentiments to preserve the Union.

Secretary of War Simon Cameron telegraphed Governor Kirkwood: "Call made on you by tonight's mail for one regiment of militia for immediate service." Doing chores on his farm outside Iowa City when he received the message, the governor wondered out loud whether he could raise that many troops, up to 1,000 volunteers. He issued the call for volunteers on April 17, and Washington County announced a meeting for that evening at the courthouse, during which members of the bar would address the citizens of the county. The meeting notice advised: "There will be no lack for listeners."[8]

Chipman addressed the citizens assembled that evening and volunteered for service that very night, along with others from the county. In early May, the Washington County volunteers received orders from the governor to report for duty in Keokuk later that month. When the townspeople learned of the imminent departure of the company, they quickly organized a dinner to honor the volunteers. The dinner was held in the courthouse square, with "some very impressive exercises," according to the county history, after which the company left for Keokuk. Chipman, a healthy 27-year-old, six feet tall and physically fit, with a medium build, was elected by his peers and commissioned as second lieutenant in Company H of the Second Iowa Infantry.[9]

Kirkwood's fear that he would not be able to raise enough troops proved unfounded as enough men volunteered to fill ten regiments, not just one. Because of the sudden need for a large number of officers, many inexperienced men were uprooted from civil pursuits. With no military experience, Chipman suddenly found himself a junior officer. He was fortunate in his early military career to be associated with an experienced and able commanding officer. Colonel Samuel R. Curtis was a graduate of West Point and held the highest military office in his class. He had practiced law in Ohio and was adjutant-general of Ohio. He served as a colonel in the war with Mexico. Eventually, he made Keokuk, Iowa, his home and, from there, was elected to Congress as a Republican in 1856, and again in 1858 and 1860. Strongly antislavery, he became a friend and supporter of Lincoln, who considered him for a cabinet position in the new administration in 1861 but ultimately selected his former political adversaries.[10]

Elected as colonel to command the Second Iowa at the outbreak of the Civil War, Curtis, 54 years old, appointed young Chipman adjutant, to assist the colonel personally — the beginning of a long military relationship. Curtis applied his education, experience, and wisdom to creating an able regiment. And he immediately recognized the need for arms. Acting quickly, Curtis procured old-fashioned bronzed muskets by slipping them out of the St. Louis arsenal controlled by secessionists.[11]

Missouri

Late at night on June 12, after six weeks of training the Second Iowa, Curtis received a telegram from General Nathaniel Lyon in Missouri, requesting Curtis to take his regiment immediately to Hannibal, Missouri, "and move over the road to St. Joseph, and put down traitors everywhere on both sides [of] the road, and if possible strike down upon Lexington." By daybreak, the regiment was ready. It embarked on the steamer *Hannibal City*, moving downriver to Missouri and becoming the first Iowa regiment to serve outside of Iowa. After disembarking at Hannibal, the regiment advanced down the road toward St. Joseph, capturing rebel flags. Terrified, disorganized rebels fled at the regiment's approach. The volunteers arrived in St. Joseph and, finding Union forces in control, camped south of town along the Missouri River. Assigned to guard the railroad line around St. Joseph under the command of the Department of Missouri, Curtis' troops were able to thwart southern attempts to destroy the bridges. The ability of the Second Iowa to secure the railroad line in northern Missouri proved a great advantage for the Union in moving supplies and soldiers. Having accomplished this, Curtis, still a member of Congress, left the regiment to participate in a special session in Washington, D.C. While there, he was promoted to brigadier general, never to return to command the Second Iowa.[12]

At the special session of Congress, Lincoln addressed the lawmakers on July 4. He recounted the series of events by which the seceding states forced the issue of war, and he debunked the theory of secession that Jefferson Davis presented to the Confederate Congress — that government by the people included the right to withdraw from the government. "It presents the question," reasoned Lincoln, "whether discontented individuals, too few in numbers to control administration according to organic law in this case, or any other pretenses, or arbitrarily, without any pretense, break up their Government, and thus practically put an end to free Government upon the earth. It forces us to ask, 'Is there in all Republics this inherent and fatal weakness? Must a Government, of necessity, be too strong for the liberties of its own people, or too weak to maintain its own existence?'" "There was no mistaking now the stupendous issue," observed Chipman about Lincoln's speech to Congress. "It meant not only the possibility of free government in America but whether it ever could exist anywhere upon the earth. It meant that the heresy of the right to secede ... should once and for all time be fought out at the cannon's mouth. Behind it of course stood the spectre of human slavery, but the great moving cause was the asserted right of a State to withdraw from the Union."[13]

Lincoln continued,

> The sophism, is that any State of the Union may consistently with the National Constitution, and therefore lawfully and peacefully, withdraw from the Union without consent of the Union or any other State. The little disguise that the supposed right to be exercised only for just cause, themselves to be the judges of its justice, is too thin to merit notice. With rebellion thus sugar-coated they have been drugging the public mind of their section for more than thirty years, and until at length they have brought many good men to a willingness to take up arms against the Government the day after some assemblage of men has enacted the farcical pretense of taking their State out of the Union, who would have, could have, been brought to no such thing the day before.[14]

While the secession, or attempted secession as Lincoln and Chipman saw it, polarized public opinion between the deep South and the free North states, the border states, the states in between, suffered conflicting sentiments. Missouri was particularly contentious. Congress had tried to settle the slavery question with the Missouri Compromise of 1820 by allowing slavery in the part of the Louisiana Purchase south of latitude 36°30' and prohibiting it north of that line. Slave-state Missouri was the lone exception. Repealed by the Kansas-Nebraska Bill of 1854 and found unconstitutional by the *Dred Scott* court in 1857, the Missouri Compromise ultimately provided only temporary relief from the grave division engendered by the slavery question. Missouri suffered from continued internal division over the issue, a flashpoint in the more general North-South rift.

After an unsuccessful attempt to compromise in Missouri, pro–Union fighters chased secessionists, including the governor, to southern Missouri. There, the governor called the legislature into session, though with less than a quorum, and this quasi-legislature passed an ordinance of secession. Jefferson Davis's government admitted Missouri as the twelfth Confederate state, but the action was futile because the governor had lost control of the state. Into the government vacuum rushed Missouri's state constitutional convention, which had been called to consider the question of secession. The convention, minus the members who had favored secession and had been chased out with the state government, took over. It installed a provisional government in July 1861, with Hamilton R. Gamble, a conservative Whig, as governor, to serve until November when the Missourians could elect new officers. As a result of successive postponements of elections, the provisional government remained until January 1865.[15]

General John C. Frémont, whom Chipman had supported for president five years earlier, commanded the Union forces in Missouri after Lyon perished in battle. Lincoln hoped Frémont would calm the volatile state. Instead, aloof and high-handed, he succeeded only in inflaming passions. On August 30, he declared martial law in Missouri. He also proclaimed that the government would confiscate all property of those who opposed the Union, "their slaves, if any they have, are hereby declared freemen." Lincoln first learned of Frémont's emancipation of Missouri slaves through the newspaper. He immediately responded:

> Should you shoot a man, according to the proclamation, the Confederates would very certainly shoot our best man in their hands in retaliation; and so, man for man, indefinitely. It is therefore my order that you allow no man to be shot, under the proclamation, without first having my approbation or consent.... The confiscation of property, and the liberating of slaves of traitorous owners, will alarm our Southern Union friends, and turn them against us — perhaps ruin our rather fair prospect for Kentucky.

But Lincoln stopped short of ordering Frémont to rescind his proclamation.

Chipman explained Lincoln's actions to the young men of the Cherry Tree Club:

> Unwilling to rebuke Frémont, Mr. Lincoln, in his kindly and conciliatory way, so characteristic of him, wrote a letter asking General Frémont to modify his order and pointing out the difficulty he was having in the border States to maintain a loyal spirit. But Frémont was obdurate and refused, believing, which was true, that the popular feeling of the North was behind him. Mr. Lincoln was, in September, 1861, compelled to modify Frémont's proclamation and make it conform to the Act of Congress and the rules of war.... And to settle the matter he declared that he "reserved to himself the right to determine whether it should become a necessity indispensable to the maintenance of the Government to exercise the supposed power of proclaiming emancipation of the slaves."[16]

Into this turmoil, Chipman's regiment was placed to help maintain the Union's interests. With Curtis' promotion, Colonel James Tuttle took command of the Second Iowa. James Baker was promoted to fill Tuttle's vacancy as lieutenant-colonel. Under Tuttle's command, the regiment spent the summer months and into the fall, in hot, cramped, unhealthy conditions, taking non-combat assignments in Missouri and Kentucky. On September 23, Kirkwood appointed Chipman major of the Second Iowa. Curtis returned to Missouri in his new role as brigadier general.[17]

Lincoln realized he could not allow Frémont to remain in Missouri and risk loss of that state to the Confederacy, even though he knew Frémont would resist being relieved. Lincoln therefore sent his long-time friend, Leonard Swett, to St. Louis to pass along to Curtis the removal order for Frémont. In his instructions, Lincoln directed Curtis not to deliver the order if, when the messenger arrived, Frémont "shall then have, in personal command, fought and won a battle, or shall then be actually in a battle, or shall then be in the immediate presence of the enemy, in expectation of a battle." Upon his arrival in St. Louis, Swett went directly to find Curtis but could not see him until the next morning.

Word of Frémont's impending removal had arrived in Missouri by other means. The newspapers in New York reported that the order was being sent to Frémont, and reporters arrived on the same train as Swett to cover the breaking news. Because the reporters, and, consequently, Frémont himself, might suspect that Swett bore the order, Curtis and Swett devised a plan to get the order into Frémont's hands. Curtis sent three different messengers with copies of the order to attempt to deliver it to Frémont, who was near Springfield. Curtis had heard that Frémont had taken precautions so that a removal order could not be delivered.

Dressed as a Southern planter, one of the messengers rode up to Frémont's headquarters and told the aides he had information from the rebel lines. The chief of staff told the messenger he could not see Frémont, but that the messenger could give any correspondence to the chief of staff. The messenger refused the offer and refused to leave. Late in the evening, the chief of staff finally escorted the messenger in to see the general. The messenger ripped the paper from the lining of his coat and handed it to Frémont, who nervously unfolded and read it. By this means, Frémont was removed from command on November 2. Lincoln sent along to Curtis his special thanks for his assistance in relieving Frémont. The president appointed Major General Henry W. Halleck over the Western Department, and Curtis continued his service in Missouri, under Halleck's command.[18]

Frémont's attempted emancipation of the slaves in Missouri exposed a division among high ranking Union officers and inflamed the passions of the men fighting under those officers. Some, including Chipman, believed strongly in the cause of emancipation. But there were many others who, though willing to fight to preserve the Union, would not countenance freeing the slaves. As Chipman told his fellow Iowans when he visited his hometown in 1863, these officers threatened "they would leave the army and take the stump against the administration and if necessary would join the southern cause before they would submit to such an encroachment of southern rights.... It was not uncommon in camp for soldiers to convene and pass resolutions against emancipation and express[] indignation at the idea of fighting side by side with slaves...."[19]

In St. Louis, the Federals confiscated McDowell's College, a medical school operated by Southern sympathizer Joseph Nash McDowell. Dr. McDowell, a tall and imposing man with long white hair and shaggy gray eyebrows, was staunchly pro-slavery and bitterly secessionist. His political rhetoric became so severe that, at one contentious gathering, he began his speech by drawing a revolver and laying it on the desk in front of him before delivering his fiery harangue. At the beginning of the war, he left St. Louis to live within the Confederacy.[20]

Only a block away from Frémont's old headquarters in the Brandt Mansion, McDowell's College was located among mansions and nice homes of the day. The soldiers, under Halleck's command, converted the college into a prison, known later as the Gratiot Street Prison. It held not only prisoners of war, but also civilian prisoners and disobedient Union soldiers. Under the strict conditions of a highly volatile city, those who showed any Southern bias were often imprisoned. Halleck forbade the display of Confederate flags in the vicinity of the prison and threatened to arrest any woman (apparently, women had been the offenders) who violated the prohibition and confiscate her carriage. Chipman saw a civilian led to the prison for cheering "Jeff Davis" in public. The Second Iowa was assigned the ignominious task of guarding the natural specimens left from the college's educational days, now in the midst of a detention center.[21]

Soon after Frémont's removal, Chipman became the subject of a tug-of-war. Halleck had assigned Curtis to command the Southwest District of Missouri, headquartered in Rolla, about 100 miles southwest of St. Louis. As a major, Chipman was important to the command structure of his regiment. But Curtis knew Chipman's intellectual and organizational abilities and wanted Chipman for his own staff. On November 12, Curtis detailed Chipman to duty on his staff as acting assistant adjutant-general. During Chipman's time on Curtis' staff and away from the Second Iowa, Curtis was occupied with the task of driving Confederate forces, under General Sterling Price, out of Missouri, which he succeeded in doing, partly because Price retreated on his own.

Chipman served with Curtis for almost two months until Tuttle, commanding the Second Iowa, complained to Halleck. A brigadier general could not, by law, retain an officer with the rank of major on his staff. Prompted by the request, Halleck wrote to Curtis telling him Chipman's rank was too high to serve as an acting assistant adjutant-general on the staff of a brigadier general: "The services of Major N.P. Chipman, Second Iowa Volunteers, are required with his regiment, and they have been applied for by his colonel. Moreover, he cannot be legally detailed as acting adjutant general. You will therefore direct him to rejoin his regiment." Curtis relieved Chipman from duty on his staff and ordered him to report to his regiment, "forthwith." The day after Halleck wrote to Curtis, Chipman was on a train to St. Louis to rejoin the Second Iowa.[22]

When Chipman volunteered for military service in April 1861, he did it with such haste that he left his law partnership unresolved. In January 1862, the partnership expired by its own terms, and Chipman found it necessary to ask for leave to go home and attend to certain financial matters left from the expiration of the partnership. He had not been away from his regiment, except on his duty assignment on Curtis' staff, during the nine months since his mustering in at Keokuk. Halleck approved a ten-day leave, and Chipman went home for a brief visit, returning to his regiment on January 31. During his leave, he wrapped up his business affairs, severing his economic ties to Washington, Iowa.[23]

Although not actively fighting, the Second Iowa suffered greatly from sickness in St. Louis. Of more than 900 men who were mustered in, less than half were fit for duty by the late summer of 1861. To add to the misery of sickness and boredom in St. Louis, the Second Iowa was publicly disgraced. A thief slipped into McDowell College and carried off some stuffed rabbits.

Critics of the St. Louis military presence pounced on the opportunity and blew the offense out of proportion, complaining loudly to the military authorities. Since the culprit was not found, Halleck blamed the regiment. He ordered the regiment, which was just then in the process of deployment to Tennessee on February 10, 1862, to march to the river for embarkation without music and with its colors tucked away. Demoralized, they trudged to the river, having found no glory but only sickness and misery in the first ten months of military service.[24]

Fort Donelson

As the Second Iowa was suffering disgrace in St. Louis, the Union troops to the south in Tennessee were on the move. Halleck, from his command post in St. Louis, showed no heart for fighting the rebels in Tennessee. Under Halleck's command, however, was General Ulysses S. Grant. Stationed in Cairo, Illinois, Grant seized the opportunity to become more aggressive. Cairo was positioned along the Mississippi River with access to the Cumberland and Tennessee Rivers, via the Ohio River. These rivers were strategically critical to the Union because they provided a route into the South. Under the control of the Union, these rivers would allow commerce to flow to the West, especially St. Louis, and make it more difficult for the Confederacy to make any advances in the West.[25]

Fort Henry and Fort Donelson, both in Tennessee, were located where the Tennessee and Cumberland Rivers flowed only a few miles apart — Fort Henry on the Tennessee River and Fort Donelson on the Cumberland River. Grant planned to capture the two forts with the help of Flag-Officer Andrew H. Foote's small fleet of ironclad gunboats. He requested permission to go to St. Louis and explain his plan to Halleck. Grant recounted that "[t]he leave was granted, but not graciously." "I was received with so little cordiality that I perhaps stated the object of my visit with less clearness than I might have done, and I had not uttered many sentences before I was cut short as if my plan was preposterous. I returned to Cairo very much crestfallen." Backed by a dispatch from Foote, Grant deigned again to ask, this time by telegraph. Halleck telegraphed permission on February 1, and Grant's troops were on the move the next day.[26]

Grant took his troops up the Tennessee River toward Fort Henry by boat and landed just downstream from the fort. On February 6, the troops were in position, and Grant ordered the advance of both the troops and the gunboats, at the same time. The gunboats traded fire with the fort and soon gained the upper hand. By the time the troops arrived after delays for thick underbrush and lack of roads, most of the garrison had escaped toward Fort Donelson. The Union cavalry gave chase but was unable to overtake the fleeing soldiers. In the river battle, a Confederate shell penetrated the boiler of one of the gunboats, the *Essex*, which exploded killing and wounding many on board. Other than that and some lighter damage to other boats, Fort Henry had been taken with relative ease. Under Grant's orders, the ironclad gunboat *Carondelet* steamed upriver, to the south, and destroyed the bridge of the Memphis and Ohio Railroad, cutting off a southern supply route.[27]

Flush with success, Grant telegraphed Halleck: "Fort Henry is ours. I shall take Fort Donelson on the 8th." This optimistic assessment of his prospects did not, ultimately, account for bad weather, which made the overland march with artillery and wagon trains to Fort Donelson more difficult, and the need to repair and reposition Foote's ironclad gunboats. But the delay allowed Halleck to send reinforcements from St. Louis. Among these, the Second Iowa, under Tuttle's command, disgraced in St. Louis, made its march to the river, bound for the fighting in Tennessee under Grant.[28]

The Confederate commander of the Western Department, General Albert Sydney Johnston, had to decide whether to make a stand at Fort Donelson or withdraw to defend Nashville. He decided to defend Fort Donelson, but sent only 12,000 of his available 35,000 to reinforce the 5,000 Confederate soldiers already there. General John B. Floyd commanded the fort, with division commanders General Simon Bolivar Buckner and General Gideon Pillow. Floyd was under indictment in Washington, D.C., for his graft and embezzlement as Secretary of War under President Buchanan. And Pillow was an insubordinate and quarrelsome Tennessee politician. But Buckner was the fittest of the three to command. A West Point classmate of Grant, he loaned money to Grant when Grant was broke and down on his luck in St. Louis before the war. Buckner took up a position, facing inland, on the Confederate right, while Pillow positioned himself on the Confederate left.

On February 7, Grant took his staff and some cavalry and rode to within gunshot of the entrenchments around Fort Donelson to reconnoiter personally. He took note of the topography and the two roads available for marching and considered his adversaries. He remembered Pillow from their service in the Mexican War and knew Pillow would not venture to fire on him even at the short distance. Grant's estimation of Floyd was that "he was no soldier" and would yield to Pillow. Grant regarded Buckner, whom he knew the best of the three Confederate generals at Fort Donelson, as the most capable.[29]

Foote's gunboats steamed down the Tennessee River from Fort Henry, up the Ohio River, and up the Cumberland River toward Fort Donelson. Meanwhile, Grant marched 15,000 men from Fort Henry east toward Fort

Donelson on February 12. The soldiers encountered no obstructions during the march, which was only about 10 miles, and they completed the march the same day. The weather was fair, which prompted many of the soldiers to throw aside their blankets and overcoats. Grant's forces set up artillery lines and used the one- and two-room homes in the area to establish hospitals. The next few days it rained and snowed, alternating between freezing and thawing, which caused great suffering for the men who had no shelter and no blankets and overcoats. With his force of 15,000, without entrenchments, Grant looked toward an entrenched Confederate force of 21,000. This disadvantage prompted Grant to wait for reinforcements to arrive.[30]

Fort Donelson was situated on the Cumberland River two miles north of the town of Dover in northern Tennessee. Upriver, to the southeast, lay the town of Nashville, an important hub of southern railroads. The fort stood on high ground, as high as 100 feet over the river. The enclosed area of the fort, really just a stockade with soldiers' huts and camp equipment, covered about 15 acres. Creeks swollen from precipitation and the backflow of the river bordered the fort on the north and south. To the west, on the side of the fort away from the river, the Confederate soldiers had constructed rifle pits outside the walls as much as two miles from the river, running generally along the crest of the high ground. They felled trees to form abatis fortifications by sharpening the ends of branches and directing the points outward from the pits. The soldiers built other rifle pits, staggered within the outer line. The area was wooded, with broken terrain — streams, ravines, and other features that produced a rough battlefield — making it impossible for commanding officers to see their own brigades from flank to flank.[31]

On the Union side, Grant positioned his division commanders. General John A. McClernand was positioned on the Union right, facing the fort. General Lew Wallace occupied the center. General Charles F. Smith took the position on the Union left.[32]

On February 13, Grant ordered an ironclad gunboat to fire on Fort Donelson. Many of the shots fell within the fort, causing consternation among the troops and diverting attention away from Grant's land maneuvers. On the next day, Halleck's Union reinforcements arrived to give Grant numerical superiority. The Second Iowa was among those reinforcements, approaching Fort Donelson on the steamer *McGill*, up the Cumberland River. The regiment landed three miles below the fort and Tuttle reported to Grant, who ordered the Second Iowa to reinforce Smith's line on the Union left, attached as part of a brigade commanded by Colonel Jacob G. Lauman. As night fell, the temperature dropped, and the regiment spent a disagreeable night without tents or blankets, bracing themselves against the cold. The ubiquitous mud, caused by the rains and snows of prior days, froze to ice.[33]

Grant planned to hold the enemy within the lines set up around Fort Donelson while the gunboats battered the fort into submission. By about 3 P.M. on February 14, Foote was ready with his gunboats for the attack. He advanced with his entire fleet and fired on the fort. The return fire proved to be more effective than it had been at Fort Henry, as the gunboats had approached the fort too closely and overshot the enemy's battery positions. The gunboats did little damage but the Confederate guns effectively riddled the gunboats, disabling the guns and damaging the boats. One by one, the gunboats drifted helplessly down the river and out of the fray. Grant watched with dismay from the shore. The next day, a messenger brought word from Foote that he had been injured but desired to speak with Grant. So Grant gave orders to his division commanders not to engage the enemy but to hold their position until further orders, and he set off to see Foote.

Finding Foote's flagship anchored about five miles downriver, Grant took a small boat out to speak to him. Foote suggested that Grant should lay siege on Fort Donelson while Foote repaired the disabled gunboats, which he believed he could have done in ten days. Grant took the matter under consideration and returned to the shore, where he was met by a frantic officer of his staff who said that the Confederates had attacked McClernand's division and caused the division to fall back.[34]

Grant's ability to command without panicking became apparent during the ensuing battle. As Foote and Grant were conferring on Foote's flagship, Foote offered and Grant accepted a cigar, which he lit and smoked on his way back to his headquarters. After meeting his staff officer who carried news of the attack, Grant galloped forward and, while giving the troops orders, continued to carry the cigar in his hand. He recounted that the cigar

> had gone out, but it seems that I continued to hold the stump between my fingers throughout the battle. In the accounts published in the papers I was represented as smoking a cigar in the midst of the conflict; and many persons, thinking, no doubt, that tobacco was my chief solace, sent me boxes of the choicest brands from everywhere in the North. As many as ten thousand were soon received. I gave away all I could get rid of, but having such a quantity on hand, I naturally smoked more than I would have done under ordinary circumstances, and I have continued the habit ever since.[35]

Grant made a hasty return to the Union entrenchments. He found no activity on the left where Smith's division, including the Second Iowa, was entrenched. But Wallace, in the center, had sent a brigade to assist McClernand to beat back the Confederate advance.[36]

The night before, after defeating Foote's fleet, the Confederate generals had conferred on their options. Despite elation over the success against the gunboats, they understood the severity of their situation, trapped in the fort where the Union army, with superior numbers, could make crippling attacks or simply wait for the Confederates to consume their provisions, endure great hardship, and eventually surrender. The Confederate generals decided to break out. All night they shifted men and resources to their left, where Pillow was positioned. As morning broke, the Confederates attacked McClernand's division. After several hours of fighting, McClernand was in no position to stop the Fort Donelson garrison from escaping to the south. Yet Pillow pulled back rather than pressing forward. Worried about the exhaustion and disorganization he saw in his troops, he doubted they could march south and overcome possible flank attacks by the other Union divisions. So he convinced Floyd, over Buckner's protest, to call off the attack and return the troops to their entrenchments. On Grant's orders, and with some moral support from Foote's wounded fleet, the Federals moved forward to retake the ground they had lost.

Up until 2:00 P.M. on February 15, most of the fighting had taken place on the Union right, where Pillow's reinforced division attacked McClernand's position. On his return to the battlefield, Grant calmly assessed the situation. He told a member of his staff: "Some of our men are pretty badly demoralized, but the enemy must be more so, for he has attempted to force his way out, but has fallen back: the one who attacks first now will be victorious and the enemy will have to be in a hurry if he gets ahead of me." Grant quickly determined that the Confederates must have shifted some of their strength to attack McClernand's position and so surmised, correctly it turned out, that an attack could be made successfully on the left. He rode his horse rapidly to Smith's position and, with his cigar still wedged between his fingers, explained to Smith the predicament of the garrison, directing Smith to charge the enemy with his entire division.[37]

Chipman and the men of the Second Iowa were fresher than most of the Union troops outside Fort Donelson. Although the night had been cold and uncomfortable, they had not been required to endure those conditions for several days and nights, as had many of the other regiments. Smith ordered Lauman to have the Second Iowa lead the charge, with other regiments in the brigade following to support.

Tuttle and his men had just eaten some salt pork and were waiting for their ration of hard bread when they were called to attention as Smith and Lauman approached on horseback and ordered a charge. Lauman said to the color sergeant, Harry Doolittle: "Harry, I want to see that flag on the fort at 4 P.M." Lauman expressed misgivings to Tuttle, thinking the enterprise was rash, a conclusion with which Tuttle, eager for action, disagreed. Yet Lauman acted on Grant's orders and deployed sharpshooters to cover the advance of the brigade. Tuttle, his officers, and the Second Iowa then led the bayonet charge up the hill, with Grant and Smith urging them to advance without

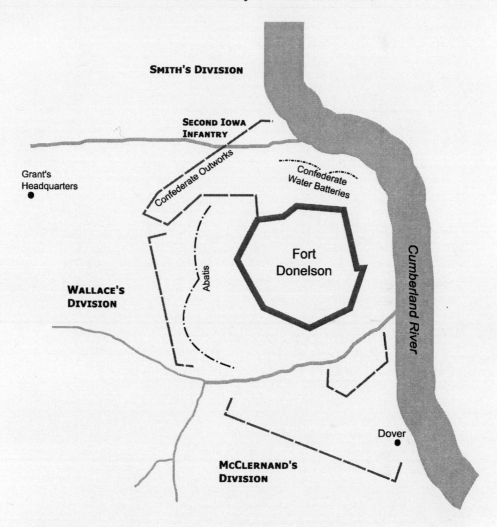

SMITH'S DIVISION

SECOND IOWA
INFANTRY

Grant's
Headquarters
●

Confederate Outworks

Confederate
Water Batteries

Fort
Donelson

Abatis

Cumberland River

WALLACE'S
DIVISION

Dover
●

McClernand's
DIVISION

Chipman fought with the Second Iowa Infantry in the Battle of Fort Donelson, Tennessee, on February 15, 1862. He was wounded as his regiment led the charge to take the fort.

stopping to fire until they had overrun the abatis fortifications. Chipman advanced in the front line of the charge, shouting encouragement to his compatriots.[38]

As the Second Iowa moved forward, it met no resistance at first. The men saw no enemy and heard no sound. Tuttle shouted, "Steady, boys," which helped the men keep their wits about them and stay in position. Through an open space, down a ravine, and up over rough ground, they had almost reached the fortifications with no sign of Confederates. No sooner had the thought crossed the minds of the men of the Second Iowa that there was no one in the fortifications than a line of guns flashed from under the felled logs of the fortifications.[39]

Through a storm of enemy fire, they put their heads down and pushed up the hill, heeding the orders not to fire until they reached the fortifications. Baker narrowly escaped death as a ball went through his cap and exited next to his temple. But Chipman was the first to fall. He was hit in the left thigh twice, which immediately incapacitated him, wrenching him to the ground. Some of his men approached to help, but Chipman refused to be carried away. Instead, he waved his sword and exhorted the men to continue the charge, to take the fort.[40]

Nearly 60 years later, in 1921, Daniel Brown, a fellow volunteer of the Second Iowa saw Chipman's name in the newspaper in an article about the Andersonville trial. He wrote a letter to Chipman: "The last time I remember seeing you was when we went up the ridge to Fort Donelson. You were wounded, and, as I passed you, you held up your sword pointing us forward."[41]

The Second Iowa reached the abatis fortifications and leaped over to find only a few rebel stragglers left to attempt to pick off the approaching troops, as the remaining rebel troops who had been positioned there were already in full retreat up the hill toward the fort. The stragglers met the business end of the regiment's bayonets. "Now give them hell," Tuttle yelled, giving the first order to fire at the fleeing Confederate troops. The Second Iowa, with the remainder of Lauman's brigade following, continued the pursuit until they reached a ridge not far from the fort. The Iowans secured the position, and Buckner, though he tried, could not dislodge them. Once the position was established and held, Tuttle retired from the battlefield to receive treatment for a wound, and Baker took command as the regiment dug in for the night, ready to continue the assault the next morning.

Now there was time to carry Chipman and the other wounded to one of the field hospitals that Grant had established. Following closely on the heels of the charge, Surgeon Well R. Marsh and Assistant Surgeon William W. Nassau gave first aid to those who had fallen. They possibly saved Chipman's life or at least his leg, as they administered medical attention on the battlefield as soon as they could move in.[42]

The Second Iowa's performance was, in Smith's words, "a very handsome exhibition of soldierly conduct." With no prior combat experience, the Second Iowa managed to stay calm and execute commands, charging the fortifications at the obvious risk of death, without pause and without firing a shot.[43]

The advance of the regimental colors symbolized the bravery and daring of the Second Iowa on its charge of the Fort Donelson fortifications. Civil War regiments always carried flags into battle. Often the flags were made by the women of the town or towns from which the regiment came, so the flag symbolized home and family. But on the battlefield, the flag, borne by the color guard, also provided a practical guide for the troops during the chaos of battle, as well as an inspiration and rallying point. Doolittle carried the Second Iowa flag as the regiment began its attack, but he was soon hit four times. As he lay wounded, Corporal Schencius Page took the flag and raced forward. But Page was mortally wounded. Corporal James Churcher seized the flag and made it to the Confederate entrenchment but was there severely wounded. So Corporal Voltaire Twombly took over. Almost immediately knocked down by a ball, he rose and advanced with the regiment until the close of the engagement. Twombly was the only member of the color guard remaining with the regiment at the end of the charge. The charge of the Second Iowa convinced Lauman that there was nothing that brave men could not accomplish.[44]

As the battle outside the fort subsided, with thousands of Confederate and Union soldiers lying dead, dying, or wounded, Floyd, Pillow, and Buckner argued over their next move. Floyd and Buckner were resigned to defeat and wanted to surrender the garrison; Pillow still wanted them to fight their way out. Floyd, fearing capture because he was wanted by the North for his scurrilous behavior as Secretary of War, slipped away in the night, quietly taking 1,500 troops with him upriver toward Nashville on two steamboats. The Second Iowa's regimental history judged that Floyd, "much more successful in the line of felony than in the military art, was anxious to save his precious body from capture." Pillow, the politician, also fled, taking a skiff across the Cumberland River and sneaking away. By morning on February 16, Buckner was left in command with his troops demoralized, all gained ground lost, and Lauman's brigade poised just outside the fort.[45]

At daybreak, Lauman's brigade heard a bugle drawing attention to the fort, where the brigade observed white flags in the inner works. An officer approached the fort, and was given a communication from Buckner to Grant seeking surrender terms from his old friend. Grant replied: "Yours of this date, proposing armistice and appointment of Commissioners to settle terms of capitulation, is just received. No terms except an unconditional and immediate surrender can be accepted. I propose to move immediately on your works." Buckner bristled at the ungenerous proposition, but surrendered nonetheless, along with up to 13,000 Confederate soldiers.

Grant rode to the position of the Second Iowa and called down to Tuttle, who had returned after receiving care for his wound: "Colonel, what regiment is that?"

Tuttle replied, "Second Iowa Infantry."

Grant wheeled around to his staff officers and said: "Three cheers for the Second Iowa."

He awarded the honor of moving first into the fort to the Second Iowa, though without the wounded Chipman. The victorious regiment, colors unfurled, marched into the stockade, amid triumphant shouts of the conquering army and celebratory salvos of artillery fire. To Twombly, of the Second Iowa color guard, went the honor of planting the regimental flag, along with the stars and stripes, on the captured fort.

The regiment that only six days before left St. Louis in disgrace stood, if but for a moment, at the pinnacle of national pride and sentiment. Halleck, who had ordered the public rebuke of the Second Iowa, reported: "The Second Iowa Infantry proved themselves the bravest of the brave; they had the honor of leading the column which entered Fort Donelson." The victory, however, came at a price. Of 630 members of the regiment who were healthy enough to join the charge, 41 died and 175 were injured. In his report, Tuttle said that Chipman was "gallant to perfection."[46]

The news of Fort Donelson's capture spread speedily through the North, by telegraph and press. Governor Kirkwood traveled to Fort Donelson to help care for the wounded. He took the Second Iowa's flag back to Iowa City, showed it off to the citizenry, and preserved it for the state historical society. The capture of Fort Donelson opened the Cumberland River for an advance on Nashville, which surrendered without a fight within nine days. But perhaps the greater importance lay in the surge of national pride and confidence it prompted in the North, which celebrated the victory with ringing church bells and cannon salutes. It also created a national hero in Grant. Every newspaper in the North celebrated his name, initiating his rapid rise which eventually sealed his reputation as the greatest Union general of the Civil War. He was soon promoted to major general and pinned with the moniker, "Unconditional Surrender" Grant.

The corollary of the North's celebration was the South's despondency. Nearly one-third of Johnston's forces had been killed, wounded, or captured. Nashville was lost. All of Kentucky and most of Tennessee were under Union control. The capture of Fort Donelson set the trend of Union military superiority in the West that, although ultimately a difficult process, eventually led to Union control of the Mississippi River.[47]

3
The Proclamation of Freedom (1862–1863)

Although a soldier in active service, both in the drudgery of day-to-day military duty and during the spasmodic periods of battle, could be forgiven if he did not pay attention to the broader issues affecting the war and its justifications, Chipman always kept abreast of the issues of sovereignty, diplomacy, and popular opinion. He maintained a keen interest in the doctrinal underpinnings of the Civil War, both during the war and after. This attention and sophistication, supported by his legal education but enlarged by his natural interest in societal issues, made Chipman useful to the leaders he served. He was more than a mindless functionary. Serving, as he did, with significant leaders — Curtis and, later, Stanton, Lincoln, and others — he could understand and apply the policy underlying each decision in carrying out the order associated with that decision.

Service with Curtis

Transported from the battlefield with other injured men, Chipman found himself on the steamer *Chancellor*, en route to Paducah, Kentucky, where Halleck had sent General William T. Sherman to forward reinforcements to Grant and to regulate traffic on the rivers to Fort Henry and Fort Donelson. Paducah was overrun with Union wounded, Confederate prisoners, and curious northerners. Hearing of the Fort Donelson battle, wives of Union officers gathered at Paducah seeking passage up the Cumberland River. Sherman took control, prohibiting citizens from going to Fort Donelson. He communicated with Grant and provided support for Grant's troops. When the *Chancellor* arrived in Paducah, Sherman sent it upriver to Mound City, Illinois, where the wounded could receive treatment at the General Hospital. Sherman wrote to Grant, "The whole country is alive to the necessity of caring for the wounded."[1]

The chaos of the Fort Donelson battle and its aftermath led to a mistaken report, somewhere in the military reporting structure, that Chipman had been killed. One week after he was injured, however, he was well enough to write to St. Louis headquarters:

> Owing to the confusion incident to the capture and surrender of Fort Donelson, I, among other wounded, was hurried off without time to ask leave of absence through the proper channel. I am now lying at the house of a friend where my wounds are being attended to. I desire to report myself and ask leave of absence until sufficiently recovered to rejoin my regiment.[2]

With time, the serious injuries to his thigh began to heal. After a few weeks, Chipman was well enough to travel, but not fit to return to active duty, so he went home to convalesce. On March 21, five weeks after the battle, he sent to headquarters a certificate from his attending physician that it would be at least six more weeks before he could return to duty. Chipman added: "No one can regret more than I the necessity of being compelled to be inactive for so long. But I shall hope to redeem the time on my return." He again wrote on April 16 — he was recovering fast, but was still on crutches. In early May, he traveled to St. Louis and continued his convalescence there. Although Chipman's recovery was eventually complete, he did not return to the Second Iowa until June 1862, four months after the battle at Fort Donelson.[3]

During the time he was away from his regiment, then part of the Department of the Mississippi, one of several geographical subdivisions of the Union Army, this one comprising everything west of the Appalachians and still under the command of Halleck, the Second Iowa spent almost a month in the relatively quiet Fort Donelson. Grant was not the only officer to receive promotion as a result of Fort Donelson's capture. McClernand, Wallace, and Smith, all brigadier generals before Fort Donelson, were promoted to major general. Tuttle became a brigadier general and took command of a brigade comprised of several Iowa regiments. Colonel James Baker took command of the Second Iowa.

In March, the regiment marched to the Tennessee River and embarked for Pittsburg Landing, in southern Tennessee. On April 6, while the Second Iowa was encamped near Pittsburg Landing under Grant's command, Confederate troops attacked. The Battle of Shiloh, named for a nearby church, raged for two days, but the Union forces eventually overcame the Confederates. The Second Iowa again distinguished itself in battle as Colonel Baker fell mortally wounded.[4]

After the Battle of Shiloh, Halleck traveled down from St. Louis to take personal command of the Union forces in Tennessee. Not as aggressive as Grant, Halleck moved the troops slowly toward the Confederate base at Corinth, Mississippi, digging trenches at each position. About the time Halleck laid siege on Corinth, Chipman arrived from St. Louis to join his comrades in the Second Iowa, where he resumed his duties as major of the regiment. The reunion, however, did not last long. Halleck promoted Chipman to colonel, retroactive to April 17, to serve as an aide on Halleck's staff. On June 13, Halleck ordered Chipman to "proceed without delay and report to [Curtis]." Finally winning the tug-of-war he lost temporarily in January, Curtis made Chipman his chief of staff.[5]

In the months after Chipman had left Curtis' staff in January, Curtis further pursued Price's army into Arkansas. At Pea Ridge, Curtis' troops defeated Price's in a decisive battle on March 7 and 8. After giving his troops some time to recover from the battle, Curtis marched through Arkansas to Helena, located on the Mississippi River, 70 miles downriver from Memphis. Curtis encountered no major resistance along the way, but he prevailed in various minor skirmishes and engagements. This march later paled in comparison to Sherman's march to the sea, but newspapers throughout the country reported the details of Curtis' exploits. With Curtis in Helena, the west bank of the Mississippi was secured at a point below Memphis and well along the way to Vicksburg, Mississippi.[6]

Although Curtis is not numbered with the great Union generals, Chipman commonly called attention to Curtis' perfect record in battle and his success in ending the Confederate threat to Missouri. On March 21, Lincoln promoted Curtis to major general. With his promotion in hand, he could validly use Chipman on his staff. He had kept track of Chipman well enough to know he was at home recovering from his Fort Donelson injuries. Sending his best regards to Chipman's family, with whom Curtis was apparently acquainted, Curtis took time out during his campaign across Arkansas and wrote to Chipman, wishing him a speedy recovery and warning him that he was actively seeking Chipman's transfer, again, to serve on his staff.[7]

Civil War generals, such as Curtis, were burdened with many command decisions and administrative actions. Decisions and actions the general was allowed to delegate, however, were frequently delegated to his chief of staff. Once a general made a decision as to a course of action, the chief of staff could take control of the subordinate details, with the authority of the general. Inspecting troops, assigning tasks, coordinating the movements of a corps or division to maintain order, gathering information through the reporting structure, and keeping the general apprised of the details, according to the general's preferences, were all within the purview of the chief of staff. This officer

An abolitionist Republican who was considered for a position in Lincoln's cabinet, Samuel R. Curtis continued to serve in Congress when Lincoln chose political adversaries instead. When the Civil War broke out, Curtis organized the Second Iowa Infantry, with Chipman as his adjutant. Later, when Curtis was promoted to major general, Chipman was his chief of staff in Missouri and, briefly, Kansas (Library of Congress).

had to be, therefore, a trusted advisor and confidant, uniquely charged with making the general look good. The service of the chief of staff allowed the general to focus on the larger demands of a campaign, with confidence that the chief of staff would keep everything running smoothly and appropriately. Properly filled, the position could be one of great personal satisfaction and achievement to the officer, as it was for Chipman while he served under Curtis.[8]

Chipman rejoined Curtis about the time Curtis completed his march to Helena. In Helena, Curtis and Chipman established headquarters in the magnificent residence of Confederate General Thomas Hindman, situated near the base of a hill that looked down on the town. From there, they sent out expeditions penetrating further into Confederate positions, capturing batteries and scouting the area later occupied by Grant's troops as they advanced on Vicksburg.[9]

The Cotton Trade

During the war, the Mississippi River, always a commercial route, remained an important lane for trade between the North and South, to the extent commerce was either allowed or accomplished surreptitiously. Helena's position along the Mississippi River ensured that this trade would pass by the city's shores. And the competition for the privilege of trading through Helena was rife with possibilities for corruption.

Foremost among the commodities traded between the North and South was cotton. The South produced cotton and needed staples such as clothing and food products. The North produced the clothing and food products required in the South but needed the cotton to support the important textile industry. As the war began, both sides banned trade with the enemy, and the North blockaded southern ports along the Atlantic coast to obstruct the South's foreign trade. With Union advances by generals such as Grant and Curtis along the Mississippi River, however, the government desired to open the trade route to those loyal to the North. This restricted trade, while satisfying some demand, drove shocking price disparities. A trader who could buy cotton at depressed prices in the South and sell it for inflated prices in the North stood to accumulate quick and considerable wealth.

Lincoln sent out agents of the Department of the Treasury to investigate merchants and determine whether they were loyal. It took time to get these agents into the field and let them perform their function. In the meantime, the cotton trade did not await the arrival and approval of the agents. The capture and occupation of Helena allowed the flow of commerce, and flow it did.[10]

At first, Curtis determined to let the trade flow through Helena freely. But he soon discovered that much of the trade was corrupt, involving spies, secessionists, and traitors. The undesirables infested his camp. Alarmed, he reversed his policy and prohibited trade except by those he licensed. He licensed only those who could prove their loyalty, creating a logistical nightmare that Chipman labored to resolve. The large number of traders denied licenses included not just southern sympathizers and rogues but also wealthy speculators who, though northerners, were unable to prove their loyalty. Some of the speculators excluded from the cotton trade accused Curtis of being in partnership with those whom he licensed — an easy and even predictable accusation. Curtis vehemently denied cotton trade partnership with anyone, yet the accusations tracked him to St. Louis and beyond over the next year.[11]

As Curtis' forces took control of the area around Helena, Confederates burned large supplies of cotton to avoid having them fall into Union hands to be used to prop up the northern economy. Slaves saved as much of the cotton as they could from the fires and transported it to Helena to trade. In Helena, Curtis allowed blacks to trade the cotton and even advised them who the honorable merchants were. When he learned that scoundrels had taken advantage of cotton-trading blacks, he forced the misfeasors to take back bad money and give the black traders good money. "[B]y this means," reported Curtis to Lincoln, "a thousand poor negroes, whose masters had run away, got means to which they were justly entitled, and have been saved from starvation." But this strategy, too, enflamed passions against Curtis.[12]

The Union Army, under the auspices of Halleck, who had been promoted to general-in-chief in Washington, sent a roving court of inquiry to investigate the management of the troops and the conduct of individual officers in the Mississippi valley. Without telling Curtis that he was under investigation, the court collected any and all gossip and rumor that anyone in Helena was willing to divulge. With the enemies Curtis had made, much of the gossip and rumor impugned Curtis. The roving court returned to Washington, with Curtis still in the dark about its visit to Helena, and reported to Lincoln. The report reflected badly on Curtis.[13]

Lincoln informed Curtis that charges had been made against him in Helena. "My dear sir," wrote Lincoln in his own hand. "I feel it my duty to you, as a friend, to tell you, that the Sec. of War and General in Chief inform me that charges have been presented against you, something about speculating in cotton, as I understand, which can not be overlooked. I am sorry to write on so unpleasant a subject. This matter will be held until I have time to hear from you. Yours truly, A. Lincoln."[14]

Lincoln did not share with Curtis the secret source of the accusations, that a court of inquiry had visited Helena. Curtis replied:

> The charge that I was speculating in cotton did not prevent me from doing just what I thought was right and proper, and I never should have responded to that charge, if it had not taken this form. I have lived too long, and have filled too many private and public places without reproach, to be afraid of lies, invented by rebel sympathizers, and exasperated knaves generally. I do not shrink from any and all fair scrutiny; I can explain any special act of mine to the satisfaction of any honest man. Conflicts with the rebels in the centre of the most violent population of the South were incident to my campaign and unavoidable. I had to deal severely with wealth and intelligence in the

heart of secession. In such a conflict, instead of support, I had some around me who were willing to avail themselves of falsehood to destroy me.

Curtis' letter did not settle the matter, which would come to a head later while Curtis commanded in St. Louis.[15]

With parts of Arkansas under Federal control, Lincoln appointed John S. Phelps as military governor. He and Curtis differed on the question of liberating slaves who escaped from their masters into Union lines, as contraband of war. Though Phelps disapproved of Curtis' practice of liberating escaped slaves, he recognized Curtis' authority over military matters and did not interfere in the summer of 1862. Curtis obtained leave to attend the Pacific Railroad Convention in Chicago, where he served as president of the body making plans for the transcontinental railroad. In his absence, Brigadier General Frederick Steele commanded in Helena. Steele and Phelps reversed Curtis' policy on contrabands and allowed slave masters into Helena to track down their "property," the escaped slaves. Curtis returned to Helena after about a month's absence and was angered to find the change in policy and his camp, in his words, "a place of dissipation and folly." He quickly cleaned up the situation, chasing secessionists and slave masters away.[16]

Emancipation Proclamation

Lincoln's pre-election speeches condemning slavery as inconsistent with the founding principles of the nation were well known. But his conduct during the war was consistent first and foremost with his desire to preserve the Union. In the summer of 1862, Horace Greeley, the influential editor of the *New York Tribune*, addressed a letter to Lincoln under the headline, "The Prayer of Twenty Millions," in which Greeley took Lincoln to task for the "the policy you seem to be pursuing with regard to the slaves of Rebels...." Greeley excoriated Lincoln for not emancipating the slaves. Lincoln replied masterfully in a letter Greeley published, a letter Chipman admired as "a fine example of Mr. Lincoln's lucidity of expression as it also is of the frankness and simplicity of his character." Lincoln reminded Greeley of their friendship and refused to take offense even if the tone of Greeley's letter was harsh.[17]

Responding to the substance of Greeley's attack, Lincoln wrote:

> As to the policy I "seem to be pursuing" as you say, I have not meant to leave any one in doubt.
> I would save the Union. I would save it the shortest way under the Constitution. The sooner the national authority can be restored; the nearer the Union will be "the Union as it was." If there be those who would not save the Union, unless they could at the same time *save* slavery, I do not agree with

them. If there be those who would not save the Union unless they could at the same time *destroy* slavery, I do not agree with them. My paramount object in this struggle *is* to save the Union, and is *not* either to save or to destroy slavery. If I could save the Union without freeing *any* slave I would do it, and if I could save it by freeing *all* the slaves I would do it; and if I could save it by freeing some and leaving others alone I would also do that. What I do about slavery, and the colored race, I do because I believe it helps to save the Union; and what I forbear, I forbear because I do *not* believe it would help to save the Union. I shall do *less* whenever I shall believe what I am doing hurts the cause, and I shall do *more* whenever I shall believe doing more will help the cause. I shall try to correct errors when shown to be errors; and I shall adopt new views so fast as they shall appear to be true views.

I have here stated my purpose according to my view of *official* duty; and I intend no modification of my oft-expressed *personal* wish that all men every where could be free.[18]

As Lincoln's official policy remained preservation of the Union, regardless of the survival of slavery, he was already formulating privately a change in that policy. When he wrote his letter to Greeley, he had presented to his cabinet a draft proclamation to emancipate the slaves. He realized, however, that to make this highly political move he needed to have the confidence and backing of the northern states. He desired to issue the proclamation from the strongest position. Yet support had been lagging because the war had not been going well of late. Lincoln pocketed the draft and waited for a Union victory to buoy public sentiment. That victory came at Antietam in September after General Robert E. Lee's army had crossed the Potomac River. Although the Union army suffered heavy casualties, Lee's army retreated across the river.[19]

On September 22, 1862, after Union success in the Battle of Antietam, Lincoln officially began the process that would change the complexion of the war for which numerous northerners, including Chipman, his family, and many of his fellow combatants, had watched, prayed, and waited, some patiently and others impatiently. He issued the preliminary Emancipation Proclamation, warning the southern states that, unless they returned to the Union, he would, in 100 days, free the slaves. On January 1, 1863, Lincoln signed the final Emancipation Proclamation.

Lincoln's proclamation was not universally welcomed in the North. Even in Iowa, where there had been such an outpouring of support for Lincoln after the South attacked Fort Sumter, many families, seeing the real cost of war, sending their sons into battle never to return, expressed opposition to Lincoln and his reasons for going to war. Similarly, the Emancipation Proclamation pushed some fence sitters into active opposition, as they saw the emancipation of the slaves as an unworthy, and even unconstitutional, reason to continue the war.

In addition to freeing slaves in states over which the United States did not have control — a symbolic but practically unenforceable act — the Emancipation Proclamation freed all the slaves that had escaped from those states north across the battle lines. Chipman exulted in the new Union policy. "Henceforward," Chipman later wrote, "the war assumed a new aspect. It had thus far been waged to save the Union with or without slavery. Now it was a war for the re-establishment of the Union — the Union without slavery."[20]

Curtis took full advantage of this opportunity and began issuing certificates of freedom to slaves who had escaped into Curtis' willing protection. He had validly harbored the escaped slaves as contraband of war, even though, under the *Dred Scott* decision, they were still deemed the property of their southern masters. Now, as a result of the South's active rebellion and the president's wartime proclamation, they could be certified as free. Chipman, acting for Curtis, was pleased to sign some of the first certificates and to help the newly freed men to find jobs. Lincoln's critics, then and later, complained that the Emancipation Proclamation, by limiting its reach to those states in rebellion, had no actual effect of freeing slaves. Curtis, Chipman, and the slaves from rebellious states who received certificates of freedom from them disagreed.[21]

Chipman reported in a speech to the citizens of his hometown,

> You know our peace brethren tell us, after they have exhausted expletives against the Proclamation of Freedom and the President, for issuing it, and grow frantic over its unconstitutionality and injustice to the South, that after all it is inoperative and a "dead letter." My incredulous, tender-footed hater of freedom, what means the influx of negroes in the north? Where do your neighbors get their colored laborers that I see so often? Where do the 20,000 black men used as fatigue men, teamsters, etc. in the army and the 25,000 colored troops now in the service come from? A regiment of whom is commanded by one of your own townsmen, a command he is not ashamed of. I'm sure. How do you explain the large falling off of the slave population in Missouri and other border states? Does the great decline in value of slave property even upon the heels of its rapid diminution and when it is needed more than ever mean nothing? I have seen cargo after cargo of this enslaved race armed with free papers go North from Helena singing, "Ain't I glad to get out of the wilderness" and "It must be now the Kingdom coming." This spring several boatloads of men, women and children were sent up to General Curtis by General Prentise from Helena to be disposed of. Coming from a state declared to be in rebellion. They were prima facie free and General Curtis made them so indeed by issuing to each free papers and finding them employers.

Chipman continued,

> I am proud that it has been mine to attach the seal of freedom to a hundred emancipating papers and to have seen by my act an hundred human beings made free. I tell you next to winning a soul to Heaven stands its temporal enfranchisement.[22]

The Department of the Missouri

Having established a Federal presence on the Mississippi River, Curtis and Chipman did not remain long in Helena. In September 1862, Lincoln, despite the accusations against Curtis of illicit cotton trading, gave Curtis command of the Department of the Missouri, headquartered in St. Louis. The department included Missouri, Arkansas, Kansas, the territories of Nebraska and Colorado, and the Indian Territory. Back in the boiling contentions of Civil War Missouri, Curtis thrived, stumbled, then flamed out.[23]

Still under Frémont's martial law order, Missouri had no practical way to resolve political disputes. As a result, personal or factional disputes, irresolvable in the voting booth, arose in the place of party disputes. Furthermore, the state constitutional convention placed Governor Gamble in power, without a popular vote. Missouri was politically dysfunctional. Two opposing factions, though both Unionist and Republican, rose to the surface and claimed the allegiance of the leaders and citizens within the state: the Claybanks and the Charcoals. The members of a third faction, known as Snowflakes and favoring secession, had either been driven out of Missouri or kept a lower profile publicly.

In Missouri, the clay is of a neutral color. The conservatives, those espousing relatively colorless views, were dubbed the "Claybanks." Those of more radical views were called the "Charcoals." Both the Claybanks and Charcoals were loyal to the Union and agreed on the main issue of preservation of the Union. They differed, however, over slavery. The Claybanks desired to preserve the Union with or without slavery. The Charcoals viewed slavery as the main evil and advocated overthrowing the institution of slavery as well as defeating the Rebels. The Charcoals had no patience for those who supported slavery or even those who did not agree that the institution must be abolished. Another source of contention between the Claybanks and Charcoals was the method of dealing with the disloyal. The Charcoals contended that all southern sympathizers should either be imprisoned or sent across enemy lines and that their property should be confiscated. The Claybanks were more willing to forgive and accommodate. They considered that many who supported slavery also opposed secession. The Claybanks allowed that former prejudices and opinions were powerful and, as long as those holding prejudices and opinions contrary to the Union did not engage in hostilities, they should be tolerated.[24]

The Claybanks and Charcoals raced to gain the ear of each military commander assigned to St. Louis, urging the commander to take the view of the pleading party. Frémont generally sided with the Charcoals, manifested most prominently in his attempt to emancipate the slaves in Missouri, though he was so aloof from the internal politics that he was popular with few. Halleck, though personally radical, courted both factions. He favored the Charcoals but did so with sufficient discretion that he did not alienate the Claybanks. Curtis, however, was himself a Charcoal with no inhibitions about demonstrating his partiality.[25]

When Curtis took command in St. Louis, he employed the aggressive tactics that had served him so well in his march across Arkansas. Among civilians, however, the heavy hand was appreciated only by the most radical of the Charcoals. He continued Halleck's policy of punishing the disloyal. He confiscated the property of many wealthy families who expressed secessionist sympathies and banished them to the South, allowing families to take one thousand dollars with them and those without families to take two hundred dollars. Curtis used the remainder of their property to care for sick and wounded soldiers.[26]

Though Chipman agreed with the philosophy underlying many of Curtis' actions in St. Louis, he was more inclined to keep his views close to the vest. For this reason, he was accepted and respected by all parties. In addition, Chipman learned from Curtis the importance of proper dress and comportment. Curtis was known for his solemn, even somewhat sedate, manner, never laughing boisterously, but easily approachable. He was kind and generous in his personal dealings and impeccable in the social graces. This portrayal could also describe Curtis' chief of staff. Kind and not of an aggressive demeanor, Chipman was known as a calm, reflective personality who never lost his temper. Curtis saw Chipman's favorable standing with the leaders of the various factions and called upon Chipman to smooth over rough relationships and accomplish things Curtis could not. It was this support and diplomacy that Curtis saw as Chipman's chief strength and the main reason, later, for objecting to Chipman's reassignment.[27]

Curtis' strictness in dealing with southern sympathizers and insubordinates and his eagerness to assist escaping slaves earned him many enemies on both sides of the battle lines. As the military authority in Helena and then St. Louis, Curtis found that those with wealth and political influence, especially slaveholders, sought to gain advantage from him. Curtis, however, would not ease his policies. His tenacious insistence on applying abolitionist policies unified his enemies as they sought to rid themselves of this unswayable department commander.

Soon after Curtis took command of the Department of the Missouri, Lincoln requested a response from Curtis concerning the charges of corruption in the management of the cotton trade. The general immediately responded, denying the charges and saying that he believed the charges were the result of a conspiracy: "When I came to this command, I found a conspiracy had been going on here [St. Louis], and at Helena, to break me down,

General Samuel R. Curtis (seated in the middle) during his tenure as commander of
the Department of the Missouri, with his staff. Chipman, chief of staff, is seated at
Curtis' right (Iowa Gold Star Military Museum).

and secure a Pro-Slavery successor at Helena. I heard that a little, drunken,
Irish strolling player whom I had employed to go into rebel corners where
rowdies enrolled their rebel bands, and who left in a pet because my quartermaster would not allow him to steal horses, had been employed by some
regular army officers to spy into matters at Helena."

An investigation into this and other agitators in the Helena camp led
Curtis to believe several Union officers had sent these troublemakers into
camp to spy on Curtis and find cause for accusations against him. Curtis came
to the conclusion that Union spies sent to Helena were part of a plan by Halleck to detect corruption in the Army, which turned out to be a basically
accurate description of the roving court of inquiry that collected the gossip
and rumor. Curtis had voiced strong objections to this system and believed
his resistance to "this detective business" had resulted in the charges. He vehemently denied any corruption or pecuniary gain from the cotton trade. "I
started in the world poor," he told Lincoln, "and hold my own sadly."[28]

Lincoln took no action against Curtis, but also did not exonerate him,
even though Curtis requested an inquiry or military tribunal to clear his
name. The charges, though unpursued, hung over Curtis' head in St. Louis.
Rumors surfaced that Curtis would lose his command based on the charges.

Charcoals lobbied Lincoln to allow Curtis to remain in command. Curtis should retain his command because the charges were unproven, they contended. Even if the charges were true, they argued, the matter was not serious enough to risk the takeover in Missouri of proslavery elements.[29]

Belle of St. Louis

The foremost concern of most Missouri citizens, as Curtis returned to St. Louis, had nothing to do with Curtis' involvement in the cotton trade. Instead, they worried about their safety from guerrilla raids. Confederate raider William Quantrill and others intent on using the war as an excuse to settle old scores and act on regional hatred made forays into southern Missouri, murdering and pillaging. Through concerted effort, Union forces drove the raiders into Arkansas, securing peace for most of Missouri. Refugees, however, poured into St. Louis, poor and homeless. The women of St. Louis took on the task of caring for these refugees through societies formed for the purpose. One of these societies, the Ladies' Union Refugee Aid Society, set up a shelter in an old St. Louis mansion.

Those who entered the city needing help could remain in the mansion long enough to be fed and clothed before taking passage to Illinois or some other northern state where they could find safety until the end of the war, when they could return to their homes in southern Missouri. Among the directors of this society was Mrs. Robert Holmes.

Many of the leading women in St. Louis also joined together in another organization, the Ladies' National League. Those enrolled pledged their sympathies and labor in behalf of the soldiers fighting for the Union. In the first year of its existence, the league raised more than $2,000, which it used to assist soldiers, freed slaves, and the refugees who found their way to St. Louis. One of the managers of this league was Mrs. Holmes' 19-year-old daughter, Mary Isabel (Belle) Holmes, Chipman's future wife. Her father, Robert Holmes, a distinguished merchant of that city, an early contributor to the Union cause, and a member of the state's constitutional convention, was president of the board of public schools. Chipman met the distinguished Holmes family through his administrative duties. He agreed with the family's beliefs and loyalty to the Union. And he quickly took an interest in young Belle.[30]

Young, energetic, and unabashedly loyal to the Union, Belle encouraged loyalty and giving in others. While other young women were more subdued and homebound, Belle worked enthusiastically to help the refugees, contributing time at the old mansion and obtaining the material and monetary contributions of St. Louisans. She had compassion for the refugees escaping the violence to the south. Two other groups whose circumstances touched Belle's

Mary Isabel "Belle" Chipman, born in 1845, married Norton Parker Chipman on
January 31, 1865. She died six days after their 54th wedding anniversary (California
State Library).

heart were soldiers' families left destitute with their main breadwinner either away at war or, worse, deceased in battle and the injured soldiers brought to St. Louis from the battlefields. She joined with other women of the city, mostly married and older than she, to form the St. Louis Ladies' Union Aid Society, similar in name to the society to aid refugees but different in purpose.[31]

The Ladies' Union Aid Society, an auxiliary of the Western Sanitary Commission, created in the first year of the war, began its activities in St. Louis but eventually made its influence felt throughout the Mississippi Valley. Belle and the other officers of the society served in the city's 14 hospitals. They were known by the baskets they carried — baskets filled with relief for the injured soldiers. The society's secretary described a typical basket:

> Within was a bottle of cream, a home-made loaf, fresh eggs, fruit and oysters; stowed away in a corner was a flannel shirt, a sling, a pair of spectacles, a flask of cologne; a convalescent had asked for a lively book, and the lively book was in the basket; there was a dressing-gown for one, and a white muslin handkerchief for another; and paper, envelopes and stamps for all.[32]

Members of the society traveled to the battlefields along the Mississippi River, to assist injured soldiers on hospital steamers and, some, still in trenches. Those not in the field or the city's hospitals met to make bandages and other supplies needed in the hospitals. They administered to spiritual as well as physical needs, distributing 125,000 pages of religious tracts and 20,000 books and papers on behalf of the United States Christian Commission. As the demand for hospital clothing overwhelmed the available supply, the society conceived a plan to meet the demand while helping soldiers' destitute families. Each Thursday, hundreds of soldiers' wives filled the rooms of the society on Chestnut Street, morning to night, to assemble the hospital clothing from materials provided by the society and receive pay for their work.[33]

The society also scoured the city for fresh food to add to the rations given to the injured soldiers to give them proper nourishment as they convalesced. Donations of food poured into the hospitals and the society provided soldiers the meal of their choice. An 1867 summary of the society's wartime activities reported:

> Bills of fare were distributed in each ward every morning; the soldiers wrote their names and numbers opposite the special dishes they desired; the surgeon examined the bills of fare, and if he approved endorsed them. At the appointed time the dishes distinctly labeled, arrived at their destination in charge of an orderly. Nearly forty-eight thousand dishes were issued in one year.[34]

Chipman was engaged in constant battle, either physical with the South or political with the Claybanks and the outright secessionist elements in Missouri, so it was refreshing to associate with Belle, who was engaged in charitable activities. In his writings, Chipman never complained of his travails during his tenure as chief of staff in the Department of the Missouri. Belle's presence in St. Louis provided a pleasing diversion for Chipman, and she admired the young colonel, so completely committed to the same cause.

Missouri Power Struggle

While Chipman found favor in St. Louis, his commander faced opposition. Curtis' Charcoal measures, particularly the confiscation and banishment policy, brought him into serious conflict with Governor Gamble. They collided early and often over military operations and federal policy, and frequently their disputes ended up in Lincoln's lap. The president described the feud as a "pestilent factional quarrel among themselves."[35]

At Gamble's prompting, Lincoln wondered if the time had come to return control over Missouri to the civil authorities. Since Frémont's order in the summer of 1861, Missouri had been under martial law. On December 17, 1862, Lincoln sent a brief telegraph to Curtis: "Could the civil authority be reintroduced into Missouri in lieu of the military to any extent, with advantage and safety?" Curtis responded strongly that peace in Missouri depended on military force. At no time in Curtis' considerable war experience in Missouri had there been more efforts to overthrow Union power. Wealthy secessionists in St. Louis stood ready to receive and succor Confederate troops should those troops be successful in breaking through to Missouri.[36]

Although Lincoln agreed to let martial law continue in Missouri, he intervened in two matters related to the administration of the law: first, monetary assessments or confiscation against secessionists and, second, the banishment of a Presbyterian minister. In these two matters, Curtis found himself at odds not only with Gamble, but also with the president. Just when Curtis needed Chipman's diplomatic talents, however, Chipman was heading, under Curtis' orders, to Arkansas to monitor the department's troops along the Mississippi River.[37]

The assessments problem preceded Curtis. Before Curtis took command of the Department of the Missouri, Brigadier General John Schofield, then in command of the District of Missouri, on August 28, 1862, issued an order creating a board in St. Louis County to assess a total of $500,000 from secessionists and southern sympathizers. The money from the assessment went to fund the state militia. The board determined who were secessionists and southern sympathizers based on the board's own knowledge or by information obtained in response to invitations to the public for information. Disputes both as to who should be assessed and how much they should be assessed arose. Gamble asserted the militia no longer needed the funding and desired to terminate the board's activities, but Curtis hesitated. Gamble, believing the measure to be one of martial law not subject to his control, took the matter to Lincoln. He told the president that, if it were within his authority, he would stop the assessments. On December 10, Lincoln telegraphed Curtis to suspend the assessments.[38]

Lincoln acted because he heard allegations of corruption in making and collecting assessments. Particularly, he heard that assessments against several people totaling $10,000 were made. Whoever collected the assessment, collected a total of $30,000 and pocketed the excess $20,000. Lincoln believed that, "true or not, in the instance, nothing but the sternest necessity can justify the making and maintaining of a system so liable to such abuses." In a letter to Curtis following his telegram suspending the assessments, the president encouraged Curtis and Gamble to join together and share information on this matter. "May I not hope that you and he will attempt this?" asked the president. The two leaders, however, continued to squabble, never satisfactorily resolving the problem.[39]

The matter of the Presbyterian minister caused a flurry of communication between St. Louis and the White House and tried the president's patience. For some time, Curtis had perceived a threat in the preaching of some St. Louis ministers who were sympathetic to the rebellion. Franklin Dick, the provost marshal general of the department, charged with the enforcement of martial law in St. Louis, encouraged Curtis to banish several ministers for disloyalty. Curtis resisted Dick's entreaties, but eventually took action when an influential Union man, George P. Strong, approached Curtis about banishing the minister of the congregation to which Strong belonged. Willing, after the various requests, to make an example of one minister, Curtis, through Dick, ordered the banishment of Reverend Samuel B. McPheeters, of the Pine Street Presbyterian Church, and his family.[40]

As Curtis found later, McPheeters may not have been the best minister to use as an example. Although his wife was a vocal rebel sympathizer, McPheeters tried to keep his feelings about the war to himself. A provision of martial law required any minister who wished to perform civil marriages to take a loyalty oath. Seeing it as his duty to enable himself to perform civil marriages, he took the oath. McPheeters' congregation was of mixed sympathies, and those who were more radically Unionist, including Strong, sought to procure from McPheeters, whom they suspected of not being true to his loyalty oath, further assurances of his allegiance to the Union. McPheeters' baptism of an infant named after Sterling Price, the Confederate general from Missouri and archenemy of Missouri Unionists, prompted Strong to action.

Although McPheeters admitted he had heard what the parents intended to name the baby prior to the baptismal ceremony, he claimed he believed it was a joke and was astonished when the name was presented to him at the ceremony. Outraged, Strong and his committee demanded that McPheeters give the congregation his written opinion and personal position on the civil and political questions facing the nation. McPheeters refused. He asserted that, as a matter of principle, his congregation had no right to a declaration of political beliefs from their pastor. Unappeased, Strong took his complaint to Curtis.[41]

Curtis allowed the banishment order, which included a clause turning over the church to the Unionists connected with Strong. It issued on December 19, 1862, and Lincoln was immediately besieged by pleas from all who had a part in the dispute and some who did not. Those in favor of the banishment argued that overturning the order would embolden the secessionists within Missouri and create danger in a state that had thus far remained loyal to the Union, though not without extreme conflict. McPheeters and his supporters asserted he was being punished for an innocent stand on principle and that he was condemned with no attempt to show he was guilty. One correspondent maintained that the McPheeters fiasco was part of a larger problem: "The military authorities here are trying an experiment, to ascertain how much oppression a loyal community can stand and still be warm supporters of the Government."[42]

Strong traveled to Washington, with a letter of reference from Curtis, to encourage Lincoln to support the military authority in Missouri. McPheeters went to Washington and, with Attorney General Edward Bates, who was from Missouri, met with Lincoln on December 27. McPheeters showed the president the loyalty oath he had taken, which Lincoln noted was "strong and specific." The pastor assured the president that he constantly prayed for the president and government in church services, a claim Strong disputed. Lincoln accurately noted that McPheeters was not charged with violation of the oath of loyalty. Reporting to Curtis after the meeting, Lincoln observed: "Now, after talking with him, I tell you frankly, I believe he does sympathize with the rebels; but the question remains whether such a man, of unquestioned good moral character, who has taken such an oath as he has, and can not even be charged of violating it, and who can be charged with no other specific act or omission, can, with safety to the government be exiled, upon the suspicion of his secret sympathies." With that, Lincoln rescinded the order banishing McPheeters but left Curtis with authority to reinstate it "if, after all, you think the public good requires removal."[43]

Lincoln concluded his letter to Curtis with his most important words of the Civil War on entanglement between church and state: "But I must add that the U.S. government must not, as by this order, undertake to run the churches. When an individual, in a church or out of it, becomes dangerous to the public interest, he must be checked; but let the churches, as such take care of themselves — It will not do for the U.S. to appoint Trustees, Supervisors, or other agents for the churches."[44]

Curtis made no effort to reinstate McPheeters' banishment. He also did not purport, any longer, to determine who controlled the Pine Street Presbyterian Church. He did, though, prohibit McPheeters from exercising any public functions, including preaching, on the ground of disloyalty, because McPheeters declined, when given the opportunity by Curtis, to answer any questions concerning his loyalty. Curtis reported the action to Lincoln: "Your Excellency will see that my questions only seek to ascertain his loyalty, and the idea of an assault on the Divinity of Christ's Church is as he apprehends quite too refined for my intellectual comprehension. If your Excellency can perceive any reasonable ground for further clemency towards this man, who very politely evades answers to questions which would either convict him of disloyalty or remove any misgivings; it will afford me great pleasure to receive Your further instruction in the premises." Lincoln gave Curtis no further instructions concerning McPheeters and, in fact, the order was allowed to stand long after Curtis had been relieved of command in Missouri.[45]

Just three days after Lincoln wrote to Curtis explaining his reasons for rescinding the McPheeters banishment order, Lincoln again sent a letter to the general:

> I am having a good deal of trouble with Missouri matters, and I now sit down to write you particularly about it. One class of friends believe in great severity, and another in greater leniency, in regard to arrests, banishments, and assessments. As usual in such cases, each questions the other's motives. On the one hand it is insisted that Gov. Gamble's Unionism, at most is not better than a secondary spring of action — that hunkerism, and a wish for political influence, stand before Unionism, with him. On the other hand, it is urged that arrests, banishments, and assessments are made more for private malice, revenge, and pecuniary interest, than for the public good.[46]

Lincoln's patience with the Missouri factions was withering. Notably, there was no political process to resolves their difficulties. Neither could they resort to the courts. Not even Halleck, then general-in-chief, sheltered Lincoln from having to manage the Missouri difficulties. Under martial law, but with both a department commander and provisional governor in place and no consensus between them, no one was in charge in Missouri. Consequently, Lincoln had to be.

Having left St. Louis to survey matters on the Mississippi River just as Curtis' problems escalated, Chipman returned to St. Louis as the crises diminished. But the damage had been done. Although Lincoln forbore another few months before relieving Curtis of command, the Missouri problems of December 1862 and January 1863 were the catalyst for Lincoln's later action. Determined to hold the peace and extricate himself from this continuing dispute, Lincoln decided to act. He had no real authority over Gamble, the provisional governor installed by the state constitutional convention, so he fired Curtis in May 1863, eight months after Curtis took command of the Department of the Missouri. Lincoln appointed Schofield, who had earlier commanded in St. Louis. The Charcoals complained, asking for reappointment of Curtis, but the president persisted in breaking up the intractable relationship between Gamble and Curtis.

Hoping to head off further refereeing of Missouri disputes, Lincoln sent Schofield a letter:

> Having relieved General Curtis and assigned you to the command of the Department of Missouri, I think it may be of some advantage for me to state to you why I did it. I did not relieve General Curtis because of any full conviction that he had done wrong by commission or omission. I did it because of a conviction in my mind that the Union men of Missouri, constituting, when united, a vast majority of the whole people, have entered into a pestilent factional quarrel among themselves — General Curtis, perhaps not from choice, being the head of one faction, and Governor Gamble that of the other. After months of labor to reconcile the difficulty, it seemed to grow worse and worse, until I felt it my duty to break it up somehow; and as I could not remove Governor Gamble, I had to remove General Curtis. Now that you are in the position, I wish you to undo nothing merely because General Curtis or Governor Gamble did it, but to exercise your own judgment and *do right* for the public interest.
>
> Let your military measures be strong enough to repel the invader and keep the peace, and not so strong as to unnecessarily harass and persecute the people. It is a difficult role, and so much greater will be the honor if you perform it well. If both factions, or neither, shall abuse you, you will probably be about right. Beware of being assailed by one and praised by the other.
>
> Yours truly, A. Lincoln.[47]

Unstated in Lincoln's letter, even if he denied relieving Curtis for wrongdoing, was that Curtis was still under the cloud of the cotton trade charges. Lincoln sent Curtis a copy of the letter to Schofield to assure him that his decision was not based on the charges, and Curtis' friends published the letter in the Missouri newspapers to relieve some of the gossip concerning the charges as a reason for Lincoln's action. But questions and incriminations persisted, with Curtis' reputation in peril.[48]

The publication of Lincoln's letter in the newspapers caused Gamble to lose some sleep. He was offended by what he considered a "most wanton and unmerited insult," so he wrote Lincoln to tell him so: "I have borne in silence the attacks ... by newspaper writers, but when the President ... in an official communication undertakes to characterise me, the Governor of a loyal state, as the head of a faction in that state, an answer is demanded...." He chided Lincoln for "judgment unbecoming your position" and complained specif-ically that, when Lincoln wrote that he removed Curtis because he could not remove Gamble, he "distinctly intimated that you would have removed me if you could...."[49]

Lincoln's response to Gamble has often been cited as an example of Lin-coln's frustration with the pettiness of military and civil leaders:

> Sir My Private Secretary has just brought me a letter saying it is a very '*cross*' one from you, about mine to Gen. Schofield, recently published in the Demo-crat. As I am trying to preserve my own temper, by avoiding irritants, so far as practicable, I have declined to read the cross letter. I think fit to say, how-ever, that when I wrote the letter to Gen. Schofield, I was totally unconscious of any malice, or disrespect towards you, or of using any expression which should offend you, if seen by you. I have not seen the document in the Demo-crat, and therefore can not say whether it is a correct copy. Your Obt. Servt. A. LINCOLN.[50]

Shell-shocked and paranoid, and perhaps too intimidated to write to Lincoln himself, Curtis prevailed on a friend, Richard McAllister, to inform Lincoln that the publication of Lincoln's letter was not Curtis' doing. To the contrary, Curtis had counseled his allies that the letter could not be published without the president's consent. Because Lincoln, himself, had shown the let-ter to others, however, Curtis believed he could, without asking Lincoln, show the letter to his own friends and political allies. McAllister claimed that how the letter ended up in the newspapers was a mystery, both to him and to Curtis.[51]

As Curtis relinquished command of the Department of the Missouri and headed home to Keokuk to await further orders, he arranged with Schofield to dispatch Chipman to City Point, Virginia, ostensibly to escort prisoners for exchange but also to meet with Lincoln in Washington and make a plea to salvage Curtis' reputation and defend him against the cotton trading charges.

4

The Great Emancipator
(1863)

"My relations with Mr. Lincoln," recounted Chipman in his later years, "were official rather than personal although they were in some degree personal, for he would have it so with those whose duties brought them close to him."[1]

When Chipman arrived in Washington at Curtis' request, he already had a high opinion of Lincoln. He followed the president's political career and campaigned in favor of the Republican Party when Lincoln ran for president. Lincoln's policies tended to be more conservative than those associated with Chipman's abolitionist background and certainly were not as radical as Curtis'. Yet Chipman had confidence in Lincoln and believed he could save the Union.

But Chipman later admitted that, despite his admiration for the president, he did not, at the time, understand Lincoln's greatness: "Let me say," Chipman told a newspaperman, "that his contemporaries cannot get the true perspective of Lincoln either as a man or of his place in history. They may contribute materials, out of which the historian may some day accomplish this, but that is all. He will be judged not by what his intimate associates saw and knew of him, either in his social or official life, for the personal equation can not be eliminated and time alone can soften the asperities and heartbreaks of the Civil War that will linger for many, many decades."[2]

Meeting Lincoln

Several months before Chipman made his first visit to Washington on assignment from the disgraced Curtis, the English novelist Anthony Trollope spent part of the winter in the capital city. In his detailed travelogue, he was critical of almost everything he saw and experienced. Six principal buildings dominated the city — the Capitol, the Post Office, the Patent Office, the Treasury, the White House, and the Smithsonian Institution. Trollope admitted there was "a certain nobility about the proposed dimensions of the avenues and squares," even if he had little hope that the vast streets and open spaces of the city could be made to live up to the lofty designs. When the streets were not frozen, they were filled with knee-deep mud. Without the moisture, the streets disintegrated into clouds of dust. "One walked through an atmosphere of floating mud," recalled Trollope, "for the dirt was ponderous and thick."[3]

The dome of the Capitol was as yet unfinished, as was the city itself. Built as the federal city, under the political control of no state, Washington was marshy and unhealthy. Speaking of the White House, Trollope noted it was not much above the level of the Potomac River and the occupants of the mansion were subject to fevers and ague. "This comes of choosing the site of a new city, and decreeing that it shall be built on this or on that spot. Large cities, especially in these latter days, do not collect themselves in unhealthy places. Men desert such localities — or at least do not congregate at them when their character is once known. But the poor President cannot desert the White House. He must make the most of the residence which the nation has prepared for him." Trollope judged that "nobody in Washington is proud of Washington, or of anything in it."[4]

Trollope saw the Washington Monument as a type of the city itself— unfinished and abandoned. "At present some third portion of the shaft has been built, and there it stands. No one has a word to say for it. No one thinks that money will ever again be subscribed for its completion. I saw somewhere a box of plate-glass kept for contributions for this purpose, and looking in perceived that two half-dollar pieces had been given — but both of them were bad. I was told also that the absolute foundation of the edifice is bad — that the ground, which is near the river and swampy, would not bear the weight intended to be imposed on it." Trollope went to the site of the monument and found cattle collected there, without a blade of grass on which to feed. It lay in an undrained, brown field, within sight of the White House. "It is still possible that both the city and monument shall be completed," observed Trollope, "but at the present nobody seems to believe in the one or in the other. For myself, I have much faith in the American character, but I cannot believe either in Washington City or in the Washington Monument. The boast made has been too loud, and the fulfillment yet accomplished has been too small."[5]

While one may dismiss Trollope's observations as condescendingly critical, Charles Dickens visited Washington in 1842 and had similar impressions of the capital: "It is sometimes called the City of Magnificent Distances, but it might with greater propriety be termed the City of Magnificent Intentions; for it is only on taking a bird's eye view of it from the top of the Capitol, that one can at all comprehend the vast designs of its projector, an aspiring Frenchman. Spacious avenues, that begin in nothing, and lead nowhere; streets, mile-long, that only want houses, roads and inhabitants; public buildings that need but a public to be complete; and ornaments of great thoroughfares, which only lack great thoroughfares to ornament — are its leading features." Dickens also had little faith in the city's future, guessing it would remain rather insignificant. "Few people would live in Washington, I take it, who were not obliged to reside there; and the tides of emigration and speculation, those rapid and regardless currents, are little likely to flow at any time towards such dull and sluggish water."[6]

As flawed and mildly disagreeable as he found Washington to be, Dickens was mortified, filled with a "sense of shame and self-reproach," when he stopped to dine in nearby Baltimore and was waited on by slaves: "The sensation of exacting any service from human creatures who are bought and sold, and being, for the time, a party as it were to their condition, is not an enviable one."[7]

Chipman arrived at City Point, Virginia with the prisoners in early June 1863. He turned the prisoners over to the exchange commissioner and went north to Washington. Preparing to meet with Lincoln, Chipman sought out Senator James H. Lane of Kansas. As chief of staff to a political general, Chipman had picked up some political insight himself. He was unknown to the president, even though Curtis was a long-time Lincoln ally. Alone, Chipman's influence with the president would be slight. So he sought out someone who was more powerful politically and, for his own reasons, would urge the president to support Curtis. Lane was recognized as the anti-slavery leader of Kansas. Honored and supported as an advocate for the new state, but considered unbalanced and pugnacious by his detractors, Lane was nevertheless dynamic and charismatic. His state had been lumped together with Missouri in the Department of the Missouri, which was acceptable to Lane and his radical colleagues as long as Curtis, their ally, commanded the department. With Curtis' termination and Schofield's appointment, however, Lane was adamant that Kansas should be free of Schofield's comparatively conservative policies. Speaking of Lane, Lincoln told his secretary, John Hay, that he liked radicals despite the trouble they caused: "They are utterly lawless — the unhandiest devils in the world to deal with — but after all their faces are set Zionwards."[8]

In a letter of introduction from Curtis to Lincoln, Curtis wrote: "Permit me to introduce my Chief of Staff Col. N.P. Chipman who visits Washington in pursuance of orders to exchange prisoners. I hope your Excellency will receive him as he is a pure patriot and a gallant soldier, devoted to our cause and your sincere friend." Having briefly presented Chipman, Curtis sought Lincoln's ear: "While a little rest after two years care and toil may be very useful to me, I hope your Excellency will not hesitate to use my services on any occasion; and especially do not make me appear as a special object of your displeasure, since as a faithful and personal friend I have devoted myself to your support, and the cause of our unhappy country since the origin of our troubles."[9]

During this June meeting, probably at the White House, Lincoln and Chipman discussed Lincoln's reasons for relieving Curtis. The president graciously and patiently explained his decision and showed Chipman a copy of the letter he had sent to Schofield. Lane, meanwhile, advocated splitting the Department of the Missouri. Either at this meeting or soon thereafter, Lincoln accepted Chipman's proposal to gather the evidence concerning the cotton trading allegations and present a defense of Curtis.[10]

Chipman's arrival in Washington to defend Curtis and Curtis' letter to the president prompted Lincoln to respond supportively and personally in a letter directly to Curtis. While the charges of cotton trading still hung over Curtis' head, Lincoln assured him that the administration had not passed judgment on those charges and "the presumption is still in your favor that you are honest, capable, faithful, and patriotic." Even so, Lincoln acknowledged that Curtis would find difficulty in accepting that his removal as department commander was not the result of the cotton trading allegations but instead for Lincoln "almost a matter of personal self-defence to somehow break up that state of things in Missouri."[11]

His business in Washington completed, for now, Chipman's service status was unsure. Schofield had ordered Chipman to return to St. Louis for duty there, but Lincoln's invitation to Chipman to present Curtis' defense threw Chipman's return for duty in St. Louis into doubt. Secretary of War Edwin M. Stanton, who had replaced Simon Cameron in January 1862, soon settled the matter when he gave Chipman a desk in the War Department, with authority to travel west to prepare his case in favor of Curtis.

"The year 1863 brought great anxiety to Lincoln and at times he almost lost hope," Chipman told the men of the Cherry Tree Club. Popular support for the war waned in the North in the early months of 1863. Peace Democrats, known as Copperheads, challenged for political power. The most famous of the Copperheads was Clement Vallandigham, from Ohio, who agitated for immediate withdrawal from the South. General Ambrose Burnside enacted a measure prohibiting within the area of his command, including Ohio, expression of sympathy for the enemy. Vallandigham intentionally violated Burnside's ban in a speech accusing Lincoln of fighting the war to free the slaves rather than to save the Union and calling for Lincoln's removal from office. Arrested and convicted in May 1863 by a military commission for "uttering disloyal sentiments," he was sentenced to imprisonment for the duration of the war. Vallandigham petitioned the federal government for a writ of habeas corpus, but the petition was denied because Lincoln had suspended the writ. When the case was taken to Lincoln, he commuted the sentence to banishment to the Confederacy. Delivered across enemy lines, Vallandigham made his way back around to Canada, where he ran a campaign for governor of Ohio and obtained the Democrats' nomination.[12]

Lincoln spoke to a deputation that arrived in Washington on Vallandigham's behalf: "Your own attitude encourages desertion, resistance to the draft, and the like, because it teaches those who incline to desert and to escape the draft, to believe it is your purpose to protect them." Lincoln added: "Must I shoot a simple-minded soldier boy who deserts while I must not touch a hair of the wily agitator, who induced him to desert? I think that, in such a case, to silence the agitator and save the boy is not only Constitutional, but withal a great mercy." Vallandigham eventually lost the gubernatorial election by a wide margin to the Republican nominee.[13]

Within days after Chipman and Lane met with Lincoln, in July 1863, riots broke out in New York and elsewhere protesting the draft. Irish immigrants, in particular, objected to conscription under the new law enacted by Congress and signed by the president. Thousands rampaged through New York, destroying property and lynching black residents. Lincoln was forced to divert troops, including some recently engaged in the Battle of Gettysburg, to New York to restore order.

Hometown Campaigning

As the local elections of 1863 approached and during the dark days of the draft riots, Chipman returned to his Iowa hometown to deliver a speech. Iowa held its mid-war gubernatorial election that year. But Chipman's speech was more generally in favor of the Republican Party and in support of Lincoln. During Chipman's visits to Iowa and, more particularly to his hometown, he perceived a shift in public opinion and declining support for Lincoln. Chipman observed that the original volunteers from Washington, Iowa "[e]nter[ed] the service with the belief that to suppress rebellion was but the work of a day and that there was no necessity for disturbing the social systems of the South or abridging their peculiar political privileges.... Indeed I think that a third of the army that were of the original 75,000 expected to return in time for harvest and seemed to regard their business more in the light of suppressing an election riot than as entering upon a war of indefinite length." By 1863, Chipman was convinced that the war could not end for several years and might not end for many years. He sadly concluded "that before our country will again be blessed with peace and harmony such as once found us, North and South, in a common brotherhood, the present generation will have passed away."[14]

With the local elections approaching and the Emancipation Proclamation on the minds and in the conversations of Iowans, a conservative movement developed — "conservative" in the sense of being resistant to further change and opposed to the radical reform of the South. Also identified as a "peace" movement, this growing group threatened to undermine the support of the troops and, to Chipman, this was intolerable. He recognized in this movement the potential for prolonging the war and jeopardizing ultimate Union victory. "Let me tell you," he warned his townspeople, "that it is not the bayonets alone that end the wars nor the lack of their vigorous use that prolongs them, but that very much rests with the public sentiment at home."[15]

Chipman took head-on the public opinion shift that had occurred since the original outpouring of support.

> We loved our country then and were ready to make any sacrifice for its preservation. Why is it the great heart of the people distrust its own impulses now? What underlies the apathy and indifference which have taken the place of the fervor of that time? Whence the open and secret opposition to the government calling for loyal leagues, the organization of a union party and the consolidation of the loyal element of the country into a political power to meet covert treason and silence coadjutors of rebellion in your midst. Why are we here to night? I know not unless it be that our national peril is still very great that an enemy in the rear moves dastardly and insidious though less powerful than the one in front, threatens us and that we desire to know and do our duty as American citizens.[16]

The peace movement back home was inconsistent with the troops' intense loyalty to the president. Even though some soldiers, including officers of high rank, openly opposed Frémont's attempt to emancipate the slaves in Missouri, by the time Lincoln signed the Emancipation Proclamation, many of those same former opponents "wrote letters to their old political friends urging not only the emancipation idea but insisting that negroes should be armed and put into the field. It was not uncommon in camp for soldiers to convene and pass resolutions against emancipation and expressing indignation at the idea of fighting side by side with slaves, yet to day they congratulate the slave who escapes into our lines and make no objection to seeing him share some of the dangers and perils of battle and disease."[17]

Chipman sought to put his audience on notice that the peace movement, which rallied for peace at any price, even allowing the division of the Union and the continued enslavement of a race, was inconsistent with support for the troops — the desire of the troops, not just their duty, was to put down the rebellion and free the slaves.

> Let me say to my conservative friend who chalks out campaigns on store boxes and meets and vanquishes the enemy every time with his little army of wooden men and sees no necessity of changing or modifying our early policy of conciliation and concession, that the smell of gun powder is a sure cure to such fallacy. [¶] After you have had a leg or two shot off you will lose some of your amiability towards rebels, you will realize that they are not fighting their way back to the government, but that they are determined on independence and separation from the government. The revolution of the army is wonderful on this subject.[18]

Chipman's description of the peace movement as composed of those who played child's games demonstrated his belief that they did not understand the true stakes of the war. They saw the war as little more than a family squabble, that their "family relations should restrain us from dealing harshly with the wayward"; instead, any familial sentiment, on the part of the South, "has entirely passed away and the true one taken its place...." Chipman assured his townspeople "that we are at war with an enemy foreign to us in everything which makes two people separate and distinct speaking the same language. There is no longer any community of interest or sympathy. They hate us and hate our institutions. They are implacable and relentless in warring upon us, and this is understood and felt by those who have occasionally been made to feel its force."[19]

Chipman's speech was not just a call for patriotism but also an unconcealed rallying cry for Republican victory in the upcoming elections. He accused the Democrats of seeking to undermine the ability to prosecute the war by opposing the draft:

> It must make the fathers of Democracy turn in their graves to see their party, once so powerful, so patriotic, so glorious prostituting itself to purposes so base, becoming the apologists for treason, openly opposing the government in efforts to maintain its own life believing their former record and blotting out in one last act of infamy the prestige of half a country. The true democrats of the country are not responsible for this degeneracy, but are loudest of all loyal men and bitterest in their denunciation of it.[20]

Chipman cautioned against taking measures against the Copperheads that might precipitate division and even war in the North. But he encouraged action:

> You have heroically given of your blood and treasure to suppress rebellion in the South, have you no practical rebuke to give traitors at home? You will

find it hard to believe that your own neighbors can be so far committed to any combination as to resort to armed resistance of law. So you were slow to believe it of the South and yet the language and threats of the one are the same as the other. Read the signs of the times. A systematic attack is made on the President by prominent politicians of New York urging compromise and peace and vague hints are thrown out of trouble in the North that must follow conscription. The President answers them by arresting and sending South a leading member of that party [Vallandigham] for preaching the treason of his coordinators more boldly than they. Persistent in their attempts to drive the administration to ruin, that same party nominates this man, tried, convicted, and expatriated for treason, for governor of Ohio and all the state conventions ratify it. What a spectacle and what a comment upon republican institutions. There ought to be some special international law to reach this man who is now uttering treasonable manifestos from Niagara Falls. These are the initial steps. The overt act was committed upon the first attempt to enforce the Conscription Act. Scenes of blood and deeds of atrocious barbarity unrivaled in our history was the last step in their great crime. The New York riots are directly traceable to the anti-war movement in the North, if not a part of the plan. See you not cause for alarm?

Chipman's 1863 political speech reflected the responsibility he felt as a lawyer to explain to his hometown the legal justifications supporting Lincoln's decisions as chief executive and commander in chief. He maintained that those who rebelled against the United States and its constitution thereby forfeited the protections of that constitution. It would serve neither national interests nor theoretical purity to allow the South to use ostensibly constitutional principles as a sword to repeal the Constitution itself. "There is no principle of national or international law," urged Chipman, "that throws the aegis of the Constitution over an enemy and protects him even after throwing off and trampling underfoot the shield it offers. 'Tis treason that talks such heterodoxy that government and that people were basely puerile and deserving contempt that would see its national charter spit upon and its ability of self protection defied."[21]

Chipman's 1863 political speech also signaled the end of one period in his life. He must have felt that he was among friends, if not exactly political allies, because he believed he could not only speak openly and harshly about the peace movement but also warn his fellow Iowans about the consequences of opposition to Lincoln and the troops. He had called the town home for 16 years. Yet his ties to the community were fading. By then, he had wrapped up his law partnership and was a full-time military man. His father and sisters remained there, but he would never return to Iowa as a resident. His stronger ties were to St. Louis, where he served with Curtis and where resided the 19-year-old Belle Holmes, his future bride, and his attachment to the nation's capital would grow from that time forward. Instead of his hometown, "Washington" would refer, ever after, to his new home on the Potomac.

Visiting his hometown gave Chipman the opportunity to take command of a company in response to a crisis. Governor Kirkwood had taken the precaution of organizing home guards in each county, military units not committed to the Union army but kept at home in case of a threat to the peace of Iowa. Only once did Kirkwood see the need to call out the home guard. It happened in August 1863, while Chipman was in Iowa. Cyphert Tally, a pro–Confederacy Iowan, addressed a political meeting in South English, near Keokuk. He was bitter about the fall of Vicksburg and the defeat of Lee at Gettysburg. Pro-Union residents called a meeting across the street, and soon the opposing parties clashed. Shots were fired by both parties, and when the dust settled Tally was dead. His followers left town, vowing to return to hang the shooters and burn the town.

The alarm went up to Kirkwood, who called upon the home guards from the various Iowa counties to report to South English. Apparently aware that Chipman was in the state, Kirkwood sent orders for Chipman to take command of the home guards. Each of the counties had a captain in command, so Chipman outranked them all. He formed a camp as the home guards began to arrive and erected a barricade where they would defend the town.

Tally's followers and other southern sympathizers gathered in the bottoms of the Skunk River, 600 or 700 strong. They demanded the arrest and trial of several of the leading citizens of South English for the murder of Tally, threatening to march on the town and hang the men if their demands were not met. A delegation was sent to make the demand to Chipman, and Chipman agreed, having the sheriff arrest several of the South English citizens for a trial during the next term of the traveling district court. This seemed to assuage Tally's followers, who disbursed. But the next night nearly 1,000 pro–Confederate rioters collected in the river bottoms and spilled into the town.

Meanwhile, Kirkwood had arrived in town and gave a rousing speech in favor of the Union. He told the rioters that the men who had been arrested would be tried, but not by the rioters. Kirkwood warned that he would not countenance a fire-in-the-rear rebellion in Iowa and, unless they disbursed by morning, he would order the troops to shoot them down like dogs. As home guards continued to arrive in South English from all parts of Iowa, the rioters, hearing about Kirkwood's fiery speech and Chipman's growing company, entirely dispersed, ending the standoff. Later, the charges against the citizens who had been arrested, as well as some of the rioters who had been rounded up, were dropped. And the Skunk River War ended before it started.[22]

Defending Curtis

A lithograph of an Abraham Lincoln portrait painted by John H. Littlefield, who had been a law student in Lincoln's law office. This lithograph hung in Chipman's judicial chambers in the California State Capitol. Chipman gave the lithograph to the Court of Appeal upon his retirement (California Court of Appeal, Third Appellate District).

By September 1863, Chipman had collected all of the evidence and character testimony about Curtis in the West, and he reported to Washington. Lincoln personally signed an order allowing Chipman access to the secret court of inquiry's report impugning Curtis, and Chipman set about analyzing the report and preparing his brief. To further justify his presence in Washington, Chipman was assigned to judge-advocate duties in the War Department and soon began work preparing a trial by military commission against a Maryland merchant accused of smuggling and communicating with the enemy contrary to the laws of war.[23]

In October, Chipman took time from his schedule to notify Curtis of the general's personal tragedy. Curtis lost his son in a massacre in Baxter Springs, Kansas. Major Henry Z. Curtis had served under Chipman on his father's staff in the Department of the Missouri. When Curtis lost his command, Major Curtis was assigned as adjutant to General James G. Blunt, who, in October 1863, was in the process of moving his headquarters from Fort Scott, Kansas to Fort Smith, Arkansas. With an escort of about 100 cavalry members, Blunt, along with Curtis and the headquarters band, traveled across Kansas on October 6. Meanwhile, Quantrill was returning out of Missouri with his raiders. Quantrill's men, most of them dressed in Union uniforms, approached Blunt's entourage. Before the Union troops realized they were being attacked, not greeted, Quantrill's men opened fire. Instead of making a stand, Blunt's cavalry escort turned tail and fled. Blunt and the younger Curtis attempted to halt the cavalry and turn them to fight, but the attempt proved futile. The Confederates pursued and killed as many as could be caught. They also murdered the band members. Blunt and Curtis, surrounded, attempted to escape. Blunt succeeded, but Curtis' horse was shot from under him. He stumbled into a creek bed and was soon captured. As they did to all of the captured Union troops, Quantrill's men executed Curtis, shooting him through the temple from close range. Although it was initially believed Curtis had been taken prisoner, his body was found the next day. Four days after the massacre, Chipman received first word of it in Washington and had the unenviable duty to send a telegram to Curtis informing him of the murder of his son.

Gathering up his courage and his lawyerly training, Chipman went to the White House for his meeting with Lincoln, but not alone. Consistent with his emerging pattern of surrounding himself with those who would give personal weight to his arguments, Chipman took two of Curtis' personal friends, Judge Jacob Brinkerhoof of Ohio and Leonard Swett of Illinois. The latter, a close friend of the president from their Illinois law practices, was one of Lincoln's chief supporters at the Chicago convention in 1860. During the Lincoln presidency, Swett became a lobbyist to the president for many causes, paid not so much because of his lawyering skills as for his access to the president.

Lincoln knew Curtis and recognized his long-time loyal support. He had considered Curtis for his cabinet before selecting his former political adversaries. So when Chipman went with Brinkerhoof and Swett to meet with Lincoln at the White House, Chipman knew he had a friendly audience in Lincoln. Nonetheless, Chipman left nothing to chance. This was perhaps the only chance to redeem his boss, who had been both brilliant and victorious in his Missouri and Arkansas military campaigns but had fallen victim to politics. Chipman gave the president a comprehensive brief reciting the facts, and he arranged for Swett, the talented and experienced attorney, to be the voice.

Lincoln proved to be even more amenable to Curtis' cause than Chipman had hoped. After pleasantries, attention turned to Swett for his oral petition. He had barely begun, when Lincoln raised his hand and said, "Hold on, Swett; hold on." Lincoln was well aware of the cotton trading allegations. He may also have been acquainted with Chipman's brief before the meeting. With this foreknowledge he was able to set the groundwork for consideration of Curtis' case by stopping Swett's presentation and, characteristically, telling two stories from the days when Swett and Lincoln practiced law in Illinois. The particulars of the two stories were not preserved. However, 46 years later, when asked by newspaperman C.K. McClatchy to recount his personal dealings with Lincoln, Chipman recalled that the stories "illustrated [Lincoln's] point that it was easier to get IN to trouble than to get OUT and, as we were insisting that Curtis should be restored to his command, they also conveyed the idea that having got OUT of trouble the person was anxious to take the chances of getting IN again." The stories not only had the effect of setting the groundwork for Lincoln's friendly review, but they also helped lighten the serious atmosphere, and to calm a young colonel's nerves. Chipman remembered: "We had our laugh over the stories and he then gave the closest attention to the cases, showing deep sympathy for the unjustly accused officer, and shortly created a new department and placed General Curtis in command."[24]

After Chipman completed his defense of Curtis, exonerating his boss, he moved back to the prosecution of the Maryland merchant accused of smuggling. The military commission convicted the merchant and confiscated a large amount of goods. Thus, in one month, Chipman impressed Lincoln and Stanton by passionately defending Curtis and then successfully prosecuting an important smuggling case.

Lincoln and Stanton

As did Grant in his memoirs, Chipman, as one of the few Lincoln acquaintances who lived well into the 20th century, found it constructive to describe Lincoln and Stanton by comparing and contrasting them:

> Stanton never unbent in his relations with subordinates.... His customary attitude ... was austere and exacting. Not so Lincoln; he made one feel that the obligation was his; that we were all engaged in a life struggle to save the Union and that mutual faith and mutual encouragement would alone crown our effort with success, and he always had a cheerful word for his subordinates, often illustrating his point with some quaint anecdote drawn from his life in the West. He was sleepless in his vigilance and watchfulness of the progress of his army, following minutely its movements and sharing deeply the effect of its reverses and victories, not the least of his anxiety always being to stiffen the courage and hopefulness of the loyal people of the North."[25]

Grant was equally reverential in describing Lincoln, although he took pains to assure the readers of his memoirs that Lincoln was no shrinking violet: "Mr. Lincoln did not require a guardian to aid him in the fulfillment of a public trust."[26]

As for his description of Stanton in contrast to Lincoln, Grant was less restrained than Chipman. He thought Lincoln and Stanton

> were the very opposite of each other in almost every particular, except that each possessed great ability. Mr. Lincoln gained influence over men by making them feel that it was a pleasure to serve him. He preferred yielding his own wish to gratify others, rather than to insist upon having his own way. It distressed him to disappoint others. In matters of public duty, however, he had what he wished, but in the least offensive way. Mr. Stanton never questioned his own authority to command, unless resisted. He cared nothing for the feeling of others. In fact it seemed to be pleasanter to him to disappoint than to gratify. He felt no hesitation in assuming the functions of the exec-

Edwin M. Stanton served as Lincoln's secretary of war during the Civil War. He ordered Chipman to report for service in the War Department after observing Chipman's defense of Samuel Curtis (Library of Congress).

utive, or in acting without advising with him. If his act was not sustained, he would change it — if he saw the matter would be followed up until he did so."[27]

Understanding this difficulty in maintaining good relations with the secretary of war, it is to his credit that Chipman not only thrived in his service in the War Department, but also gained admiration for Stanton, even if the secretary was not lovable. Chipman, though not timid, was also not aggressive in his demeanor. Calm and composed, even under stress, Chipman never lost his temper. Perhaps it was this personality trait, more than any, that helped Chipman function well in the War Department through the end of the war.

The Gettysburg Address

Stanton quickly showed his confidence in the young lawyer at a desk in the War Department by assigning him as a personal escort to Lincoln on his journey to the cemetery dedication in Gettysburg, Pennsylvania. Many times in the remaining 60 years of Chipman's life, journalists and masters of various ceremonies who described or introduced Chipman noted his presence on the platform when Lincoln gave the Gettysburg Address.

Stanton was protective of the president and often assigned members of his staff to guard Lincoln. Chipman was an understandable choice. He was young and healthy, six feet tall and battle-tested. He was skilled in executive communication from his duties as chief of staff for Curtis. Chipman saw the assignment as his ordinary duty, not as a special privilege. Stanton's purpose in sending Chipman, a member of his own staff, related to the constant communication between the president and the secretary of war. While Lincoln was in Gettysburg, Stanton kept him apprised, by telegraph, of the latest war news and even relayed to Lincoln the news that Lincoln's son Tad, who had been sick when Lincoln left Washington, was doing better. The secretary of war made Lincoln's traveling arrangements, suggesting at first that the party travel to Gettysburg the morning of the dedication but rearranging the travel for the day before the dedication, at the president's insistence.[28]

The first week of July 1863, Union forces under the command of General George G. Meade met General Robert E. Lee's Confederate troops at Gettysburg, Pennsylvania, well into Union territory. After several days of fierce fighting, Meade prevailed and Lee retreated. While 23,000 Union soldiers were killed or wounded; the toll on the Confederates was even worse: 28,000 casualties. The Civil War lasted almost another two years, but Meade's victory at Gettysburg, along with Grant's capture of Vicksburg, Mississippi, that same month, was the crucial turning point toward eventual Confederate surrender.

As the armies left Gettysburg, they left a scene of carnage and decaying flesh. As scattered attempts to bury the dead proved inadequate, citizens appealed to Governor Andrew Curtin for assistance. He responded by putting David Wills in charge. A civic leader and owner of the largest house on the town square, Wills formed a commission to collect money from the states and clean up the Gettysburg battlefield. The commission created a national cemetery — the first national cemetery, as Chipman, who would figure prominently in the national remembrance of the Union dead, later noted.[29]

Wills "felt the need for artful words to sweeten the poisoned air of Gettysburg." He invited Edward Everett, former congressman, governor, secretary of state, and president of Harvard University and the preeminent orator in America, to provide a patriotic address at the dedication of the cemetery. The dedication was originally scheduled for October 1863, and the invitation to Everett was made in September as the work of burying the bodies went forward. Everett, however, needed more time to do careful research and craft his customary masterpiece. So Wills rescheduled the dedication for November 19. No earlier than late October but not formally until November 2, Wills invited Lincoln to attend the dedication along with his cabinet, even though the cemetery was sponsored not by the federal government but by the 17 Northern states that had lost citizens in the battle.[30]

Chipman believed the text of Wills' invitation to Lincoln was important because it not only limited Lincoln to "a few appropriate remarks" but may have suggested to Lincoln some of the language he used in the remarkable address. The invitation read: "These grounds will be consecrated and set apart to this sacred purpose, by appropriate ceremonies on Thursday, the 19th instant. Hon. Edward Everett will deliver the oration. I am authorized by the Governors of the several States to invite you to be present and participate in the ceremonies which will doubtless be very imposing and solemnly impressive. It is the desire that after the oration, you, as Chief Executive of the Nation, formally set apart these grounds to their sacred use by a few appropriate remarks. It will be a source of great gratification to the many widows and orphans that have been made almost friendless by the great battle here, to have you here personally; and it will kindle anew in the breasts of the comrades of these brave dead, who are now on the tented fields or nobly meeting the enemy in the front, a confidence that they who sleep in death on the battlefield are not forgotten by those highest in authority; and they will feel, that, should their fate be the same, their remains will not be uncared for. We hope you will be able to be present to perform this last solemn act to the soldier dead on this battlefield."[31]

Chipman responded to McClatchy's 1909 inquiry concerning Chipman's recollection of the speech. "[I]t seems to me possible," he posited, "that in [the invitation] Mr. Lincoln found the source of the inspiration so manifest in his marvelous Gettysburg speech." Some of the themes reflected in the invitation also appeared in Lincoln's speech, such as dedication and consecration. While Wills' invitation used these terms only superficially, as one would expect them to be used in reference to a battlefield cemetery, they may have suggested to Lincoln the transcending values of which he spoke on that November day: "But, in a larger sense, we can not dedicate — we can not consecrate — we can not hallow — this ground." Wills' desire not only to honor the dead but to buoy "the comrades of these brave dead" may have suggested to Lincoln his inclusion of those who survived the battle: "The brave men, living and dead, who struggled here, have consecrated it, far above our poor power to add or detract."[32]

Lincoln traveled to Gettysburg on November 18, one day before the cemetery dedication, because he feared he would be unable to make the trip in time on the crowded rails on the morning of November 19. The traveling party included, as Chipman recalled, "The President, members of his Cabinet (not all of them), members of Congress and many others...." The trip took six hours, with transfers in Baltimore and Hanover Junction. When Lincoln arrived in Gettysburg in the afternoon, Wills and Everett met him at the station and escorted him to Wills' home on the town square, just two blocks away, where Lincoln stayed the night.[33]

On November 19, Lincoln joined the procession from the town square to the cemetery. He sat on a raised platform with other dignitaries and security personnel, including Chipman. Everett addressed the crowd of at least 15,000, delivering his carefully scripted account of the Battle of Gettysburg. Focusing on the brevity but greatness of Lincoln's subsequent address, some have denigrated Everett's speech as long and laborious. Chipman's recollection of the speech, however, was of admiration: "Mr. Everett spoke first and

Chipman (circled at left) on the speaker's platform with Lincoln (circled at center) at the Gettysburg National Cemetery, on November 19, 1863. This is the only known photograph of Lincoln on the speaker's platform, probably taken before his speech (National Archives).

for two hours held his vast audience spellbound by the nobility of his sentiments and the rare power of his art. It was a most valuable contribution
descriptive of that great battle, of the origin and character of the war, and the
object and consequences of victory."[34]

Everett closed, and the crowd showed its appreciation. "When the richly
merited applause had ceased," recalled Chipman, "Mr. Lincoln rose, glanced
over the heads of the assembled multitude, adjusted his glasses and with a
clear, but unimpassioned voice, read this matchless tribute to the glorious dead
whose graves were around him and whose immortal spirits, he seemed to feel,
were hovering over him."[35]

"Four score and seven years ago," began Lincoln,

> our fathers brought forth on this continent, a new nation, conceived in Lib-
> erty, and dedicated to the proposition that all men are created equal.
>
> Now we are engaged in a great civil war, testing whether that nation, or
> any nation so conceived and so dedicated, can long endure. We are met on a
> great battlefield of that war. We have come to dedicate a portion of that field,
> as a final resting place for those who here gave their lives that that nation might
> live. It is altogether fitting and proper that we should do this.
>
> But, in a larger sense, we can not dedicate — we can not consecrate —
> we can not hallow — this ground. The brave men, living and dead, who strug-
> gled here, have consecrated it, far above our poor power to add or detract.
> The world will little note, nor long remember what we say here, but it can
> never forget what they did here. It is for us the living, rather, to be dedicated
> here to the unfinished work which they who fought here have thus far so
> nobly advanced. It is rather for us to be here dedicated to the great task
> remaining before us — that from these honored dead we take increased devo-
> tion to that cause for which they gave the last full measure of devotion — that
> we here highly resolve that these dead shall not have died in vain — that this
> nation, under God, shall have a new birth of freedom — and that government
> of the people, by the people, for the people, shall not perish from the earth.[36]

The *New York Tribune* and other newspapers reported that the crowd
applauded five times during the speech and at the end there was "(Long continued applause.)" Eyewitnesses, however, described the applause as a formal
applause, paying tribute to the occasion. Chipman recalled an even more
solemn and subdued, yet appropriate, response: "A suppressed murmur of
approval, as though that vast assemblage had simultaneously drawn a deep
sigh was all the response that greeted the speaker."[37]

Persistent myths have surrounded the Gettysburg Address since soon
after Lincoln gave it. Lincoln prepared the speech on the train while traveling to Gettysburg. Lincoln gave the speech without notes. The speech fell
flat on the audience, and Lincoln, himself, thought it was a failure. "The fact
is, the reputation of no other speech in all American history has ever been so
warped by misconception and myth," says Lincoln scholar Harold Holzer.

Chipman was aware of these myths and, in the early twentieth century, as one of the last living of the people to accompany Lincoln on the platform during the speech, he felt the duty and desire to expose the myths. As late as 1922, when Chipman was 88 years old, he was still setting the record straight.[38]

Particularly pernicious, in Chipman's mind, was the myth that Lincoln did not properly prepare for the important remarks he would make at the cemetery dedication. A senator in attendance thought the speech was extemporaneous. A biographer claimed that Lincoln wrote the speech on the train on the way to Gettysburg. Chipman responded: "My belief is that Mr. Lincoln felt the significance of the event and prepared what he would say." "It is certain that he had notice of what was expected of him," asserted Chipman, "and it is improbable that he left Washington wholly unprepared with manuscript and did not know pretty nearly what he intended to say."[39]

Addressing the question of whether Lincoln had prepared the speech in advance, specifically, Chipman noted that Lincoln read from "two sheets of note paper." Describing the speech more generally, Chipman told the men of the Cherry Tree Club, "I stood by his side at Gettysburg when he delivered that marvelously beautiful tribute to the noble dead who lay at his feet. I saw him when with clear and almost angelic voice he urged his care-furrowed face towards the sky and uttered those immortal lines, speaking as one inspired, and as though in the very presence of the throne of God!" His statement that Lincoln's face was turned "towards the sky" is not inconsistent with reading the speech from "two sheets of note paper." It is reasonable that Lincoln memorized parts of it and did not peer down at the paper the whole time he spoke. While one may dispute how much of the speech Lincoln read from his two pages of note paper, it is beyond cavil that Lincoln went to Gettysburg with a speech well-prepared.[40]

If Chipman found it inconsistent with Lincoln's personality and Chipman's observations that Lincoln either prepared on the train on the way to Gettysburg or did not prepare at all, giving the speech extemporaneously, Chipman found it more distressing that the American public would think that Lincoln's speech was not well received: "Comments, mere speculation, have been made that 'it fell flat upon the audience'; that there was but slight indication of applause and that Mr. Lincoln himself felt that he had made a failure." Holzer explained the genesis of the long-standing myth: "We probably owe the legend of Lincoln's lack of enthusiasm for his own performance at Gettysburg almost entirely to Ward Hill Lamon, one of the most consistently undependable sources in the annals of Lincoln biography. It was Lamon who claimed that when Lincoln took his seat after the address, he confided sadly: 'That speech won't *scour*! It is a flat failure, and the people are disappointed." And it was Lamon who added that when they returned to Washington, Lincoln repeated: 'I tell you, Hill, that speech fell on the audience like a wet blanket. I am distressed about it. I ought to have prepared it with more care.'"[41]

"All this is idle," Chipman chided.

> No one knew better than [Lincoln] the power and force of thought well expressed; it would be an impeachment of his clarity of judgment to suppose he did not feel that he had said the right thing for the occasion and in his happiest vein. I have no distinct recollection of the matter further than I have stated. [¶] It was not a speech to elicit an outburst of applause, and to have so received it, would have belied the solemnity of the language and the manner in which he read it, for it was plain that the deepest emotions of his sympathetic nature were profoundly moved. One would as soon think of applauding the Lord's Prayer or Saint Paul's sermon on the immortality of the soul so comforting at our burial services.[42]

As a witness to the speech and its reception, Chipman denied that it was poorly received. Accompanying Lincoln back to Wills' home, Chipman overheard Everett express sentiments that Everett later repeated in a note. Lincoln warmly congratulated Everett for his oration, but Everett remonstrated, "Oh Mr. Lincoln, you said more in two minutes than I said in two hours."[43]

The impact on Chipman of the Gettysburg cemetery dedication went well beyond Lincoln's extraordinary comments. Ever after, Chipman, following Lincoln's lead, exerted great vigor in memorializing those who fought to save the Union. Two years later, he prosecuted the cruel commandant of the Andersonville Prison, where thousands of prisoners of war died unnecessarily. He participated in creating the Grand Army of the Republic, the private association for Union veterans of the war. He played a prominent role in founding Memorial Day, ensuring that the memory of the Civil War's fallen heroes would be preserved in a day dedicated to decorating their graves and remembering their sacrifices. And he chaired the committee to celebrate the first Memorial Day at what was to become another national cemetery at Arlington, Virginia. These were all actions of a man deeply impressed by the solemnity and importance of that November day in 1863.

As one who had put his own life on the line, who had charged up the hill at Fort Donelson despite the possibility, even the likelihood, he would be wounded, perhaps mortally, Chipman appreciated the ultimate sacrifice these soldiers had made and many others would make before the war ended. For the rest of his life, by both actions and declarations, he carried on with the spirit of Lincoln's words. Chipman remembered and honored the full measure of devotion through which the fallen had consecrated and dedicated not just the hallowed ground of the cemetery but the whole of the United States.

5

Wartime Washington
(1863–1864)

So Curtis was reinstated to command, though not to the same command. He took command of the Department of Kansas, headquartered at Fort Leavenworth, about 30 miles northwest of Kansas City, a new department that Lincoln and Stanton established in the West. Chipman went to assist Curtis in Kansas, although temporarily.

In the process of regaining command, Curtis eventually lost his right hand man. Lincoln and Stanton had taken note of the 29-year-old colonel who showed some effective advocacy skills. Impressed by his zealous and loyal defense of Curtis, as well as his prosecutorial debut in the War Department, they quickly decided that Curtis would no longer need Chipman's services in the West.

Chipman found it unfortunate that he would be ordered even further from the battlefield. Leaving the Second Iowa to be Curtis' chief of staff was a difficult move because Chipman felt he was abandoning his comrades who remained in the trenches. Now, leaving Curtis was also a test for Chipman. He had devoted his service and allegiance to the old Iowa general and had supported him through the loss of his command and the loss of his son. Regardless of the eventual advantages of service in the War Department and personal contact with the likes of Lincoln, Stanton, and Grant, Chipman regretted leaving Curtis.[1]

The Department of Kansas

Replacing Curtis did not end Lincoln's difficulties in Missouri. Schofield meddled in Missouri politics in ways unacceptable to Lincoln, so Lincoln determined to make another change. He and Stanton relieved Schofield of command and split the Department of the Missouri, appointing Curtis to command the newly created Department of Kansas and General William S. Rosecrans over Missouri. Regarding the cotton-trading accusations against Curtis, Lincoln, referring to his meeting with Chipman, Swett, and Brinker-hoff, "fairly presum[ed]" Curtis was innocent. "[A]s he is my friend," he told Stanton, "and, what is more, as I think, the countr[y's] friend, I would be glad to relieve him from the impression that I think him dishonest, by giving him a command." Lincoln figured that, even if this were not advantageous militarily, it served his purposes of keeping the peace and giving Curtis "great relief."[2]

Curtis' new command placed Chipman's situation in doubt again. For several months, Chipman had occupied the desk in the War Department, handled judge-advocate duties, defended Curtis to the president, and carried out personal orders from Stanton, including his Gettysburg assignment. Whether Chipman would serve the rest of the war in Washington or return to the West to lead Curtis' staff became the subject of another tug-of-war for Chipman's services during the winter of 1863-64. Chipman requested relief from his judge-advocate duties so he could return to the field as Curtis' chief of staff in the Department of Kansas. Curtis pressed the issue with the secretary of war, but Stanton allowed only a 30-day leave so Chipman could help Curtis organize the new department.[3]

In January 1864, Chipman went to Fort Leavenworth. Curtis restored to Chipman the full authority of a trusted chief of staff. Much needed to be accomplished as the usual course of a newly formed department had proceeded without the essential care of a chief administrator. Chipman surveyed the forts and troops in Kansas, relocated some of the troops, assuring vigilance among regiments, and obtained intelligence reports on the location of guerrillas in the state.[4]

This last duty was of particular concern to Curtis, as about 200 Confederate guerrillas remained in the state. Chipman embarked on a tour of troublesome areas, traveling to Olathe and returning to Fort Leavenworth via Lawrence. When he arrived again at Fort Leavenworth, Curtis was at Fort Smith, Arkansas. Chipman telegraphed him: "Returned via Lawrence. Quiet on border. Excitement allayed. Our troops vigilant; bushwhackers put on defensive. Bring 2 clerks from Eighteenth Iowa. Hope you will strengthen your escort. Guerrillas harassed and may swing around south of Fort Scott."[5]

After his advocacy on behalf of Curtis, Chipman was eager to help Curtis succeed in his new command and equally eager to have Lincoln approve. The Kansas Legislature passed a joint resolution expressing support for Curtis. Enclosing the resolution, Chipman wrote to John Nicolay, the president's personal secretary: "I think His Excellency the President will be glad to know not only that his selection of a military commander for this Department is entirely acceptable to the people, but that the almost unanimous feeling of the citizens of Kansas points to him as the rightful successor to the next Presidency." Whether this meant that Kansans supported another term for Lincoln or thought Curtis would be the next president was not clarified. In light of Chipman's political loyalty to Lincoln, it seems unlikely he meant Curtis would take Lincoln's second-term opportunity.[6]

On his way back to Fort Leavenworth from his tour of the department, Curtis paused in Fort Scott to send an urgent entreaty to Stanton: "I am highly pleased with the compliment you paid to my chief of staff, Col. N.P. Chipman, by ordering him to return to do service at your headquarters at the end of thirty days, but with great reluctance I must beg you to direct his services to continue with me for the present. He is the only man I have who understands my department office duties since the untimely death of my son and assistant adjutant-general, Major Curtis."

If Curtis thought to gain Stanton's sympathy, he may have, by detailing Chipman's strengths, sealed Stanton's decision to return Chipman to the War Department. "Besides," continued Curtis, "Colonel Chipman has a mature judgment, and acquaintance with political and personal feuds in this country, the actors being friends whom I respect, but whose partisan strifes I desire to avoid, and in my absence from headquarters he will carry on current business correctly without giving offense to any." Curtis described the necessity he had found of visiting personally the various parts of the new department and the utility of leaving Chipman at Fort Leavenworth to handle administrative duties during his absence. "I hope therefore," Curtis concluded, "you will allow Colonel Chipman to remain with me to assist in the administrative duties of this department. By complying with this request, Mr. Secretary, you will greatly oblige me, and add to many personal considerations for my requests for which I am greatly obliged and truly grateful."[7]

Not known for accommodation of personal requests, Stanton flatly rejected Curtis' appeal. Chipman returned to Washington.

Washington

In the dark, winter days of 1864, when Chipman returned to Washington from Kansas, Washington suffered from cold as much as from the deprivations of war. Noah Brooks, the Washington correspondent for the *Sacramento Daily Union*, described a city snowed in. Members of Congress struggled to find their ways back to the capital from the holiday recess. Attendance was slim at the first session as the roads were blocked with snow and several members were stranded on a ferry boat frozen in its place on the Susquehanna River. Even the severe cold could not stem the diseased, contagious conditions of the city. As poor whites and former slaves found refuge in Washington, the crowded conditions exacerbated the already unhealthy environment. As Chipman settled back into city life, a smallpox scare gripped Washingtonians. Senator Lemuel J. Bowden of West Virginia contracted the disease and succumbed to its effects. Congress immediately sought to establish new sanitary regulations for the city, as if it could legislate away the filth and disease.[8]

The continuing cold brought a new concern. The Potomac River froze, so that wagons could cross from Alexandria, Virginia. Above Washington, the ice was strong enough to bear a crossing of Confederate troops, if the Confed-

Chipman in his Civil War uniform in 1865, the year he prosecuted Henry Wirz, the commandant of the Andersonville Prison. Portrait by Mathew Brady (Library of Congress).

erate leaders should attempt it. The ice also prevented transport of provisions for the troops guarding Washington from the harbor of Alexandria. Brooks observed: "Never before — no, not even within the memory of the oldest inhabitant himself— has there been such a cold term as the present, and everybody goes about asking everybody if he ever knew the like."[9]

Chipman's duties in Washington were mainly in the office of the judge advocate general. This office, which had existed in the Revolutionary War, was reauthorized by Congress in July 1862. Congress additionally authorized the Bureau of Military Justice, attached to the War Department, in June 1864. The Bureau held court-martial proceedings against military personnel and trials by military commission against those accused of treason. Lincoln appointed Joseph Holt as judge advocate general when the office was created. In all, 39 officers, including Chipman, served in the corps of judge advocates from the creation of the office through the end of the war.[10]

Holt, a Democrat from Kentucky at the beginning of the war, campaigned for James Buchanan in 1856, and served under Buchanan as postmaster general and, briefly, secretary of war, ending with the start of the Lincoln administration. When the war began, he changed his position, becoming a fervent Unionist, convinced that secession would result in perpetual national weakness, incessant conflict, and expensive vigilance. His changing attitudes did not extend, however, to emancipation of slaves, at least not in the early war years. He criticized Frémont's attempt to emancipate slaves in Missouri and applauded Lincoln's decision to relieve Frémont of his Missouri command. Gradually, Holt's views became more consistent with the Radical Republicans who opposed slavery vehemently. He was considered as a vice-presidential candidate in 1864, and Lincoln indicated he had no quarrel with the prospect. But ultimately Andrew Johnson was selected at the convention. Chipman named Holt as one of only two men — the other Stanton — who approached Lincoln in "unbending and unceasing devotion to the restoration of the Union."[11]

While Chipman served in the War Department, Grant came to Washington. As the war progressed, generals rose and fell in prominence. The most noteworthy rise of an officer was that of Grant. From when Chipman served under him at Fort Donelson through Grant's eventual capture of Vicksburg on July 4, 1863, Grant was the most impressive Union general in the West. Because Lincoln was frustrated with the inability of other generals to make any progress against Lee in Virginia and eager to bring east the success Grant had enjoyed in the West, he worked with Congress to reauthorize the rank of lieutenant general, George Washington's old title, and gave Grant that rank, making him the highest ranking Union general. In March 1864, Grant became general-in-chief of all Union forces. Halleck, who previously held that office, became chief of staff.

Instead of taking up residence in Washington and sending his dispatches to the front, Grant set up his headquarters in City Point, just east of Richmond and Petersburg, with the Army of the Potomac. He put Sherman in command of the West and prepared a plan to defeat Lee, with his Army of Northern Virginia, and take Richmond, the Confederate capital. His coordinated strategy included campaigns on several fronts, as well as destruction of rail lines, roads, crops, and other resources essential to the South. He stayed in close communication by telegraph with Lincoln and the remainder of the Union forces. Lincoln regularly visited the telegraph office in the War Department. Chipman occasionally observed the president as he followed the progress of the war from the telegraph office. Lincoln amazed Chipman, who remembered: "He was sleepless in his vigilance and watchfulness of the progress of his army, following minutely its movements and sharing deeply the effect of its reverses and victories, not the least of his anxiety always being to stiffen the courage and hopefulness of the loyal people of the North."[12]

Of his coordinated strategy, Grant wrote in his memoirs: "My general plan now was to concentrate all the force possible against the Confederate armies in the field. There were but two such, as we have seen, east of the Mississippi River and facing north. The Army of Northern Virginia, General Robert E. Lee commanding, was on the south bank of the Rapidan, confronting the Army of the Potomac; the second, under General Joseph E. Johnston, was at Dalton, Georgia, opposed to Sherman who was still at Chattanooga. Beside these main armies the Confederates had to provide troops to guard the Shenandoah Valley, a great store-house to feed their armies, and their line of communications from Richmond to Tennessee."[13]

Philip Sheridan was another officer who rose to Union Army prominence. He graduated from West Point in 1853, but he held only low-level positions in the army before and during the first part of the Civil War. Assigned to quartermaster duties under Halleck in the West, he eventually asked to be transferred when he encountered difficulty with Curtis. Once he had the chance to show his mettle in battle command, however, Sheridan rose rapidly to command the cavalry of the Army of the Potomac under Grant and, later, to command the Army of the Shenandoah, charged with capturing and rendering the important valley useless to the Confederacy. His success made his a popular name in Washington. He was the more distinctive because of his diminutive size—five feet, five inches—but long body and arms. Chipman recalled that "[o]n horseback he looked to be quite a tall man."[14]

When Sheridan arrived from the West, he accepted an invitation from the president to a reception at the White House. Chipman knew Sheridan from their time in the West, but Holt had not met him and was anxious to make his acquaintance.

Chipman did not see Sheridan in the room, so Holt found Lincoln and asked: "Mr. President, I wish you would point out General Sheridan to me."

Lincoln straightened up and looked around the room above the heads of the others already assembled. He did not see Sheridan either, so he replied: "I don't see him, General, but I will tell you how to find him. When you see an officer who can reach down and pull on his boots without stooping, that's Sheridan."[15]

Prisoner Exchanges

One of the pressing issues facing the elected officials in Washington and the War Department in the spring of 1864 was the exchange of prisoners of war with the Confederacy. The dispute over prisoner exchanges between the Union and the Confederacy figured prominently in the conditions leading to Chipman's prosecution of Henry Wirz, the commandant of the Andersonville Prison, after the war. Cessation of prisoner exchanges resulted in a rapid increase in Union prisoners of war held in the South. Were it not for this rapid increase and the consequent prison overcrowding at a time of dwindling economic resources in the South, the deprivations of Andersonville probably would not have occurred. Using this reasoning, some have asserted that the North was responsible for the conditions at Andersonville because it would not exchange prisoners with the South during the last year of the Civil War. This is a claim that Chipman argued against for the rest of his life, devoting a chapter to prisoner exchanges in his book, *The Tragedy of Andersonville*.[16]

At the beginning of the war, prisoner exchanges were handled informally by parole — a traditional European system. Prisoners gave their word they would not rejoin the fighting until an exchange took place between the Union and Confederate commanders. They were released to go home until the Union and Confederacy could agree on their exchange for enemy prisoners who had also been paroled. The federal government did not officially condone these exchanges, but allowed them. As the war escalated, the potential for abuse in the loose parole system became evident. Some soldiers impressed into service submitted themselves to capture intentionally so they could go home. Although paroled soldiers not yet exchanged could not return to military service, they were sometimes used in duties that relieved others to go to battle. Additionally, questions arose concerning whether some enemies, especially guerrillas, should be treated as prisoners of war or simply as criminals. This latter problem perplexed Chipman, especially as he assisted Curtis in dealing with captured guerrillas who, though fighting on behalf of the Confederacy, did not observe the traditional laws of war.[17]

The federal government avoided, for a time, any formal exchange agreement, desiring not to acknowledge the Confederacy as a legitimate government. But practical considerations finally overrode these concerns, and the Union and the Confederacy entered into a cartel — a formal prisoner exchange agreement. In the summer of 1862, each government appointed exchange commissioners and agreed to exchange physically at City Point, Virginia and Vicksburg, Mississippi. Tables for the value of prisoners assigned the number of enlisted men to be exchanged for the various officer ranks. Surplus prisoners from the equal exchange were paroled until they could be included in a formal exchange. Pursuant to this cartel, Chipman took prisoners from St. Louis to City Point in June 1863, at the time Curtis was relieved of duty in Missouri.

The Confederacy tended to benefit more from this cartel because it had fewer men available to conscript into service and therefore could not afford to lose them as prisoners to the North. The Confederacy, itself, believed it received the greater benefit from the prisoner exchanges. Colonel Robert Ould, the Confederate exchange commissioner, boasted that the South was sending "miserable wretches" to the North in exchange for "some of the best material [he] ever saw."[18]

Nevertheless, as the Union gained the advantage in battles in Gettysburg and Vicksburg, and the South's reinforcements became scarce, the Confederacy violated the cartel. In the Union's victory at Vicksburg, large numbers of Confederate troops were taken as prisoners of war and paroled in the South. The Confederate general unilaterally declared these troops exchanged and used them in battle at Chickamauga — an important Confederate victory.

On October 20, 1863, Halleck wrote to Grant, who was then at Louisville, Kentucky:

> It is now ascertained that the greater part of the prisoners paroled by you at Vicksburg (July 4th), and General Banks at Port Hudson, were illegally and improperly declared exchanged, and forced into the ranks to swell the rebel numbers at Chickamauga. This outrageous act, in violation of the laws of war, of the cartel entered into by the rebel authorities, and all sense of honor, gives us a lesson in regard to the character of the enemy with whom we are contending. He neither regards the rules of civilized warfare, nor even his most solemn engagements. You may, therefore, expect to meet in arms thousands of unexchanged prisoners released by you and others on parole, not to serve again until duly exchanged.[19]

The South's violations of the cartel, the North's evaluation that the cartel favored the South, and, finally, the Emancipation Proclamation contributed to the end of the prisoner exchange cartel. The federal government's original policy was to prevent slaves from coming into Union lines and to return those who did to their owners. The purpose was to maintain the loyalty of border-state slaveholders.

General Benjamin F. Butler, serving in Virginia, came up with a theory that would allow the Union to harbor escaped slaves while still assuring loyal slaveholders that the aim of the government was not to abolish slavery. Because slaves were property, as the Supreme Court decreed in the *Dred Scott* case, the Union seized them from the enemy as "contraband" of war, just like any other enemy property useful to the Union. Chipman found this theory despicable, even if it was useful: "It has always seemed to me that a much broader principle was applicable to these unfortunate human beings, which would carry with it, under the existing circumstances, a right to freedom, and to be treated by us as entitled to such right, and not merely as property contraband of war."[20]

As had the Confederates, the Union benefited from the support the slaves gave the active military — building, maintaining, feeding, washing, and doing other tasks. Additionally, and perhaps more importantly, this deprived the slaves' masters of their services. In December 1861, Secretary of War Simon Cameron reported to Congress that the escaped slaves "constitute[d] a military resource, and being such, that they not be turned over to the enemy, is too plain to discuss." Congress responded with a resolution that the resources of the military should not be used to return escaped slaves to their masters.[21]

The next logical step was to enlist black men in active combat. Long before enlistment of "contrabands" became generally accepted in the Union ranks, Union General David Hunter, in South Carolina, organized former slaves into a fighting regiment. Called on by Congress to explain his departure from Union policy concerning "fugitive slaves," Hunter responded with reasoning that intrigued Chipman. Hunter noted that there were no fugitive slaves within his ranks because it was the masters, not the slaves, who had fled, in the face of Union advance: "[N]o regiment of 'fugitive slaves' has been or is being organized in this department. There is, however, a fine regiment of persons whose late masters are 'fugitive rebels'— men who everywhere fly before the appearance of the national flag, leaving their servants behind them to shift as best they can for themselves." In any event, reasoned Hunter, he had been authorized to utilize the services of anyone loyal to the Union and there had been no limitation based on skin color, so he formed the regiment under official authority.[22]

From June 1862, when Hunter responded to Congress, to September when Lincoln issued the preliminary Emancipation Proclamation and January 1863 as Lincoln signed the final proclamation, the idea of arming the freed slaves gained in popular northern support, even if the support was not universal. Lincoln's proclamation declared that former slaves "of suitable condition, will be received into the armed service of the United States to garrison forts, positions, stations, and other places, and to man vessels of all sorts in said service." Chipman justified this stand "on principles of international law [and] of self-preservation...." "[A]nd on the part of the slaves," Chipman continued, their enlistment "was as an acknowledgement of a reciprocal obligation due for the protection and freedom bestowed upon them."[23]

The Confederate response was vindictive, though consistent with its policy of preserving slavery and punishing anyone who would interfere. The rebel congress determined that any white Union officer captured in command of black troops would be guilty of inciting insurrection and executed as a felon. The black troops would either be restored to their masters or put to hard labor. This threat of punishment against white officers was carried out in June 1863. One of Confederate General Richard Taylor's brigades attacked a Union garrison made up almost entirely of black soldiers at Milliken's Bend, above Vicksburg. Outmanned and outgunned, the Union troops fought bravely, even ferociously, after it became known that their fellow black soldiers taken prisoner were murdered by the Confederate troops. They successfully repelled the attack and received commendations from Grant and the War Department. It was reported that some of the white officers who were captured were formally hanged by Taylor's order.[24]

With these developments, the federal government faced a dilemma. It could submit to the South's determination not to treat black soldiers as prisoners of war captured in battle by continuing prisoner exchanges or it could demand appropriate treatment of blacks. The latter position would effectively end prisoner exchanges if the Confederacy held to its position, which it did. Grant determined that the United States could not abandon the black troops and therefore ordered cessation of exchanges. Of this decision, Chipman recorded: "A government that would withhold its protection from such men and such of its defenders would be unworthy fighting for. It cannot for a moment be admitted that our government was wrong in the stand it took on this issue. It would have been a dastardly betrayal of its duty to defenders of the Union to have yielded its position and conceded to the rebel government the right to treat our officers as felons and enslave our soldiers."[25]

After consultation with Stanton, Grant, on April 17, 1864, suspended all prisoner exchanges until the North and South could agree on the status of black prisoners and of the prisoners paroled from Vicksburg and Port Hudson. The population in prison camps, both North and South, swelled dramatically. The South desperately sought further exchanges, though without resolving the questions Grant raised, so the North refused.

On August 18, four months after the interruption of the cartel, Grant wrote: "It is hard on our men held in Southern prisons not to exchange them, but it is humanity to those left in the ranks to fight our battles. Every man we hold, when released on parole or otherwise, becomes an active soldier against us at once either directly or indirectly. If we commence a system of exchange which liberates all prisoners taken, we will have to fight on until the whole South is exterminated. If we hold those caught they amount to no more than dead men. At this particular time to release all rebel prisoners the North would insure Sherman's defeat and would compromise our safety here."[26]

Chipman worried that the world would remember Grant's statement, just quoted, as the primary reason for the interruption of the prisoner exchange cartel without considering the South's violations of the cartel and treatment of black troops and their white officers. After the war, rebel sympathizers erected a monument honoring the commandant of the Andersonville prison. On it, they inscribed Grant's statement, selectively deleting references to the South's violation of the cartel and Grant's conclusion that continuation of the cartel, with the South utilizing all paroled prisoners, though unexchanged, would result in the South's extermination. "It is cowardly and atrocious at this day," Chipman maintained, "to attribute blame to our government for the wanton cruelties to prisoners at Andersonville, in its stand taken with reference to colored troops and their officers, the justice and humanity of which no one not blinded by hatred and prejudice can gainsay."[27]

Early's Raid on Washington

In the summer of 1864, as the war approached Washington, Chipman's value as a lawyer in the Bureau of Military Justice declined as his usefulness as a veteran of battle and a chief of staff grew. It began when Grant, as part of his strategy to weaken the South, sent General Hunter and his forces to the Shenandoah Valley to destroy that source of Confederate sustenance and tear up the Virginia Central Railroad. The Shenandoah Valley was not only a fertile region loyal to the Confederacy but also a natural highway into the North, the route by which Lee's army had encroached into the North the prior summer, culminating in the Battle of Gettysburg. With Lee hunkered down against Grant along the Richmond and Petersburg front, Hunter swept through the valley, his forces destroying and looting, and occupied Lexington. They burned the Virginia Military Institute, which was also the site of a substantial arsenal. Hunter's success forced Lee to send General Jubal Early from the Richmond and Petersburg front — part of Grant's plan to weaken Lee's defenses. On June 17, Early met Hunter near Lynchburg, part way between Lexington in the Shenandoah Valley and the Richmond and Petersburg front, but Hunter had made the critical mistake of advancing without sufficient ammunition. After a fierce engagement, Hunter withdrew to the west, which eventually forced him to take a roundabout route by way of the Ohio River and the Baltimore and Ohio Railroad to return to the Potomac. Early chased him for two days, well into West Virginia, then returned to the Shenandoah Valley.

Hunter's expulsion from Virginia and the Shenandoah Valley created an open corridor through the valley to Washington, and Early took it. This permitted Lee to turn the tables on Grant and force Grant to send some of his troops to defend the capital. But Grant's reinforcements under General Horatio Wright, advancing north, were not on a course to reach Washington before Early. In Hunter's absence, General Lew Wallace, commanding a smaller, less-experienced force at Baltimore, went to meet Early at the northeast end of the Shenandoah Valley. At the Monocacy River, in Maryland, northwest of Washington, Wallace battled Early. As expected Early prevailed with his larger and more experienced corps, but the engagement cost Early a day on his march. A grateful Grant praised Wallace's effort, in the face of "almost forlorn hope": "If Early had been but one day earlier he might have entered the capital before the arrival of the reinforcements I had sent. Whether the delay caused by the battle amounted to a day or not, General Wallace contributed on this occasion, by the defeat of the troops under him a greater benefit to the cause than often falls to the lot of a commander of an equal force to render by means of a victory."[28]

Government clerks, mechanics, and carpenters joined the inexperienced guards garrisoned in Washington in the numerous small forts spread around the city. On July 11, 1864, Early, with his tired army, numbering about 12,000, arrived at the fortifications northeast of the city. The improvised garrisons made their best showing of force, dissuading Early from immediately attacking. Lincoln, himself, went out to Fort Stevens to examine the action.

Washington was so unprepared for an attack that the military authorities were in the dark concerning the strength of the Union troops in and around the city. In the evening, Stanton hastily called for Chipman and instructed him to survey the strength of capital troops under the command of General Alexander McCook and report on the extent of fighting that occurred during the day. Chipman spent most of the night moving among the fortifications to get an accurate number of troops and pulling together a detailed report of engagements between Union and Confederate forces. Chipman's report, delivered the next morning, revealed that McCook's troops numbered less than 8,000, as opposed to Early's 12,000. Aside from scattered skirmishing, there had been no engagements. Chipman informed Stanton that "[a] rebel sharpshooter just wounded severely a soldier standing on the parapet of Fort Stevens."[29]

During Chipman's nocturnal survey of troops, reinforcements under Wright began to arrive from Virginia. They were battle-tested veterans, capable of defending the capital much better than the ragtag garrison that demonstrated for Early the day before. On the morning of July 12, Early's troops were rested and in place to attack, but the city was now well protected. His report finished, Chipman returned to Fort Stevens, where he saw his first combat since being wounded at Fort Donelson 29 months earlier. Observers reported that more than just soldiers like Chipman rushed to Fort Stevens. Curious citizens came in carriages, on horseback, and on foot to see the war up close for the first time, the president among them.

Lincoln's secretary, John Nicolay, saw those July 1864 events from much the same perspective as Chipman. "Certain writers," wrote Nicolay, "have represented the government as panic-stricken during the two days that this menace lasted; but neither Mr. Lincoln, nor Secretary Stanton, nor General Halleck, whom it was been even more the fashion to abuse, lacked coolness or energy in the emergency. Indeed, the President's personal unconcern was such as to give his associates much uneasiness."[30]

Margaret Leech, Civil War historian, commented: "The capital, in 1864, was too sophisticated for panic. No city ever heard the noise of cannon in its suburbs with a greater appearance of *sang-froid*.... Sight-seers were still thronging out toward Fort Stevens, some of them seeking word of relatives and friends.... They were so numerous that they interfered with the movement of the army wagons, and orders were issued to turn them back.... Nonchalance had become the fashion in Washington." The Lincolns rode in a carriage out to Fort Stevens with several members of the cabinet and of Congress. Again, as he had the day before, Lincoln watched the battle from the fort, clambering to the top of the parapet to get a better view. Within three feet of the president, a surgeon was killed by a Confederate sharpshooter's bullet. Lincoln's tall figure stuck out in the crowd, making an easy target for the next marksman. Seeing the president, Wright sent his aide Oliver Wendell Holmes, the future Supreme Court justice, to chastise the president. "Get down, you fool!" yelled Holmes.[31]

Although there was some confusion among Union troops because of misunderstandings about who was in command and of what troops, some of the reinforcements, though intended to be kept in reserve, moved into the front positions. At Fort Stevens, some of the artillery was manned by injured gunners from Washington hospitals. Though disorganized, the defense was effective. After a one-day battle, Early lost his nerve and retreated. As dusk fell, the city saw clouds of dust kicked up in the distance as the Confederate troops receded toward the northwest.[32]

The dead and wounded were carried back into the city, and it began to dawn on the previously unconcerned citizenry how close the capital had come to capture. Early told his staff officers: "We didn't take Washington, but we scared Abe Lincoln like Hell." "If General Early had had the nerve and had pushed his army after the battle of Monocacy," assessed Chipman, "he could have marched into the city with little resistance or loss. A day's delay gave Grant the opportunity to send Wright's corps from City Point, and Washington was saved. Indeed, but for General Wallace's gallant resistance at Monocacy, Washington and Baltimore would have temporarily been occupied by the rebel army and the rebel prisoners at Point Lookout set at liberty."[33]

6

Restoration of the Union (1864–1865)

General Jubal Early's advance up the Shenandoah Valley, assault on Washington, and escape back through the valley reemphasized the strategic importance of the valley, not just as an avenue to the North, but equally an economic boon to the South. Grant realized that he had to neutralize the valley, thus preventing further threats to Washington and eliminating the rejuvenating resources the valley had provided to Lee. The valley had also become politically important. Further failure there could hamper Lincoln's chances of reelection in November 1864. During the critical months between July and November 1864, Chipman participated, militarily and politically, in the events, many of them in the valley, that turned the ultimate course of the war and public opinion in the North in favor of Lincoln.

Increasingly, in the summer and fall of 1864, Secretary Stanton took Chipman away from his duties in the Bureau of Military Justice and sent him into the field both to act as messenger between Washington and the field generals and to be the eyes and ears of Stanton and Lincoln concerning the unfolding events close to Washington and into the valley.

Once the threat to Washington, itself, had been eliminated and Sheridan had achieved success in the valley, so long desired by the Union, Chipman returned to his duties in the bureau and spent the rest of the war in Washington, except for a brief leave to marry Belle Holmes in St. Louis. As the war ended and Lincoln was assassinated, Chipman viewed these events from an intimate Washington standpoint.

Sheridan in the Shenandoah

The speed and accuracy with which Chipman responded to Stanton's requests for information concerning the defenses of Washington as Early approached moved Stanton to pull Chipman closer to him in the ensuing months. As Early retreated up the Potomac River and back toward the Shenandoah Valley, Stanton wanted frequent and reliable updates on Early's location and the Federals' pursuit. He and Lincoln sent Chipman into the field as their personal liaison, then awaited his dispatches in the War Department.

General Hunter was in command of the troops chasing Early, but there was insufficient communication from Hunter to Stanton, at least in Stanton's estimation. The troops were scattered and the strength of the troops under the command of Hunter was unknown. Chipman's assignment was to go into the field, assess the strength and success of the troops, and send frequent telegrams to the War Department. On July 14, Chipman went to Baltimore's Camden Station and then traveled to Monocacy on the Baltimore and Ohio Railroad. At each stop, he informed Stanton of the location, strength, and leadership of Union troops. His last telegram of the day, from Monocacy, informed Stanton that he was awaiting horses to continue on to the valley.[1]

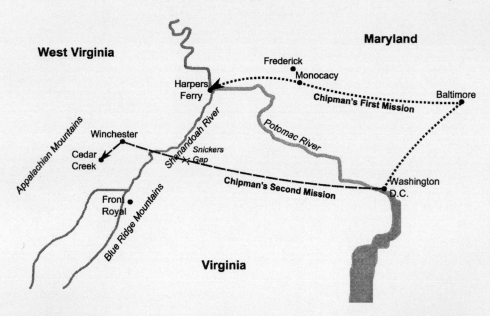

In July 1864, Stanton sent Chipman on a mission to reconnoiter Early's retreat after attacking Washington (Chipman's First Mission). In August 1864, Lincoln and Stanton sent Chipman on a mission to the Shenandoah Valley to warn Sheridan of Confederate reinforcements entering the valley (Chipman's Second Mission).

Chipman traveled through the night and obtained better information concerning Hunter's activities in the valley. Enemy forces were still retreating, with a small number left to guard the train of wagons carrying the plunder from the North, but Union troops were too tired to attack. By 8 A.M., Chipman was at Harpers Ferry, at the confluence of the Shenandoah and Potomac Rivers, along with Hunter. Having established communication lines between Hunter and Stanton and apprised Stanton of the location and strength of the Union forces, Chipman reversed course to return to Washington, taking no time to rest.[2]

With Hunter's forces aligned mainly on the north side of the Potomac and Early's on the south, no progress was made in July toward the Union's objectives in the valley. Early's presence continued to threaten the North. On July 30, Early sent General John McCausland, with his Confederate cavalry, into Chambersburg, Pennsylvania to demand a ransom of $500,000 in currency or $100,000 worth of gold. McCausland crossed the Potomac, entered Chambersburg, and made Early's demand. When the town would not oblige, McCausland burned much of the town and escaped back into Confederate lines. This incident, perhaps as much as any, succeeded in drawing Grant's attention away from Richmond and Petersburg. Ready to commit an adequate number of troops and aggressive leadership to the valley, Grant went personally to Monocacy to meet General Sheridan, Hunter's replacement, and give him his orders.[3]

Sheridan had continued to make a name for himself commanding the cavalry of the Army of the Potomac through the spring and early summer of 1864. General George G. Meade, Sheridan's immediate commander, tried to restrict Sheridan's role and reprimanded him for shoddy reconnaissance, so Sheridan went over Meade's head to Grant and secured permission to run raids on Confederate positions. He took credit for eliminating Confederate cavalry commander J.E.B. Stuart, who was known for his raids into the North, which terrorized northerners and boosted southerners' morale. Stuart's cavalry engaged Sheridan's, but a Union sharpshooter found Stuart, who died a day later in Richmond. While Sheridan's raids were not fully successful, overcoming Stuart was symbolic of the rise of Union cavalry and decline of Confederate cavalry.

To respond to the continuing threat of Early's presence in the valley, with its access to Washington, Grant put Sheridan in command of the Army of the Shenandoah. Grant knew that Sheridan's success was important for the protection of Washington and the elimination of the valley as a resource for the South, but also because the 1864 election was approaching and, as the war went, so went Lincoln's popularity.

On August 4, Grant and Sheridan met at Monocacy. After the meeting,

Philip Sheridan led Union forces in the Shenandoah Valley in the summer of 1864, rendering the valley and its resources unavailable to the Confederacy (Library of Congress).

Sheridan left immediately to take command of the troops, enlarged with troops from other commands, and prepared to attack. Already alarmed at the Union troop buildup, Early began to retreat through the valley. On August 10, Sheridan's troops advanced and, for the next two days, Sheridan pushed forward and Early retreated, offering little resistance.[4]

On August 12, however, Sheridan paused because rumors reached him of possible reinforcements to Early's command. Having advanced into valley, where the residents were loyal to the Confederacy, Sheridan knew his supply and communication lines were at risk. Sheridan was also concerned about the location and activities of Confederate officer John Mosby and his guerrillas. A native of Virginia, Mosby was known for his surprise raids on Union positions, even inside enemy lines, and his ability to disappear into the country-side, prompting the nickname, the "Gray Ghost." On the day Sheridan stopped moving up the valley, Mosby, with 330 men, entered the valley through Snicker's Gap, behind Sheridan's position, and, the next day, attacked a wagon train of Union supplies on its way to Sheridan. Mosby's victory over the wagon train was complete. More than 500 mules, 36 horses, and 200 head of cattle were captured, with more than 200 Union soldiers. Many Union soldiers died in the attack, and 100 wagons were destroyed. Mosby's men reveled in wearing the bright new uniforms of the captured Union officers. At the approach of the parade of captured loot, prisoners, and these rebel soldiers clad in Union uniforms, the residents weren't sure whether to stand and cheer or to run.[5]

The rumors that caused Sheridan to halt were based on fact. Back at City Point, Grant's headquarters in Virginia, Grant had received intelligence that Sheridan's activities in the valley had already had one desired effect: Lee had sent some of his troops from Richmond to reinforce Early. Grant sent a telegram to Halleck in Washington. The telegram instructed Halleck: "Inform Sheridan that it is now certain two divisions of infantry have gone to Early, and some cavalry and twenty pieces of artillery. This movement commenced last Saturday night. He must be cautious and act now on the defensive until movements here force them to detach to send this way. Early's force, with this increase, cannot exceed 40,000 men, but this is too much for Sheridan to attack."[6]

Halleck took Grant's telegram to Stanton, and Stanton informed Lincoln. In the late night hours of August 12, Chipman received a note from the adjutant-general's office to meet Stanton there immediately. He arose, dressed, and hurried to the meeting. Upon his arrival, he found Lincoln, Stanton, and Halleck waiting for him. Stanton explained Chipman's mission. Grant's intelligence report was to be delivered to Sheridan in person. Sheridan was vulnerable and, without the intelligence, he was open to catastrophic attack. The arrival of the additional Confederate forces into the valley on Sheridan's flank would allow Early to practically surround Sheridan. As a result of Sheridan's advance into the valley, he was not available for telegraphic communications because the Union's telegraph lines did not extend that far.

Lincoln interrupted Stanton's directions and impressed on Chipman the importance of his mission. Others had failed to get to Sheridan with routine communications, but this message was critical.[7]

Lincoln asked Chipman if he thought he could get through to Sheridan.

"It won't be my fault if I fail," responded Chipman, duly impressed by the solemnity of Lincoln's inquiry.

"Don't say fail," chided Lincoln. "That word is not in a soldier's dictionary."[8]

Stanton had already put into action a plan to get Chipman to Sheridan. He ordered a good and reliable cavalry regiment to be ready: "The regiment should be fully provided with ammunition, and, if necessary, sufficient must be taken from other regiments to complete its supply. The escort will take the shortest route to and through Snicker's Gap. Colonel Chipman will reach your headquarters this P.M., and it is desirable that there be no delay in the movement of the regiment after he reports."[9]

Chipman left Lincoln, Stanton, and Halleck, and went to the outskirts of Washington, where he met his escort regiment. Following Stanton's instructions, they cut across Virginia with the intent to enter the valley through Snicker's Gap, rather than going to the north end of the valley. Although faster for the horseback messenger, it was more difficult and, as Chipman was to find, more dangerous.

The intelligence shared with Chipman before he left Washington did not include the presence of Mosby's guerrillas in the north end of the valley. Moving through Snicker's Gap on August 13, Chipman did not know he was right on the heels of Mosby, who had just finished capturing the wagon train. After Chipman entered the valley and as he approached Winchester, his escort regiment was alerted to trouble ahead when the men heard shooting. Mosby had ambushed another, smaller wagon train. Chipman's mission was to deliver the message to Sheridan, not to engage the enemy, so his strategy was avoidance and progress up the valley, to the south. Capture would mean failure, and Chipman's direction from Lincoln was not to let that happen.

This was Mosby Country, the territory of the modern-day John Mosby Highway, where the guerrillas knew every nook and cranny and the residents wanted nothing more than for Mosby to ride through. Some of the guerrillas had already shot at the escort regiment from a distance. With some of the guerrillas in sight, about a half mile away, on horseback, Chipman asked a resident whether he had seen Mosby's men that day.

"Oh no sir, there are none of them in this neighborhood," said the resident.

Pointing to the horsemen, Chipman demanded, "Who are these men?"

"I don't know. I reckon they are some of the neighbors going to town," ventured the resident.

Chipman knew the resident was lying, and he told him so.

Continuing on, but still without the information they needed on Mosby's whereabouts, Chipman asked a group of villagers. But he received no better response than he had received from his previous contact.

Realizing it would be impossible to get accurate information from the locals in a conventional way, by asking, Chipman settled on a more productive plan. When the regiment came to a mountaineer's hut, Chipman knocked on the door. There was no answer. He broke the door down and, after a search, found the frightened owner, with his wife and half a dozen children, in the attic. They hauled the man down. Chipman drew his gun on the man and, doing his best imitation of a southerner and "in language less polite than profane," as Chipman later remembered, demanded to know whether there were any "Yanks" in the area and when "our Major Mosby passed along." The ruse worked despite Chipman's obvious Union officer's uniform because Mosby's men regularly imitated Union troops. Chipman told an audience in his Iowa hometown just a couple months later that "after some hesitation, and being convinced from our manner that if we weren't guerillas we ought to be, he told me all about the whereabouts of the guerilla we most desired to avoid."[10]

Early on the morning of August 14, Chipman arrived at the main Union Army encampment near Cedar Creek, found Sheridan, and delivered his message. Staying with Sheridan, he sent the escort regiment back to Washington with a note to Stanton: "Arrived this A.M., 6 o'clock, having marched 90 miles in 24 hours. Mosby's gang hung on our flank between Goose Creek and Snicker's Gap, firing into our rear at the Gap."[11]

"What News Now?"

The information that Chipman delivered to Sheridan in the dispatch from Grant proved indispensable to Sheridan. In his final report of his activities in the valley, made after the war, Sheridan recounted:

> The receipt of this dispatch was very important to me, as I possibly would have remained in uncertainty as to the character of the [Confederate] force coming in on my flank and rear until it attacked my cavalry, as it did on the 16th. I at once looked over the map of the Valley for a defensive line — that is, where a smaller number of troops could hold a greater number — and could see but one such. I refer to that at Halltown, in front of Harpers Ferry. Subsequent experience has convinced me that no other really defensive line exists in the Shenandoah Valley. I therefore determined to move back to Halltown, carry out my instructions to destroy forage and subsistence, and increase my strength.[12]

After delivering his message, Chipman remained with Sheridan for two weeks until August 29, when Stanton sent Chipman a telegram saying, "There seems to be no further occasion for you to remain at Harpers Ferry and you are much needed here." During those two weeks, Chipman kept Stanton and Lincoln apprised of the situation in the valley. Sheridan gradually moved back to Harpers Ferry, moving just a short distance each day and showing Early by his demonstrations that he was ready for a fight at any time. The Union troops carefully watched Snicker's Gap and other routes by which Early's army might try to get through to Washington again. The troops also guarded against any further incursions into Pennsylvania.

Sheridan's confidence was infectious, and those under his command were sure they could prevail in battle. Sheridan's men were also of the mistaken impression that their force was larger than it actually was. Somehow, this mistaken impression made it to Early in the form of intelligence, thereby dissuading him from attacking, even when he had numerical superiority. Although it was Sheridan who was retreating and actual battle was limited to long-range firing and scattered skirmishes, it seemed to Chipman that because Early was afraid to attack and could no longer approach Washington or plunder Pennsylvania, the advantage and, indeed, the victory in this campaign was the Union's.[13]

With daily reports from Harpers Ferry, even multiple reports on some days, Chipman could not assuage the voracious appetites of Lincoln and Stanton for information. Stanton could be cranky when the telegrams were slow in coming and did not contain as much information as he felt there should be. On a day when Chipman made no report because he had nothing to report, Stanton telegraphed at 8 P.M., "What news have you to-day? We have heard nothing." Chipman responded, reiterating the position of the troops and relating that he had not learned of anything going on at the front. On another day, Chipman sent a telegram at 5 A.M., reporting that all was quiet on the front and passing along a dispatch from a cavalry officer who was guarding the flank. Later in the day, Stanton shot back a message chastising Chipman for leaving out some details. A quick learner, Chipman's later dispatches included the details Stanton craved. Despite his criticisms, however, Stanton expressed appreciation to Chipman for his service at Harpers Ferry.[14]

Lincoln, known for his frequent visits to the War Department telegraph office, kept a close watch on the correspondence between Chipman and Stanton, showing his interest in Sheridan's success in the valley. On August 20, Chipman and Stanton exchanged several telegrams, Chipman reporting and Stanton giving directions and asking questions. The next day, fighting became somewhat heated on the front, but Chipman's instructions were to stay at Harpers Ferry and not to venture out to the front. At about 3 P.M., there came to Chipman a three-word telegram from Lincoln, himself: "What news now?" Chipman was accustomed to communications with Stanton, but not so much with the president. Within a short time, Chipman sent his report directly to the "President of the United States," stating, "Without myself having been to the front, from the best sources of information the following is true: Two rebel divisions came down the Martinsburg road; attacked suddenly a part of Sixth Corps at inspection and at first drove them. Our troops rallied and in turn drove the enemy. The force engaged increased on both sides and was apparently kept up pretty hotly for three hours, not extending, however, to general engagement. Artillery firing still continues and seems to have shifted to the left of Charlestown. Cannot hear the musketry at this writing. Will have messenger from the front soon."[15]

Chipman's response to Lincoln must have prompted some discussion between the president and his secretary of war because, within a few hours, Stanton notified Chipman, "You may go to the front if you wish, keeping me advised of the condition of things." Within the next day, Chipman had not only gone to the front but had traversed the entire front line, collecting all the news he could find for Washington.[16]

During his time at Harpers Ferry and on the front, Chipman developed a friendship with and admiration for Sheridan. Often at Sheridan's tent at the break of dawn with instructions from Stanton or to get from Sheridan what information he could, Chipman earned Sheridan's confidence and trust. A more self-conscious leader may have felt threatened by the presence of one who reported straight to that leader's superiors, but Sheridan thrived on the close connections that the telegraph and a diligent go-between provided. He used well the intelligence that he obtained from Grant through Washington. Chipman reported to Stanton that "Sheridan's army is in splendid condition," and even ventured to predict that "Sheridan will begin from this time to harass [the enemy], and cannot fail to inflict severe punishment before they leave the Valley."[17]

Although it took the rest of the summer and most of the fall, Chipman's prediction was borne out as Sheridan moved up the valley, inflicting losses on Early's army, laying waste to the crops upon which much of not only the valley but also Richmond subsisted, and tearing up the railroad and waterways that delivered those crops. By October, Sheridan had prevailed in the valley and returned to fight under Grant at Richmond during the final stages of the war.

Nicolay summed up the success and effect of Sheridan's work in the valley:

> General Sheridan, being placed in command of the Middle Military Division and given an army of thirty or forty thousand men, finally drove back the Confederate detachments upon Richmond, in a series of brilliant victories, and so devastated the southern end of the valley as to render it untenable for either army; and by the destruction of the James River Canal and the Virginia Central Railroad, succeeded in practically carrying out Grant's intention of effectually closing the avenue of supplies to Richmond from the northwest.[18]

Sheridan's victory in the valley, combined with other Union victories, sealed Lincoln's reelection bid against General George B. McClellan. In the November election, Lincoln, with his running mate, Andrew Johnson, received 212 electoral votes to McClellan's 21. On Election Day, McClellan resigned his high commission, which was then given to Sheridan, a situation which Nicolay saw as "a fit type and illustration of the turn in the tide of affairs, which was to sweep from that time rapidly onward to the great decisive national triumph."[19]

Grant recognized that the successes of Sherman in Georgia and Sheridan in the Shenandoah Valley did more to aid Lincoln's reelection than "all the speeches, all the bonfires, and all the parading with banners and bands of music in the North."[20]

Victory Over the Rebellion

Before the election, Chipman obtained leave to travel west. Since his return to Washington from Kansas, he had left the capital only on official duty. The short respite from duty allowed him to visit home and family, and to campaign on behalf of Lincoln. It gave him great pleasure to deliver a speech to the same hometown crowd that had cheered his speech almost four years earlier when the town responded with gusto to Lincoln's call for volunteers.

It is also gave Chipman the opportunity to visit St. Louis during this leave, to see Belle Holmes, as he and Belle planned their January wedding.

No longer needed in the field, Chipman returned to his work in the Bureau. The Union made steady progress toward victory, and the North rallied behind Lincoln and the troops. In the dead of winter, Chipman returned to St. Louis. He married Belle on January 30, 1865. Reverend Samuel Niccolls, in his first year of a 50-year ministry, performed the ceremony in the Presbyterian Church in St. Louis. With no time for a honeymoon, they returned to Washington, where Belle set up housekeeping.[21]

In early April, all eyes were on the news from Virginia. As Grant prepared to take Richmond, he invited Lincoln and Stanton to his headquarters. Lincoln departed soon after his second inauguration, but Stanton fell ill and stayed in Washington. Always concerned for the president's safety, Stanton, still ill but active nonetheless, communicated by telegraph to ensure Lincoln's safe arrival. Anticipatory calm replaced the usual political contempt and criticism in the capital. On Sunday, April 2, Lee sent a note to Jefferson Davis, who was at church, that Richmond must be evacuated. As the Confederate government moved out, Grant's army moved in, taking the city on April 3. Lincoln wired Stanton in the War Department that Richmond was captured.

On duty in the War Department telegraph office, 16-year-old Willie Kettles handled the telegram. Upsetting an inkwell, he passed the news to another telegraph operator who threw open the windows and shouted the news to the people on the street below: "Richmond has surrendered!" The news quickly reached Stanton who found Kettles, opened the window, hoisted the startled telegraph operator, and announced to the growing crowd, "My friends, here is the young man who received the telegram which tells us of the fall of Richmond!"[22]

Thousands swarmed outside the War Department to drink in the news and celebrate. Beside himself with joy, Stanton ran through the halls and embraced members of his staff. He ran down Chipman and dragged him to the front of the building. Stanton spoke to the throng assembled outside the War Department. Doing his best to bridle his enthusiasm, he invoked divine guidance "to teach us how to be humble in the midst of triumph." Presenting Chipman to the revelers, Stanton demanded that Chipman address the people. Chipman obliged, and joined in the reverie, caught up in the elation of the moment, yet amazed at the secretary's departure from his customary austere and exacting attitude.

All of Washington spilled out into the streets, celebrating and giving thanks. Eight hundred guns fired salutes — 300 for Petersburg and 500 for Richmond.[23]

In the days that followed, Washington was decorated in colorful flags, patriotic mottoes, and lighting of every type. Even the capital's citizens who secretly sympathized with the South joined in the reverie of relief at the end of hostilities in Virginia. "[I]f all who lighted up such mottoes are sincerely loyal," observed Noah Brooks, "Washington has been dreadfully slandered. I am very sure that there were not a few illuminated houses and stores the owners of which would have cheerfully eaten every candle that they lighted up if they could have thereby prevented the victory they have celebrated. But we will not cavil at their coerced loyalty; I guess they are glad the war is over, anyhow." Voicing a different opinion, Vice President Andrew Johnson ranted from the portico at the Patent Office that Jefferson Davis should be hanged for treason.[24]

On April 9, Grant telegraphed Stanton from Appomattox Court House: "General Lee surrendered the Army of Northern Virginia this afternoon on terms proposed by myself." The news of the surrender did not set off the same hysteria that greeted the news of the fall of Richmond. But Lincoln's return from Virginia that evening prompted crowds to gather at the White House, demanding to hear from their commander-in-chief. He made an appearance, to peals of passionate cheering, but preferred to defer his remarks to a later, more formal, pronouncement. The Chipmans, too, were caught up in the spirit of the celebration and participated at times, but Chipman's work in the bureau remained pressing. So Belle, with her friends, carried on without the dutiful colonel.[25]

Lincoln's Assassination

As Washington celebrated, a measure of relief graced the president. In his last sitting for photographer Alexander Gardner, Lincoln's face, especially his eyes, showed the effects of four years of wearying concern and taxing emotion. Yet it also showed a serenity not before evident. Chipman recalled: "[F]rom the day of the second inauguration Mr. Lincoln was to be given less than five weeks to live. But he was to have the satisfaction of witnessing the crowning glory of his Administration — the overthrow of rebellion, the re-establishment of the Union, and the extirpation of slavery forever from our fair land. His last days were filled with anxious thoughts and with a full comprehension that the termination of the war would bring with it new and profoundly complex and difficult problems of government. He was now about to enter upon the great work he foresaw in closing his second inaugural address — 'To finish the work we are in, to bind up the Nation's wounds, to care for him who shall have borne the battle, and for his widow and his orphans, to do all which may achieve and cherish a just and lasting peace among ourselves and with all Nations.'"[26]

Lincoln went to Ford's Theater to see *Our American Cousin* on the evening of April 14. The Grants had declined the invitation to accompany the Lincolns. As had Chipman on Lincoln's trip to Gettysburg, Major Henry Reed Rathbone, a War Department officer, accompanied the president and Mrs. Lincoln to the theater. Chipman and James Hudnut, his assistant, excused themselves from the ongoing festivities to burn the late-night oil in the bureau.[27]

The Lincolns arrived after the play had already started. As the audience perceived the president's presence in the box above the stage, they cheered, halting the play for the acknowledgment. John Wilkes Booth, an actor of some renown, entered the president's box during the play, shot the unsuspecting president in the head, and swung his knife at Rathbone, before jumping to the stage and fleeing from the city. Chaos ensued in the theater and spilled out into the streets. Doctors attended the president and had him carried to the Petersen House across the street. Almost simultaneously, a Booth accomplice attacked Secretary of State Seward in his home, where he was recovering from injuries sustained in a carriage accident. Wild rumors circulated through the city that the entire cabinet had been murdered and that Johnson and Grant were also victims. But the attacks were limited to those at the Ford Theater and the Seward residence.

At the bureau, Belle Chipman and some of her friends with whom she had been celebrating burst into the room where Chipman and Hudnut were writing. Belle's face presaged the terrible news, and Chipman was alarmed by her appearance alone.

"Oh dear!" she exclaimed. "They shot the President in the theater!"

The news was shocking. "The excitement of battle," wrote Hudnut to Chipman 56 years later, in 1921, "was nothing compared to the excitement of that night." Wishing to do something but not knowing what could be done, Chipman immediately dispatched Hudnut to the theater to determine the president's condition. The young clerk waded through the crowds to the vicinity of the residence where Lincoln lay and returned to Chipman with grim news.

Chipman and his party, feeling helpless, went into the streets, as did much of Washington. "The streets were filled with people," recalled Chipman, "and there was a sort of ominous rumbling — the sort of rumbling that comes with riots. There was a tremendous crowd before the theater — thousands had gathered there, and there was a suppressed seething. Some were talking in low voices that were weird-sounding in the silent crowd. Some were crying, and the eerie wails rose and fell on the streets like wind."[28]

Stanton sprang into action, taking charge at the Petersen House. He ordered witness statements, put the military on alert, and sent a dispatch calling Grant back to Washington from Philadelphia. He notified Chief Justice Salmon P. Chase that his services would be needed to swear in Johnson as president on the now-inevitable passing of Lincoln. The next morning, Lincoln drew his last breath and, shortly, his heart stopped beating at 7:22. "Now he belongs to the ages," pronounced Stanton. As Washington prepared for the funeral of the beloved president, Chase administered the oath of office to Johnson.

The assassination of Abraham Lincoln was no benefit to the South. "It was a dreadful hour," declared Chipman, "when the assassin struck down this hero of heroes. The blow was given in the name of the rebellion, but it was a blow that even rebellion disowned and repudiated, for it was a blow portentous of evil in the South."[29]

Johnson's Offer

As President Johnson scrambled to piece together his administration, he offered to Chipman the office of private secretary to the president, the prestigious position held by Nicolay and Hay during the Lincoln administration. The offer presented a real dilemma to the young officer who was on the verge of resigning from the military and was planning his future.

When Chipman graduated from law school, returning to Iowa to practice law was a logical step. He grew up there and had many friends and connections. When Lincoln issued the call for volunteers after the attack on Fort Sumter, reporting for duty came naturally to the patriotic young lawyer. His positions of service within the military, even though they constituted a steep rise to stations of importance and responsibility, were not the result of his aspiring to standing. Instead, his desire was to return to the field and serve with his regiment. Johnson's offer was a departure from Chipman's rise to prominence in military service because, for one thing, he had the option of accepting or declining.

Offering the position was also a risk for Johnson. Chipman's loyalty to Lincoln and the Republican Party were no secret by then. Johnson, although loyal to the Union, came from the South and was a Democrat. Yet Johnson's willingness to take such a risk on Chipman is understandable in light of Chipman's demonstrated loyalty to those in command. His service to Stanton in the War Department, despite Stanton's difficult personality, proved that his dedication to duty and his patriotism far outweighed any partisan tendencies.

Faced with the first career decision of his married life, Chipman turned to his wife for advice, a strategy he followed through the rest of his life. Anything he decided would affect her as well. Belle advised against accepting the position. The atmosphere in Washington was still tense, especially with the assassination of Lincoln and the search for conspirators and southern sympathizers. Belle feared for her husband's safety, and, being from a strictly Republican background, she disliked Johnson's politics.

Chipman also was inclined not to accept the position. He knew the stresses and dangers associated with such service. But, more importantly to Chipman, as he told friends later, he held serious doubts about Johnson's abilities and temperament, which doubts, to some extent, resulted from Chipman's comparison of Johnson to Lincoln, regarded by Chipman as the best ever to serve. His political differences with Johnson settled the issue in Chipman's mind. In relating this experience to friends much later in life, Chipman expressed relief that he made the decision not to serve with Johnson. If he accepted, he told his friends, he would have been loyal to his chief and his public reputation would have been tainted as a result. Presented with the opportunity at the age of 31 to become the most intimate assistant of the president of the United States, Chipman declined the honor, telling Johnson that he preferred to resume the practice of law.[30]

7

The Tragedy of
Andersonville (1865)

As the Civil War reshaped the nation and its future, so it reshaped the lives of countless Americans. Chipman entered the war years as a new attorney in a small western town. Chipman's star was rising quickly in that limited sphere. He was chosen to speak at the town meeting called in response to the Confederate attack on Fort Sumter and Lincoln's call for volunteers. He had no influence and few connections outside the area of Iowa where his family had settled. With schooling behind him, he was still young, single, mobile, and enthusiastic. Perhaps most significant for his era, he was passionately Republican, a Lincoln devotee. Norton Parker Chipman, however, was as yet unknown to the national leaders of his day.

All that changed by the time of Lee's surrender at Appomattox. By then, Chipman had already spent considerable time in the seat of government, assisting the highest officials of the Union. He served on the immediate staff of Stanton and carried Lincoln's correspondence to his field generals. He had garnered a reputation of loyalty and competency among the military elite.

His personal life had also evolved. The young, single recruit of 1860 had become a mature, married, high-ranking officer. He received a brevet promotion to brigadier general of volunteers in March 1865, an honorary promotion in title only for gallant service in the Bureau of Military Justice. And, although his life had changed drastically, he was as yet to embark on the role that made him a household name in the nation struggling to heal from the deep wounds of civil strife as he prosecuted the commander of the most infamous prisoner of war camp in the South.

Captain Henry Wirz commanded the Confederate prisoner of war camp in Andersonville, Georgia, and, when the war ended, the North prosecuted him for war crimes, including the deaths of thousands at Andersonville. Thirty-one-year-old Chipman gained national fame as the prosecutor in Wirz's trial. Although the investigation and prosecution of the case took only about six months, even today it is the single event for which Chipman is most known to those who recall his name.

The Horrors of Andersonville

After the Union's victory, Chipman intended to leave the military and hang out his shingle in Washington. But the business of the Bureau of Military Justice intensified rather than diminishing. General Holt and his office of young lawyers undertook the prosecution of the Lincoln assassination conspirators, with Holt taking the lead chair. Lincoln was shot on April 14, 1865. John Wilkes Booth was caught and killed on April 26. Meanwhile, the facts of the conspiracy were quickly coming to light and the coconspirators were rounded up for trial. On May 10, less than one month after the assassination, trial against the coconspirators began. Not involved in the courtroom proceedings, Chipman took a supporting role.

As the trial progressed, a new matter required the serious attention of the judge advocate general. Many Confederate officers and officials fled, while no one pursued. But there were several prominent exceptions. Some were arrested, including Jefferson Davis, president of the Confederacy. On May 10, the same day the trial of the Lincoln assassination conspirators began, Davis was captured in Georgia. Transported to Virginia, he was imprisoned in Fortress Monroe, where he stayed for two years while the government tried to decide his fate.

Another Confederate officer captured in the days after the end of the Civil War was Captain Wirz. Built in the latter part of the Civil War to accommodate the rise in the prison population brought on by the suspension of the prisoner exchange cartel, the Andersonville Prison was used starting in February 1864. The prisoners endured the greatest hardships during the hot summer months of that year. Though the size of the prison was sufficient for perhaps 10,000 prisoners, the Confederacy incarcerated more than 22,000 Union soldiers there before making any effort to expand the facility. During the summer, the prison was enlarged and eventually contained 34,760 prisoners in August. From February 1864 to April 1865, the period of Andersonville's use as a prison, almost 50,000 Union soldiers were imprisoned there, of which more than 13,000 died, about one-quarter of the prisoners. During the month of July 1864, prisoners died at a rate of more than 56 per day. Under Wirz's Andersonville command, more Union soldiers died there than were killed in action on the Union side in the combined battles of the Second Bull Run, Antietam, Chancellorsville, Gettysburg, the Wilderness, and Appomattox.[1]

The conditions at Andersonville were no secret to Richmond. The surgeon-general of the Confederacy, rather than acting to ameliorate the deplorable conditions in the prison, saw the situation as a fortuitous opportunity to study typhus, typhoid, and malarial fevers. He sent a subordinate doctor to make the investigation but not to provide relief. The doctor's detailed report chronicling the atrocities at Andersonville was sent to Richmond.[2]

The general feeling of reconciliation felt in the United States after the war did not extend to Wirz. In Lincoln's second inaugural address, just a month before the Civil War ended, the president urged forgiveness: "With Malice toward none, with charity for all, with firmness in the right, as God gives us to see the right, let us strive on to finish the work we are in, to bind up the nation's wounds." But as the fighting stopped and prisoners were released from Andersonville and other southern prisons, northerners were horrified by the condition of the returning prisoners. The American poet Walt Whitman saw some of these men in Washington, emaciated and barely alive, and recorded his own thoughts, which turned out to be more prophetic than was Lincoln's theme of forgiveness. Whitman wrote: "There are deeds, crimes that may be forgiven but this is not among them. It steeps its perpetrators in blackest, escapeless, endless damnation."[3]

Whitman described the terrible scene: "The releas'd prisoners of War are now coming up from the Southern prisons. I have seen a number of them. The sight is worse than any sight of battle-fields or any collections of wounded, even the bloodiest. There was, (as a sample,) one large boat load, of several hundreds, brought about the 25th, to Annapolis; and out of the whole number only three individuals were able to walk from the boat. The rest were carried ashore and laid down in one place or another. Can those be *men*— those little livid-brown, ash-streak'd, monkey-looking dwarfs?— are they really not mummied, dwindled corpses? They lay there, most of them, quite still, but with a horrible look in their eyes and skinny lips, often with not enough flesh on the lips to cover their teeth. Probably no more appalling sight was ever seen on this earth. (...Over 50,000 have been compell'd to die the death of starvation — reader, did you ever try to realize what *starvation* actually is?— in those prisons — and in a land of plenty.) An indescribable meanness, tyranny, aggravating course of insults, almost incredible — was evidently the rule of treatment through all the Southern military prisons. The dead there are not to be pitied as much as some of the living that come from there — if they can be call'd living — many of them are mentally imbecile, and will never recuperate."[4]

The Andersonville Trial

Chipman recalled the circumstances necessitating Wirz's postwar prosecution: "The Andersonville horror had made so deep an impression upon the nation that when it was known that Wirz, the keeper of that prison, was under arrest, his trial became imperative." The reports of the prison filtered north and created outrage. However, despite the reports, "few persons [in] the North, not even the prisoners themselves, were aware that over 13,000 had died miserably at that horrible place, and few had any conception that a great crime had been committed." Holt recommended to Stanton that, because Holt was occupied in the Lincoln conspirators' trial, Chipman should take the lead in preparing the prosecution's case against Wirz. Chipman, Holt, Stanton, and Johnson suspected that the blame for the conditions at Andersonville extended far beyond the commander of the prisoner, all the way up

Secretary of war in the Buchanan administration before the war, Joseph Holt was appointed judge advocate general by Lincoln. He prosecuted the Lincoln conspirators and supervised Chipman's prosecution of Henry Wirz (Library of Congress).

the line of command to the president of the Confederacy, himself. As Chipman investigated, his suspicion turned to conviction that even Jefferson Davis was responsible for the suffering of Union soldiers at Andersonville. Chipman's charge, however, was to prosecute Wirz, not higher Confederate officials. The question of what to do with Davis, languishing at Fortress Monroe, was before Johnson and his cabinet.[5]

When Chipman had completed his preparation, the War Department assembled a military commission to try Wirz as judge and jury. General Lew Wallace, the later author of *Ben Hur*, presided over the commission, which consisted of Wallace and eight other Union officers. The commission included generals who had distinguished themselves in battle, lawyers of proven ability, and future politicians. General Gershom Mott was severely injured more than once during the war. General John W. Geary, a lawyer, was San Francisco's first mayor, from 1850 to 1851, and territorial governor of Kansas from 1856 to 1857. After the war, he served two terms as Republican governor of Pennsylvania. General Lorenzo Thomas, the Adjutant General of the Army, was a recognized authority in military law and the rules of war. General Francis Fessenden was a lawyer. General Edward S. Bragg, also a lawyer, commanded the Iron Brigade. After the war, he was active in Wisconsin politics as a Democrat and served several terms in the House of Representatives. General John F. Ballier of Pennsylvania later owned a hotel in Philadelphia. Colonel Thomas Allcock was an artillery officer. General John H. Stibbs of Iowa was the youngest officer on the commission at 26 years of age. As the last surviving commission member in 1911, he remembered Chipman in favorable terms as "a man of superior education and refinement, and withal one of the most genial, kind-hearted, companionable men I have ever had the good fortune to meet."[6]

Upon learning of the composition of the military commission, the *New York Times* speculated that the high rank of the commission members, higher than those who heard the case against the Lincoln assassination conspirators, indicated the commission would try "a more important prisoner than the miserable Wertz [*sic*]," referring to possible prosecution of Jefferson Davis.[7]

The trial was a local and national sensation in the summer of 1865. The commission convened in the courtroom of the Court of Claims in the national Capitol. *Harper's Weekly* described the courtroom as "large and well furnished," having a large table at one end, where the commission sat, with Chipman at the foot of the table, facing Wallace, who was at the head. Two large windows lighted the room and provided a view of the "leafy and pleasant park west of the Capitol." Crowds of spectators assembled to get a glimpse of the infamous Wirz, who had not before been seen publicly in Washington. News correspondents sent daily, detailed reports of the proceedings to major newspapers, where the reports ran on the front pages.[8]

Wirz was brought before the commission in August, and Chipman's charges were read for the nation to hear. News of the facts included in the charges sent, in Chipman's words, "a thrill of horror throughout the United States." The charges fell into two categories: (1) conspiracy to deprive prisoners of food and shelter, resulting in injury and death, and (2) murder.[9]

The conspiracy count alleged in graphic detail the conditions Wirz and the other conspirators allowed to exist in the prison — unwholesome quarters, exposure to winter cold and summer heat, impure water and rotten and scant food, and gross overcrowding, which conditions killed 10,000 Union soldiers. One thousand more died because the corpses of their brethren were left to rot among them. Wirz carried out cruel and uncivilized punishments, such as binding prisoners together and forcing them to carry large metal balls, confining prisoners to stocks that immobilized their heads and limbs for many hours without food or drink, shooting any prisoner who crossed a line, called the "dead-line," within the stockade, hunting down escaped prisoners using bloodhounds that would inflict serious injury on the escapees, and vaccinating the prisoners with poison, all of which injured or killed many more Union soldiers.[10]

The murder count alleged that Wirz killed prisoners by shooting, stomping, confinement in stocks, binding neck and feet with ball and chains, siccing ferocious dogs, and beating over the head with a revolver. The charges detailed the deaths of 13 prisoners by these means.[11]

As surprising to the public as the details of deprivation and murder that occurred in the Andersonville prison was the list of prominent coconspirators. Accused of conspiring with Wirz, though not subject to prosecution, were Jefferson Davis, Robert E. Lee, John Winder, and James A. Seddon, who had been the Confederate secretary of war. The commission arraigned Wirz on the charges and adjourned until the next day.

In its front-page report of the first day of proceedings, the *New York Times* introduced Chipman to its readership: "Col. Chipman, the Judge-Advocate, is a lawyer of fine ability, and pleasing, dignified address, who tries his case with impressive earnestness, but justly and fairly."[12]

As the commission prepared to reconvene the day after arraigning Wirz on the charges, a package was placed in Chipman's hands. From Stanton himself, the package contained orders to disband the military commission and for Chipman to report immediately to the War Department. Chipman believed Stanton had been apprised of every step in the preparation of the case, but Chipman's allegations naming Davis, Lee, and Seddon apparently surprised Stanton. He was disturbed by the development, unusually so, in Chipman's estimation. Stanton directed Chipman to prepare new charges without the Confederate high officials named.[13]

Stanton's response to the original charges was a setback for Chipman, signaling either that Chipman did not understand the intention of the Johnson administration with respect to prosecuting top Confederate brass or that the administration was ambivalent and did not have a clear intent. Chipman intended to show at trial what he felt he had discovered during his investigation, complicity in the intentional deprivations of Andersonville by the highest Confederate officials. He had briefed Holt on the full details of his investigation, and Holt supported the scope of Chipman's effort. But Stanton did not agree. After discussions within the War Department, Stanton approved new charges which added lesser Confederate officials as coconspirators and deleted the names of the high Confederate officials, referring vaguely to "others unknown."[14]

The military commission, with the same members, was reconstituted, and Wirz was arraigned on the new charges. Wirz objected to the new charges, arguing he could not be prosecuted for three reasons: first, he had been promised, when he was captured, that he would be released under the surrender terms after he responded to questioning; second, he could not be prosecuted anew, under double jeopardy principles, because he had been previously arraigned before the military commission was disbanded; and third, the charges did not allege an offense punishable under the laws of war.[15]

As for the promise that Wirz would be released under the surrender terms after questioning, Chipman argued to the commission that, even if such a promise was made, the officer had no power to absolve Wirz of the crimes he committed. Therefore, any order to release Wirz was necessarily rescinded. Chipman also argued that the terms of the South's surrender did not provide for general amnesty and pardons. Indeed, after the war, the president was besieged with requests for pardons from rebel soldiers and citizens.[16]

On the double jeopardy issue, Chipman responded that under precedent of the Bureau of Military Justice and pursuant to Holt's written decision in a prior case, jeopardy does not attach when a prisoner is arraigned. It attaches, instead, when a full trial is held, meaning that a trial on the new charges did not constitute double jeopardy.[17]

Finally, Chipman argued that, whether Wirz's actions, as alleged in the charges, violated the laws of war, was precisely the question to be answered by the commission, after hearing the evidence and argument. He left it to the commission to examine the charges and decide for itself if it sufficiently alleged crimes in violation of the laws of war.[18]

After hearing rebuttal from O.S. Baker, who, along with Louis Schade, represented Wirz through most of the trial, the commission took Wirz's objections to the charges under consideration. When it reconvened, the commission overruled Wirz's objections without comment, apparently agreeing with Chipman's arguments. Wirz pled not guilty, and the trial began.[19]

According to Chipman, the long trial "taxed the physical and nervous forces of all who took active part in it to the verge of exhaustion." Wirz's health declined, and he often reclined on a lounge and put a handkerchief over his face, making it appear that he was oblivious to what was going on in the courtroom. From August to October, more than 145 witnesses testified, mostly for the prosecution — nearly 100 of them former Andersonville prisoners, but also Confederate guards, officers, and surgeons.[20]

Evidence of Deprivations

Chipman's evidence concerning the deprivations inflicted on the Union soldiers at Andersonville concentrated on establishing that the conditions were so bad that any reasonable person would infer that Wirz and his coconspirators meant to injure or kill those soldiers. From the evidence of the overcrowded conditions, the contaminated water and inedible food, the exposure to the elements, and the inadequate medical care, the trier of fact would conclude that Wirz and the Confederate authorities intended to starve large numbers to death and render many others unfit for service, to give the Confederacy an advantage in the war. The conditions, or the manner in which the prisoners were cared for, also conserved resources for the rebel army and the citizens of the Confederate states.[21]

When the stockade (the enclosure) was built, the land was denuded of timber. No shelter was provided within the stockade and, because there was no timber, the prisoners were unable to build shelter for themselves. Originally, the stockade enclosed about 18 acres, intended to accommodate 10,000 prisoners. By June 1864, it contained 22,000 prisoners. The stockade was then enlarged. After expansion, the prison, essentially a large human corral, consisted almost exclusively of a wall placed around approximately 27 acres of bare land. The average area per prisoner was less than six feet by six feet. Every daily activity had to be undertaken in these small confines — cooking, washing, exercising, and sleeping, as well and urinating and defecating.[22]

Through this inadequate stockade ran a polluted stream. Before reaching the stockade, the sluggish stream first served the Confederate guards. After leaving the guards' camp, the stream passed by the cookhouse. Garbage, grease, and other byproducts of the cooking process were dumped into the stream. Finally, in this polluted state, the stream flowed into the stockade, where the prisoners needed the water for drinking, cooking, cleaning, and bathing.[23]

The food rationed to the prisoners was often unfit for human consumption and, at times, rations were withheld completely. Commonly, the daily ration included a third of a pound of bacon and one and one quarter pound of corn meal. The corn meal was very coarse, containing more of the cob than just the edible corn. The meal was sometimes moldy. It was cooked into cakes, but rarely cooked well enough that it was cooked through. The rations caused chronic diarrhea, leading to malnutrition and starvation. Generally, no fruits or vegetables were provided to the prisoners.[24]

The scanty and impure rations were stopped altogether when a squad could not account for every man in the morning roll call. The prisoners were divided into squads of ninety and were required to account for each man. When they did not account for every man, and it was easy in the mass of humanity to lose track of a man, their rations could be cut off.[25]

The men in the stockade had only so much shelter as they could rig from what they had on hand, which generally was nothing, but could be a blanket or a hole in the ground. Lumber that might have been used to build structures within the stockade was appropriated to other uses. Most had no protection from the rain, cold, sun, and heat. And their clothing was either filthy or completely gone, leaving them naked.[26]

The health of the prisoners was compromised by their physical confinement and lack of exercise and ravaged by scurvy, diarrhea, dysentery, and gangrene.[27]

The Confederate doctor sent to observe the Andersonville prison, Dr. Joseph Jones, described the health conditions:

> In the stockade, with the exception of the damp lowlands, bordering the small stream, the surface was covered with huts, and small ragged tents and parts of blankets and fragments of oilcloth, coats, and blankets stretched upon sticks. The tents and huts were not arranged according to any order, and there was in most parts of the enclosure scarcely room for two men to walk abreast between the tents and huts. I observed men urinating and evacuating their bowels at the very tent doors and around the little vessels in which they were cooking their food. Small pits, not more than a foot or two deep, nearly filled with soft offensive feces, were everywhere seen, and emitted under the hot sun a strong and disgusting odor. Masses of corn-bread, bones, old rags, and filth of every description were scattered round or accumulated in large piles.[28]

Dr. Jones continued:

> Each day the dead from the stockade were carried out by their fellow-prisoners and deposited upon the ground under a bush arbor, just outside the southwestern gate. From thence they were carried in carts to the burying ground, one-quarter of a mile northwest of the prison. The dead were buried without coffins, side by side, in trenches four feet deep.
> The low grounds bordering the stream were covered with human excrements and filth of all kinds, which in many places appeared to be alive with

working maggots. An indescribable sickening stench arose from these fer-
menting masses of human dung and filth.[29]

Between the war injuries with which some of the men came to Andersonville and the diseases they contracted from the conditions in the prison, a
large proportion of the men needed medical care. But the small hospital could
only accommodate the most gravely ill. As many men died in the stockade as
in the hospital.[30]

Dr. Jones described the poor care and rampant disease that doomed most
men who were treated in the hospital.

> The police and hygiene of the hospital was defective in the extreme.... Many
> of the sick were literally encrusted with dirt and filth and covered with ver-
> min. When a gangrenous wound needed washing, the limb was thrust out a
> little from the blanket, or board, or rags upon which the patient was lying,
> and water poured over it, and all the putrescent matter allowed to soak into
> the ground floor of the tent.... Where hospital gangrene was prevailing, it was
> impossible for any wound to escape contagion under these circumstances.
> The results of wounds in the hospital were of the most unsatisfactory char-
> acter, from this neglect of cleanliness, in the dressings, and wounds them-
> selves, as well as from various other causes....[31]

Regarding these deprivations and their significance to the prosecution
of Wirz for the deaths of the men so deprived, Chipman argued that Wirz
and his superiors were responsible for the lives of the prisoners: "If a guardian
charged with the duty to feed his ward deliberately starves him to death, it
is murder. In time of war captive prisoners become wards of the enemy."
Chipman used this reasoning, along with voluminous evidence from former
prisoners, Confederate soldiers, and Confederate doctors, to prove his case as
to the joint liability of Wirz and higher Confederate officials for the deaths
that occurred at Andersonville. "[P]risoners of war are entitled to such human
treatment as may be consistent with their safe-keeping and as may be reason-
ably within the power of the enemy to give," reasoned Chipman. "It is never
allowable to kill them outright, when once captured, much less to subject them
to slow death by torture or starvation. When I say that this rule of conduct
in time of war was flagrantly violated at Andersonville, I state not alone a
conclusion or inference from the evidence, but I state what was the opinion,
given under oath, of the rebel surgeons on duty there."[32]

As well as depriving the prisoners of food, shelter, clothing, and medical care, more active cruelty also caused injury and death at Andersonville
in large numbers. As punishment for various offenses, such as trying to escape,
the Confederates bound prisoners together and forced them to carry large
metal balls and confined prisoners to stocks that immobilized their heads and
limbs.[33]

Guards at Andersonville also shot prisoners for crossing a line within the stockade, even if the prisoners were not attempting to escape. Known as the "dead-line," this line over which the prisoners were warned not to cross, was about 20 feet inside the stockade wall. The line was marked by a rail in most places, but in others, for example, where the stream entered the stockade, the line was imaginary. Whenever a prisoner crossed the line, whether by accident or on purpose, one of the sentinels positioned in a guard tower shot the prisoner, without warning. Some men crossed the deadline purposely to end their suffering. Sentinels watching the deadline also had orders to fire on any prisoner who attempted to speak to the guards.[34]

Despite the presence of the deadline and other measures to keep the prisoners inside the stockade, occasional attempts were made to escape. When Wirz or the guards learned that a prisoner had escaped from the stockade or the hospital, dogs were used to track the man down. The dogs were not immediately called off when the prisoner was found and captured; instead, the dogs were allowed to attack the man, often tearing away his clothing and ripping into the flesh. Just like any other wound sustained by the prisoners, the dog bites frequently led to gangrene and death because of the unsanitary conditions. Wirz often participated personally in tracking down the escaped prisoners with dogs.[35]

Dr. Jones concluded that most of the deaths were due to "the accumulation of the sources of disease, as the increase of excrements and filth of all kinds, and the concentration of noxious effluvia, and also to the progressive effects of salt diet, crowding, and the hot climate." Another confederate doctor believed that 75 percent of those who died could have been saved with proper care, such as food, clothing, shelter and medical treatment.[36]

Having charged the deprivations and cruelties in the first count against Wirz as a conspiracy, Chipman argued that Wirz was not alone responsible for the many injuries and deaths of Union soldiers. Some of the most persuasive evidence Chipman presented at trial was the report of Dr. Jones to his superiors. The conditions at Andersonville were known to the leaders of the Confederacy at Richmond and were the subject of newspaper comments. Confederate General John H. Winder had responsibility over Andersonville prison and was well aware of the conditions and events there. Winder, who died before the Andersonville trial, was stationed in Richmond, where he reported directly to the Confederate war department, until late in the war, when he moved his headquarters to the vicinity of the Andersonville stockade.[37]

As Chipman prepared this damning evidence of conspiracy for trial, Wirz protested that he was not responsible for the overcrowding and lack of food, shelter and clothing at Andersonville. During the trial, Wirz again denied his own responsibility for the conditions at the prison, but added that he was not attempting to blame any other specific person: "It is not for me to suggest where the culpability or responsibility lay."[38]

Evidence of Murder

The evidence showed that cruelty inflicted on the Union soldiers at Andersonville not only happened on Wirz's watch but much of it was pursuant to his orders. Wirz directed punishment to be meted out in various ways. Stocks were constructed, which held the arms out in each direction. Put into the stocks, some of the men could stand on their feet; some could only touch their toes on the ground. Other stocks secured the feet, thus elevating the feet, and the hands were secured with balls and chains. Men were left in this condition, exposed to the sun and rain. Other men were chained in groups, by their necks in a circle. Their hands were cuffed together, and balls and chains were attached to their feet. The men were left in this condition as long as Wirz determined, sometimes up to two weeks.[39]

The dogs were used, on Wirz's orders, to track escaped prisoners. They sometimes maimed the prisoners, also causing death indirectly from gangrene. Wirz directed the dog handlers to allow the dogs to injure the prisoners.[40]

The deadline inside the walls of the prison was used as an excuse to shoot prisoners who crossed it, with the reward from Wirz of a 30-day furlough to the guard who accomplished the deed. One man was shot in the head for reaching across the deadline to obtain a morsel of food. Another man rolled across the deadline in his sleep and was shot in the back, killing him instantly.[41]

Several witnesses testified concerning a one-legged prisoner known as "Chickamauga," who was shot by a guard on Wirz's orders. Some of the prisoners believed Chickamauga had been spying for the Confederate guards and had reported the prisoners' efforts to dig tunnels out of the prison. Confronted about their suspicions, Chickamauga sought help from a guard. In doing so, he crossed the deadline, where none of the other prisoners dared follow him and asked the guard to summon Wirz. When Wirz rode up on his horse, Chickamauga asked to be taken out of the stockade for protection. Without responding to the request, Wirz said to the guard: "Shoot that one-legged Yankee devil." Chickamauga turned on his crutches to go away, but the guard shot him in the head, killing him.[42]

Wirz also killed prisoners, himself. He stomped recalcitrant prisoners, beat them over the head, or, more often, simply shot them. Noting the number of Union prisoners who died at Andersonville, Wirz boasted that he was of more service to the Confederacy by killing more Yankees than Lee was killing at Richmond.[43]

In closing argument, Chipman recounted for the commission the evidence that Wirz acted with malice, not innocently, in causing injury and death to Union soldiers:

> The prisoner now before you, despite all his pretended protests at the time, despite the individual and widely separated instances of humanity which have been paraded here [Wirz had presented evidence that several times he acted kindly toward prisoners], remained ... "the tool in the hands of [his] superiors." [Citation omitted.] He had introduced himself to the prisoners by stopping their rations the first day he was on duty; he had instituted, between that time and the time of General Winder's arrival, a system of the most cruel and inhuman punishments; he had made his name a terror among the prisoners, and his society a reproach to his comrades upon whom he inflicted it; he had established the dead-line and all its accompanying horrors; he had given the prisoners a foreshadowing of the stock, of the balls and chains, of the chain-gang, of starvation as a punishment, and all that black catalogue of cruelty and suffering unknown even to a "Draconian code"; he had declared to several of the prisoners engaged in the burial of the dead, "This is the way I give the Yankees the land they came to fight for"; he had scores of times told the prisoners, when maltreating them, that he intended to starve them to death; he boasted that "he was doing more for the Confederacy than any general in the field'; he had paraded the chain-gang for the amusement of his wife and daughters; he had with drawn pistol told a prisoner who dared to complain of the rations, "Damn you, I'll give you bullets for bread."[44]

Conclusion of the Trial

After the prosecution and defense both rested, the commission invited the prosecution and defense to submit written arguments, as was the custom. Also customary was for the defense to submit the first argument, to which the prosecution would respond. Counsel for Wirz asked for two weeks to prepare the argument. When the commission offered only 12 days, defense counsel withdrew, complaining that it was not enough time. The commission therefore turned to Chipman for the summation of the evidence and law from the trial.[45]

Chipman submitted a comprehensive closing brief, detailing the facts and law. After the commission deliberated, it announced its verdict: guilty of conspiracy to injure the health and destroy the lives of Union prisoners and guilty of 11 counts of murder. In specifying the basis for the conspiracy finding, the commission listed as coconspirators Jefferson Davis, James A Seddon, and others, but not Robert E. Lee. The commission sentenced Wirz to be hanged.[46]

Because any execution by a military commission required the approval of the president, Holt prepared a full and thorough report of the commission proceedings to submit to Johnson, detailing the evidence supporting the verdict and the defenses interposed by Wirz. Johnson issued his order on November 3, 1865: "The proceedings, findings, and sentence of the court in the within case are approved, and it is ordered that the sentence be carried into execution, by the officer commanding the department of Washington, on Friday, the 10th day of November, 1865, between the hours of 6 o'clock A.M. and 12 o'clock noon."[47]

Around 10 A.M. on the date appointed by the president, Wirz was taken to the gallows constructed in the yard of the Old Capitol Prison, practically in the shadow of the Capitol, where the United States Supreme Court courthouse now sits. A crowd gathered inside the yard and outside the walls men climbed trees to get a view of the execution. As onlookers chanted, "Remember Andersonville," Wirz was hanged. His body was interred at the Washing-

Henry Wirz was hanged on November 10, 1865, in the yard of the Old Capitol Prison. The United States Supreme Court building now stands on this site (Library of Congress).

ton Arsenal next to the grave of George Atzerodt, one of the Lincoln assassination conspirators, though it was later removed to a cemetery.[48]

The evidence against Wirz was overwhelming but the attitude of the Johnson administration and the country was mixed concerning whether and how to punish rebels who committed treason or war crimes. Revisionist historians have called the weeks of prosecution evidence unreliable and the trial a circus. But contemporary observers left accounts detailing the convincing nature of the evidence and the solemnity of the proceedings. Whitelaw Reid, a prominent newspaperman and later a candidate for vice president, noted: "The proofs of his guilt were overwhelming. The man not convinced by them would be the man to doubt whether there was sufficient historical evidence of our ever having had a war with Mexico. But there were others, as guilty as he, guiltier indeed in that they made him a tool to do deeds to which they would not stoop themselves. They should have been seated by his side, to make the trial other than a bitter mockery of justice."[49]

Surely, errors occurred over the course of the long trial. The perfect trial is but an ideal. An important principle of American jurisprudence, one which the critics of the judgment against Wirz have generally failed to consider, requires the court and those who review the judgment — including, in this case, the commission, Holt, and Johnson — to determine whether there was a miscarriage of justice — that is, whether the accused would have been convicted if the errors had not occurred. Chipman discussed this principle in his closing brief to the commission: "It would be strange indeed if this record of five thousand pages, of sixty-three days of weary, laborious trial, presented no wrong rulings, no improper exclusion or admission of evidence in a greater or less degree pertinent to some issue made; but I assert with all confidence and with honest belief, that the interests of this prisoner have not been and cannot be affected injuriously by such action in any instance that can be named."[50]

Davis' Defense of Andersonville

Debate over whether Wirz should have been prosecuted and whether he was just a convenient scapegoat continued over the next few decades. General Stibbs, a member of the commission, defended the verdict: "I do not see how it would be possible for an intelligent, unprejudiced, fair-minded reviewer to conclude that such a court could or would have rendered a verdict that was not in full accord with the evidence presented. I assure you no attempt was made to dictate or influence our verdict, and, furthermore, there was no power on earth that could have swerved us from the discharge of our sworn duty as we saw it. Our verdict was unanimous; there were no dissenting opinions, and for myself I can say that there has been no time during the forty-five years that have intervened since this trial was held when I have felt that I owed an apology to any one, not even to the Almighty, for having voted to hang Henry Wirz by the neck until he was dead."[51]

While Stibbs' statement reflected generally the feeling of northerners, many southerners disagreed. Jefferson Davis led a chorus of critics denouncing the trial and execution of Wirz. Although Davis was imprisoned in Virginia and eventually indicted for treason, he was never tried. A group posted bail for Davis in 1867, and the government dropped the case in 1869. A free man, Davis took advantage of the opportunity to voice his opinions on many issues emanating from the war. One of those issues was the Andersonville trial, in which he was named as an uncharged coconspirator in the verdict of the commission after trial, even though his name had been deleted from the charges against Wirz at the beginning of the trial.

In the last year before Davis died in December 1889, he resolved to publish a defense of the Confederacy's actions with respect to Andersonville. This defense was prepared for *The North American Review*, a northern magazine; however, when the editor made edits that Davis found unacceptable, Davis withdrew the article and took it to *Belford's Magazine*, a short-lived Chicago publication, where the editor agreed to publish the article unaltered.[52]

Davis' article, titled "Andersonville and Other War-Prisons," ran after Davis' death, in January and February of 1890. In it, Davis developed three themes: first, he blamed the Union for the need for war prisons because the Union suspended the prisoner exchange cartel; second, he asserted that the conditions at Andersonville were not as bad as was reported to the North; and third, he claimed Wirz's trial was unfair.[53]

According to Davis, the South sought and obtained the North's agreement to exchange prisoners because that is how civilized nations conducted war. "When the United States authorities," continued Davis, "refused to fulfil their obligation to continue the exchange and parole of prisoners, the number of Northern captives rapidly accumulated beyond the capacity of the prisons at Richmond, and also beyond the ability of the commissariat to supply them. In the absence of any prospect of relief from these embarrassments the removal of the prisoners [out of Richmond] became necessary." Over time, the North's refusal to renew the exchange cartel led to a population larger

Opposite: A cartoon by Thomas Nast contrasting the sickness, starvation, and death experienced by the Union soldiers in the Andersonville Prison with the health, plenty, and luxury of Jefferson Davis during his confinement at Fortress Monroe after the war (Library of Congress).

THE REBEL LEADER, JEFF DAVIS, AT FORTRESS MONROE.
HEALTH, PLENTY, LUXURY.

than the prison could adequately accommodate. The South did not augment the accommodations because it continued to believe the North would relent. The North's continued refusal was, in Davis' words, "a degree of cold-blooded insensibility which we had not anticipated."[54]

Concerning the conditions at Andersonville, Davis claimed that starvation was not the problem. Instead, the deadly problems were "acclimation, unsuitable diet, and despondency," which were "not in our power to remove." The only remedy for these problems was "the honest execution of the cartel." As the war progressed toward a conclusion, the South's ability to meet the needs of both soldiers and prisoners diminished. "We did not clothe the ragged," admitted Davis, "neither had we boasted of our ability to do so."[55]

Davis defended Wirz, finding fault with the trial and noting evidence that may have tended to show innocence. The process by which Wirz was convicted and executed was flawed because Wirz was captured and imprisoned after being promised freedom. Also, two witnesses who could have given evidence in favor of Wirz were turned away by Chipman. Davis concluded that Wirz was innocent and died a martyr.[56]

Davis recounted a story that had become well known, even though it did not tend to prove Wirz's innocence. A night or two before Wirz's execution, the narrative goes, three unidentified men went to Wirz's cell. They offered Wirz his freedom if he would testify in a trial against Davis. Wirz refused because he did not know Davis personally. Wirz is reported to have told a fellow prisoner after the visit that, "if they expected with the offer of my miserable life to purchase me to treason and treachery to the South, they had undervalued me." After telling the story, Davis commented: "Thus ended the attempt to suborn Captain Wirz against Jefferson Davis. That alone shows what a man he was."[57]

Twenty-five years had passed since the close of the Civil War and the trial and execution of the Andersonville commander, and Chipman hoped it would be unnecessary to open the wounds associated with the "human suffering upon a stupendous scale." Better to let the healing process continue. However, healing could not be found, in Chipman's opinion, when Davis' allegations had opened the wounds again. Chipman felt compelled to answer Davis' article with a work of his own. From his home in northern California, Chipman published a short response, not much more than a pamphlet, *The Horrors of Andersonville*. Chipman eventually enlarged the pamphlet into a full 521-page volume, *The Tragedy of Andersonville*, in 1911. This work included large amounts of testimony presented at the trial and was published soon after the United Daughters of the Confederacy erected a monument at Andersonville honoring Wirz and repeating on its plaques some of the claims Davis made in *Belford's Magazine*.[58]

Davis' major thesis in the *Belford's Magazine* articles was that the conditions at Andersonville were caused by the North's suspension of the prisoner exchange cartel. Chipman noted that "Mr. Davis seems to have been obsessed with the idea that the cartel was the cause of all this suffering." This obsession, argued Chipman, was without foundation. Grant's decision to suspend the prisoner exchange cartel was not only justified, but also the only proper course. It was the South, not the North, argued Chipman, that violated the terms of the cartel. The North could not turn a blind eye to the South's misuse of the cartel to use soldiers in battle who had not been properly exchanged. And the North could not countenance the South's refusal to treat captured black soldiers and their white officers as other captured soldiers, instead threatening to put captured black soldiers to hard labor and return them to their masters and to execute their white officers. Morally, the North could not continue the cartel under those conditions.[59]

And even if further prisoner exchanges would have alleviated the problem of the large prison population in the South, common decency required Davis and the Confederacy to care properly for prisoners they chose to keep. "[I]n no event can it be allowed that the fact that Mr. Davis had more prisoners then he wished to feed relieved him from the duty of feeding them," said Chipman.[60]

While the question of cartel observance and the problem of the South's treatment of the Andersonville prisoners were issues of general concern, Chipman took offense, specifically, when Davis accused him of not affording Wirz a fair trial. Davis accused Chipman of two types of misdeeds: turning away two witnesses (Father Peter Whelan and Colonel Robert Ould, the Confederate exchange commissioner) who would have testified in defense of Wirz and suppressing testimony of a witness (Colonel D.H. Chandler) who could have given testimony favorable to Wirz. According to Davis, Whelan would have testified that he visited both Wirz and the prisoners at Andersonville. Wirz was an "irritable but kind-hearted men, especially toward the sick," according to Whelan. He thought the charge that Wirz had beaten the prisoners was unjust because Wirz's shoulder had been broken and he did not have the power to strike. Ould, on the other hand, appeared in Washington in response to a summons by Chipman on behalf of Wirz. He intended to testify concerning the South's offers and efforts to renew the prisoner exchange cartel, but Chipman rescinded the summons and did not allow Ould to testify. As to Chandler, Davis asserted that Chandler would have testified that Wirz did all that he could to improve the conditions at Andersonville; however, Chipman asked him just one question, whether the conditions at Andersonville had been reported to Davis. When he answered that he had reason to believe no such report had been made to Davis, Chandler was excused without giving his testimony favorable to Wirz.[61]

The charges of evidence suppression, responded Chipman, were not only unfounded but constituted "perversion of fact" and called into doubt Davis' own veracity. In fact, Whelan was allowed to testify at length in defense of Wirz. Ould's testimony was excluded by the commission on Chipman's objection that evidence concerning the prisoner exchange was irrelevant to the charges presented to the commission concerning the conspiracy and murder counts. This was a position Chipman took consistently through the trial—that the North's suspension of the prisoner exchange cartel was no defense to the conditions at Andersonville. And Chandler, the last witness whose testimony Davis alleged had been suppressed, answered much more than just the one question asserted by Davis. Chandler's prolonged testimony, said Chipman, "show[ed] a condition at the prison which he reported to the secretary of war, Mr. Seddon, to be a 'disgrace to the Confederacy.'" Chandler's testimony, with other evidence, supported a "plainly deducible" inference that Davis was aware of the conditions and deprivations at Andersonville.[62]

Finally, Chipman responded to the story circulating in the United States and repeated by Davis that three men visited Wirz the night before his execution and tried to get him to implicate Davis in exchange for his freedom. Chipman observed that the story "has no especial bearing upon the justness of the verdict of the Wirz trial." Concerning the merits of the story, Chipman reasoned: "[H]istory is not made of such unsubstantial figments of the imagination as came secondhand to Mr. Davis in this unconfirmed and anonymous manner. In truth, the government needed the support of no such witness as Wirz would have been. No human being, under the circumstances surrounding him, would have believed Wirz's testimony. Besides no such confession was necessary. Wirz had claimed at his trial that he was obeying the orders of his superiors, and that the Richmond authorities were responsible and not he, as will appear in the course of this volume. It is unbelievable that so dastardly a proposition came from Federal authority, and it finds place in this publication only because it apparently has some believers and because Mr. Davis had the audacity to give it currency by his public indorsement."[63]

More than a century after Wirz was convicted and executed and Davis published his final defense of Andersonville, Alan Dershowitz, famed American lawyer and law professor, wrote an introduction for a collector's edition of Chipman's *The Tragedy of Andersonville*, in which Dershowitz concluded that "[t]he totality of the evidence speaks for itself and it speaks convincingly of Wirz's moral and legal guilt." Placing Wirz's conviction and execution in a wider historical context, Dershowitz continued: "We must never forget, of course, that military history is generally written by the victors rather than the vanquished. This is even truer of postwar military trials. No Union camp commander was placed on trial for the killing of Confederate prisoners, nor was any Union general tried for the destruction of civilian cities. [¶] The trial, conviction and execution of Captain Wirz is an important episode in the development of the laws of warfare. Tragically, it did not prevent other atrocities in subsequent wars."[64]

8
The Capital of the United States (1865–1872)

Though not as violent as the war years, the years following the Civil War proved tumultuous and politically difficult. After a brief honeymoon period during which Washington politicians worked in harmony, Congress battled Johnson for control over reconstruction of the southern states. Johnson took the initiative, seeking to impose his view of reconstruction by executive order. But Radical Republicans controlling Congress pushed Johnson to approve reforms in the South that would obliterate the old order under which secession and slavery were sanctioned.

Congress demanded action to protect the civil rights of former slaves, "freedmen," in the parlance of the day. Slavery had been abolished, but new laws in the South took away from freedmen many of the gains they had made. The Radical Republicans succeeded in passing the Civil Rights Act of 1866 to protect the freedmen's rights. When Johnson vetoed the act, Congress overrode the veto, establishing its advantage in the political battles of the era.

Amidst this turmoil, Chipman and Belle settled into civilian life in the nation's capital. He intended to stay out of politics, build a patent law practice, and enjoy the social status that his service in the war and his contacts with the president, the secretary of war, and prominent military leaders had earned him. When it was extensively circulated that Chipman was a candidate for clerk of the House of Representatives, Chipman denied it, telling the *New York Times* that he had no desire to leave private life to return to public service. But it was hard to stay neutral. Congressional power grew with the Republicans' veto-proof majority, and Johnson attempted to circumvent the laws passed over his veto by issuing executive orders.[1]

As the contempt that Congress held for Johnson increased and the public generally agreed with Congress, Johnson took some missteps that lead to active opposition from Grant, perhaps the most popular man in the United States at the time and Chipman's friend and political ally. When the House of Representatives impeached Johnson in 1868, Chipman jumped in to assist the House members trying Johnson in the Senate, thus cementing his opposition to Lincoln's successor, from whom he had rejected the offer of the personal secretary position three years before. Chipman's more direct involvement in politics by assisting the House managers in Johnson's impeachment trial began a turbulent period of his life, comprising just seven years, during which he campaigned on behalf of Grant, accepted appointment as secretary of the District of Columbia, and, ultimately, won election as the District of Columbia's delegate to the House of Representatives, a position from which he retired in 1875.

Washington Society and Politics

Mark Twain's novel about life in the United States after the Civil War and, specifically, about greed and graft in Washington provides a true-to-life glimpse of the era, even if the characters are fictional. *The Gilded Age*, which Twain co-authored with Charles Dudley Warner, so accurately reflected the era that the period after the war became known as the Gilded Age, a time of progress and expansion, marked by extravagance and excess.

Twain's description of Washington society captured the spirit of the times, as well as the predicament of those attempting to qualify themselves in the capital's social circles. He observed three categories of social elite: the Antiques, the Middle Ground, and the Parvenus. The Antiques were the "cultivated, high-bred old families who looked back with pride upon an ancestry that had been always great in the nation's councils and its wars from the birth of the republic downward." At the other end of the aristocratic spectrum was the "Aristocracy of the Parvenus," those who attained social status by wealth. As Twain portrayed these two aristocracies, "[t]he aristocracy of the Antiques ignored the aristocracy of the Parvenus; the Parvenus laughed at the Antiques, (and secretly envied them.)"[2]

The aristocracy of the middle — Twain's "Middle Ground" — was the most powerful. It included influential representatives of the states serving in both the legislative and executive branches. "These gentlemen and their households were unostentatious people; they were educated and refined; they troubled themselves but little about the two other orders of nobility, but moved serenely in their wide orbit, confident in their own strength and well aware of the potency of their influence. They had no troublesome appearances to keep up, no rivalries which they cared to distress themselves about, no jealousies to fret over. They could afford to mind their own affairs and leave other combinations to do the same or do otherwise, just as they chose. They were people who were beyond reproach, and that was sufficient."[3]

No longer a military man and living in a city to which he came by assignment, Chipman did not match completely any of the categories into which Twain's characters nicely fit. Instead, Chipman went to Washington with some of the traits of at least two of the three aristocracies, as well as some commonness that made him appear his blood was not blue at all.

Chipman came from a prominent colonial family. His grandfather's cousin, Nathaniel Chipman, was one of the architects of Vermont's admission into the Union in 1791 and authored an influential text on government, which Thomas Jefferson kept on his bookshelf. More notable even than Nathaniel were Chipman's direct-line ancestors, some of whom participated in the first European migrations to America. John Howland came to America as John Carver's servant on the Mayflower in 1620. Three years after his arrival, he married Elizabeth Tilley, daughter of John and Elizabeth Tilley, all of whom were original *Mayflower* immigrants. John and Elizabeth Howland's daughter, Hope Howland, married John Chipman in Plymouth in 1646. John and Hope Chipman were Norton Parker Chipman's fourth-great-grandparents.[4]

Another of Chipman's ancestors, Reverend John Lathrop, was a seventeenth century Puritan preacher in England. Incarcerated for his religious teachings, he was freed temporarily to comfort his dying wife only because he pledged to return to jail. After she died, he returned to jail to fulfill his pledge. Later, he was freed to care for his motherless children and, in 1623, took them to America, where he became an influential religious leader.[5]

Chipman's family inherited from its forefathers the adventurous spirit of those Europeans who settled and colonized the East Coast of America and, later, pushed the frontier westward. From his early education and encouragement, Chipman adopted the attitudes of the northern states of the Union with regard to the moral and political issues of the day. In particular, Chipman was taught both at home and at school that slavery was morally wrong. His training also instilled in him a sense of the importance of the union of states, which led to his rapid and complete support of Lincoln's determination to save the Union. These two family tendencies, westward expansion and loyalty to nation, became motivating ideals throughout Chipman's life. Chipman's ancestry was a defining factor in his devotion to the Union and a connection to the Antiques of Washington society.

Despite Chipman's ancestral heritage, he fit in better with the aristocracy of the middle, even if he did not arrive in Washington as the representative of one of the states or as an executive branch official. He must have felt comfortable with his decision to stay in Washington and open his law practice there because he could have as easily gone back to Iowa where he knew he had friends, family, and professional connections. It may be that Belle was influential in that decision making process. She had become friends with Julia Dent Grant and other wives of the military and governmental elite. Although, like Chipman, she was from out west, her family was sufficiently wealthy that she had learned to enjoy the culture and sociality available in Washington. Settled in to married life and life without the military command structure, Chipman could concentrate on his law practice.

The Chipmans experienced personal tragedy in 1867. A son was born to them that year and died in infancy. The records do not reflect that the little boy was named, leading one to conclude that he died before the Chipmans had a chance to give him a name. This son was the Chipmans' only naturally born child. They later adopted two girls.[6]

Chipman enjoyed access to and association with the elite Union generals of the Civil War, including Grant and Sheridan. In September 1867, Sheridan visited Washington, where Chipman showed him around.

Sheridan had served as military governor of Texas and Louisiana, but Johnson relieved him, over Grant's protest, when Sheridan replaced civilian authorities who impeded reconstruction. Of the conflict between Sheridan and Johnson, Sheridan recorded in his memoirs: "In administering the affairs of those States, I never acted except by authority, and always from conscientious motives. I tried to guard the rights of everybody in accordance with the law. In this I was supported by General Grant and opposed by President Johnson. The former had at heart, above every other consideration, the good of his country, and always sustained me with approval and kind suggestions. The course pursued by the President was exactly the opposite, and seems to prove that in the whole matter of reconstruction he was governed less by patriotic motives than by personal ambitions. Add to this his natural obstinacy of character and personal enmity toward me, and no surprise should be occasioned when I say that I heartily welcomed the order that lifted from me my unsought burden."[7]

On his way to his new assignment as commander of the Department of the Missouri, Sheridan reported to Washington. Word circulated widely that Sheridan would speak from his balcony at the Willard Hotel. For hours before the scheduled appearance, throngs gathered outside the hotel and on the other balconies. The crowd was larger than had been seen in Washington in years for such an event. Veterans' groups marched in procession to the hotel; political associations showed their colors; and bands played martial music. Admirers lined the corridors of the hotel and showered Sheridan with bouquets as

After the Civil War, Chipman remained in Washington, D.C., where he practiced law and participated in national and local politics (Library of Congress).

he passed. Such was the reception of a Civil War hero in Washington during the difficult years of reconstruction.[8]

At nine in the evening, gas lamps lighting the street, Chipman appeared on the hotel balcony with Sheridan leaning on his arm. Cheers issued from the crowd in waves, resounding again and again. When the ovation subsided, Chipman addressed the mass. He related to his audience that he met Sheridan five years earlier, in Missouri, when Sheridan was assigned as chief commissary of Curtis' troops. "But ministering to the bodily wants of our soldiers was too constrained a sphere for one of such pluck and mettle," recalled Chipman. He summarized Sheridan's rise to fame as a cavalry officer, the honors bestowed on him by Lincoln, who loved Sheridan as a son, and his recent leadership in New Orleans against the remnants of the Confederacy. Turning the crowd's attention to the general, Chipman exclaimed: "With hearts full of thanks to you General Sheridan for your noble defence of the right under circumstances such as never before tried your courage, your patriotism and your ability, we congratulate and welcome you among us." Sheridan spoke only briefly, thanking the crowd and assuring his audience that he would always remember the honor paid him that night. Sheridan visited the War Department, reporting to Grant there. He also "paid the usual conventional compliment of a visit" to the president, reported the *New York Times*, "but the interview was so exceedingly formal that it did not occupy more than five minutes."[9]

As rancor built between the Republican-led Congress and Johnson, Congress asserted its power by passing the Tenure of Office Act in 1867. This law would prevent the president from removing a cabinet officer without congressional consent. Congress overrode Johnson's understandable veto. In spite of Congress, Johnson wanted Stanton to resign as secretary of war so he could replace him with Grant. This was not an altogether unpopular move. Even though Congress opposed Johnson's request, Grant maintained a place of prominence and popularity in the postwar nation. When Stanton refused to resign, Johnson waited until Congress adjourned and then suspended Stanton, who protested but eventually submitted "to superior force," as he saw it. Grant took over as secretary of war, but, when Congress reconvened in December 1867, it refused to conform to Johnson's wishes. Johnson felt he could force Stanton to seek judicial recourse and obtain a decision on the constitutionality of the Tenure of Office Act, which recourse would be slow and the outcome uncertain. Grant, however, brought the power struggle to a head by vacating the office, leaving Stanton the legal officeholder.

For Grant's part, this was more of a political move to antagonize Johnson than a legal opinion concerning the validity of the law. As president, Grant later refused to submit to the requirements of the Tenure of Office Act and signed the bill repealing it. The rift between Johnson and Grant was more than just political but extended also to the important Washington social scene, of which the Chipmans were a young and important part. They, and many others, believed the many parties hosted by the Grants in the mansion of the General of the Army were more prominent and popular than those hosted in the White House.

Directly challenging Congress and the Tenure of Office Act, Johnson tried to have Stanton removed from the War Department. The attempt failed, and Congress jumped on the asserted illegality of Johnson's action to initiate impeachment proceedings in the House. On February 24, 1868, the House passed a resolution impeaching Johnson by a vote of 126 to 47. Trial in the Senate began on March 13, presided over by Chief Justice Salmon P. Chase. Congressman John A. Logan, a former Union general and, like Chipman, wounded at Fort Donelson, served as one of the House managers, the members of the House of Representatives who prosecuted the impeachment trial in the Senate. Although Chipman maintained his private law practice during this time, most of his time was spent assisting Logan in crafting and drafting legal arguments. On May 16, the Senate voted 35 in favor of and 19 against conviction, one vote short of the two-thirds majority needed to convict and expel Johnson from office.[10]

Memorial Day

In the spring of 1868, as the Senate was trying Johnson, the war was more than two years past. The events of the war remained fresh in Chipman's mind. Along with thousands of other Union veterans, Chipman joined the Grand Army of the Republic. By that spring, he was adjutant-general of the Grand Army, serving with the commander-in-chief, Congressman Logan. Chipman soon found that the prior administration had been mismanaged. "The records which came into my hands furnish no evidence of there having been reciprocal relations kept up between the Posts and Departments and National Headquarters," reported Chipman to the 1869 national encampment. Logan and Chipman worked together to turn the Grand Army into a disciplined organization, modeled after the Union Army. Though nonpolitical in theory, the Grand Army was active in Republican politics. "What such an army would accomplish when properly drilled," wrote Grand Army historian Stuart McConnell, "was already apparent to these political officers from their experience in marshaling the massive 'soldier vote' for Lincoln in 1864 and Grant in 1868. Military discipline meant success at the polls."[11]

In his Grand Army role, however, Chipman saw more than just political advantage. He also saw the opportunity to honor fallen comrades. One of Chipman's fellow Civil War veterans wrote from Cincinnati describing a practice followed in Europe. The custom among some of the Europeans was to strew flowers on the graves of the national heroes. Chipman's friend wondered if the practice might be appropriate to commemorate Civil War heroes. The idea immediately appealed to Chipman. It was a fitting opportunity for the Grand Army to institute a tradition to perpetuate the memory of those who paid the highest price to preserve the Union.[12]

The practical obstacle facing Chipman was the rapid approach of summer. Many of the finest flowers were already in bloom or would soon bloom and, before long, there would be a less than desirable supply of flowers. On May 5, though in the midst of the impeachment trial, Chipman prepared a rough draft of a Grand Army order declaring May 30 as the day set aside for decorating the graves of Civil War veterans. He would have designated May

31, the last day of the month; however, the 31st fell on Sunday in 1868, and Chipman thought it more appropriate to engage in such activity on Saturday. Logan was occupied in Congress, so Chipman took the draft order to him there. Logan made some minor changes and promptly approved the order. He directed Chipman to issue the order at once. Chipman took the order to the Associated Press and it went out to the rest of the country by telegraph and mail.[13]

The Grand Army order directed members to decorate "the graves of comrades who died in defense of their country during the late rebellion, and whose bodies now lie in almost every city, village, and hamlet churchyard in the land." "Their soldier lives," continued the order, "were the reveille of freedom to a race in chains and their death a tattoo of rebellious tyranny in arms. We should guard their graves with sacred vigilance. All that the consecrated wealth and taste of the Nation can add to their adornment and security is but a fitting tribute to the memory of her slain defenders. Let no wanton foot tread rudely on such hallowed ground. Let pleasant paths invite the coming and going to reverent visitors and fond mourners. Let no vandalism of avarice or neglect, no ravages of time, testify to the present or to the coming generations that we have forgotten as a people the cost of a free and undivided Republic."[14]

The Grand Army appointed Chipman chairman of the Committee of Arrangements for the coming observance at Arlington National Cemetery, in which were buried scores of Civil War veterans, including the remains of 2,111 unknown soldiers. On Wednesday, May 27, Chipman delivered invitations: "You are cordially invited to attend the ceremonies of Decorating the Graves of Union Dead, on Saturday, 30th instant, at one o'clock, P.M., at the National Cemetery, Arlington."[15]

Belle served on the Committee of Decorations. She and many of the wives of prominent generals and politicians, including Mrs. Grant, Mrs. Logan, and Lucretia Garfield, wife of James A. Garfield, later to be the 20th president of the United States, met on Friday, May 29, at the Foundry Church to receive donations of flowers and arrange them. Citizens of Washington and public gardens donated a profusion of flowers and wreaths, transported to the cemetery by ambulances.[16]

On Saturday, a crowd of about 5,000 gathered at Arlington in front of the mansion. Reverend Byron Sunderland, who had met with Lincoln personally and encouraged him to issue the Emancipation Proclamation, opened the services with prayer. After a hymn, James Garfield, then a member of the House of Representatives, delivered an oration. A procession formed and proceeded through the gardens south of the mansion while children and orphans of Civil War veterans strewed flowers on the graves they passed. The proces-

sion stopped at the tomb of the unknown Civil War soldiers, which was decorated while the Fifth Cavalry Band played the Dead March. After another
hymn and prayer, another member of Congress read Lincoln's Gettysburg
Address. The crowd then dispersed to all parts of the cemetery to complete
the task of decorating the graves. Finally, the band played the Star-Spangled
Banner as a signal to all to return to the stand, where the exercises were closed
with a benediction and prayer. The *Washington Evening Star* reported the ceremonies the same day and congratulated Chipman on the solemn and impressive exercises.[17]

The 1868 celebration, at Arlington and many other cemeteries throughout the country, was not the first in which Civil War graves were decorated.
As early as 1866, several localities held such tributes. Disturbed at the sight
of bare graves, women who had visited the graves of Confederate soldiers
from the Battle of Shiloh placed flowers on those graves. The town of Water-
loo, New York, held a ceremony on May 5, 1866, honoring Civil War veterans. The Grand Army's order resulted in ceremonies in 27 states of the Union
in 1868, and enlarged to 31 states in 1869. For many years, May 30 was the
date of Decoration Day, and later Memorial Day, ceremonies and observances.
By the late 1800s, most states had set aside the day as an official holiday. After
World War I, the holiday was expanded to honor those who had died in all
American wars. And in 1971, Congress passed a law fixing Memorial Day on
the last Monday of May each year.

In 1922, the *Washington Times* published an account of the origin of
Memorial Day, as related by Logan's widow, presenting a view that the con-
cept of Memorial Day was all Logan's idea. A member of Congress from California, Charles F. Curry, brought the article to Chipman's attention, and
Chipman replied to Curry, enclosing a printed speech he had given in 1884
in Sacramento concerning the holiday's origin. The idea had come from the
Cincinnati veteran, specifically, and from the existing tradition, in Europe and
the United States, of decorating the graves of deceased veterans. Chipman
wrote that he had "great regard for Mrs. Logan" and would never "enter any
controversy with her," but he desired to set the record straight. By unanimous consent of the House of Representatives, Curry was allowed to read into
the *Congressional Record* Chipman's letter and 1884 speech, along with a brief
summary of Chipman's accomplishments.[18]

Delegate to Congress

Chipman's political future changed in November 1868 when Grant, who,
incidentally, was Chipman's distant cousin through the lineage of John Lath-

rop, was elected president, defeating former New York governor Horatio Seymour by a somewhat narrow popular vote margin but an Electoral College landslide, 214 to 80. And Chipman's closeness to Grant soon became evident when Grant called upon him to defend a mutual friend.

Grant had appointed Ely Samuel Parker as commissioner of the Office of Indian Affairs, a cabinet level position. Parker was a full-blooded Iroquois, a Seneca chief. While serving as adjutant to Grant during the Civil War, Parker attended the meeting at Appomattox Court House and drafted the surrender agreement which Grant and Lee signed. As Indian commissioner, Parker succeeded in rooting out much corruption in the federal agency and brokered agreements between Indian tribes and the federal government. His and Grant's political enemies, however, brought charges against him in the Committee on Appropriations of the House of Representatives. The accusers claimed that Parker misappropriated funds. Grant asked Chipman to defend Parker. With his customary diligence and attention to detail, Chipman gathered the facts, crafted his legal arguments, and presented his case to the House committee. As a result, the committee exonerated Parker of all charges.[19]

Left: Ulysses S. Grant signed this John H. Littlefield lithograph for Chipman. It hung in Chipman's chambers, and still hangs, along with the lithograph of Lincoln, in the chambers of the presiding justice of the California Court of Appeal, Third Appellate District (California Court of Appeal, Third Appellate District). *Right:* A Seneca chief, Ely S. Parker was Grant's military secretary and was the scribe when General Robert E. Lee surrendered to Grant. Later as the commissioner of Indian Affairs, Parker was accused of corruption. Chipman successfully defended him during a congressional inquiry (Smithsonian Institution).

With a change in the form of government in the District of Columbia came the opportunity for Grant to entice Chipman into government service. He appointed Chipman as secretary of the District of Columbia. The position of secretary of the District of Columbia had been created as part of a move to a territorial form of government for the nation's capital. Until after the Civil War, the municipalities in the District of Columbia, including Washington and Georgetown, were governed by elected officials, even though Congress held ultimate control. Unlike the well-defined relationship between the federal government and state governments, the relationship between the district municipalities and Congress was more of a dual authority and responsibility, with Congress retaining the last word but exercising the prerogative only infrequently. This ill-defined arrangement resulted in power struggles and finger-pointing. As economic conditions deteriorated and lawlessness increased, especially during the 1850s and 1860s, Congress faulted the local authorities for failing to keep order and promote economic well-being and eventually based its move away from district self-government on this supposed failure.

After the Civil War, the war to preserve the Union and abolish slavery, came the question of whether the blacks should be allowed to vote. Eight northern states enfranchised blacks to some extent, and Congress signaled its interest in doing the same in the District of Columbia, which would have the practical effect of fortifying the Republican vote. Before Congress could act, the municipalities called a special election, in December 1865, to present the issue to the current voters. A bipartisan electorate voted clearly against black suffrage. In Washington, the vote against black suffrage was 6,591 to 35. The result in Georgetown was unanimous: no votes in favor of black suffrage and 712 votes against. As Congress proceeded surely, though slowly, toward black suffrage, some citizens of the district let it be known that they would prefer to disenfranchise themselves rather than submit to equal suffrage.

A bill enfranchising blacks in the District of Columbia passed both houses in December 1866, and went to Johnson. As Congress expected, he vetoed the bill. As Johnson expected, Congress promptly overrode the veto. With easy requirements of one year's residence and 21 years of age, 5,000 black men qualified to vote. In the spring of 1868, Democrat John T. Green ran against Republican Sayles J. Bowen for mayor. For the first time in United States history, the election was decided by the black vote with Bowen, the former postmaster general who favored the advancement of blacks, narrowly defeating Green. The results prompted civil unrest, and citizens of both parties feared violence in the district. The memories of the recent war, however, made even the strongly adverse partisans reject renewed aggression on the issue of race.

Despite their newfound electoral equality, the black population of the District of Columbia was anything but equal in economic and social status. Many of them were refugees from southern states who arrived in the district both during and after the war to escape the deprivations of the South. Some of them were old and disabled, with no provision for their care. In the winter, scores of these refugees were found in distress, even frozen or starved to death, in their makeshift cabins. Some found freedom in this condition more distressing than slavery had been.

The plight of poor blacks was just one issue plaguing the district. About the time Grant took office, a movement to relocate the seat of government to St. Louis gained momentum. One of the chief arguments in favor of the move was the condition of the city.

Historian James Huntington Whyte described what the capital looked like in 1865: "The dome of the Capitol was at last finished, but the Washington Monument was only a pile of masonry, the funds for its erection long since exhausted.... Pennsylvania Avenue had been paved with cobblestones by the Federal Government, though, as a result of wartime traffic, its gravel surface had become a mass of ruts and potholes. On many of the side streets pigs, goats, cattle and geese roamed unmolested and occasionally strayed into the open vestibules of private homes. Drainage was by means of surface gutters which were overgrown with weeds and filled with green-scummed slime. Crossing the streets in irregular ruts, they obliged the drivers of vehicles to come to a cautious stop before bumping over them. At night the city was so badly illuminated that few ventured to take their carriages outside the center of the city. John Randolph's dictum of three decades before that 'a Washington pedestrian should provide himself with an overcoat, a duster, a pair of rubber shoes and a fan' was still valid in 1865."[20]

Grant opposed relocation of the capital. Instead, he saw in the deplorable condition of the city an opportunity to relieve some of the suffering of the black residents. He could put them to work on grading the streets, building the sewer system, creating and repairing sidewalks. Grant's opposition to relocation took the form of ameliorating the conditions that prompted distaste for the city. The work began, though slowly for want of funding, which depended almost entirely on congressional largesse.

In 1870, Congress, recognizing the ineffectiveness of the dual authority form of government, focused on organizational change. Competing versions of a new "territorial" government for the district passed the Senate and House. The Senate version provided for a legislature, along with a governor and secretary, all elected by the voters. It also provided for a non-voting delegate in Congress, as other territories had. The House amendments allowed the president to appoint a governor. It split the legislature into two houses, giving the president the authority to appoint the members of the upper chamber and leaving the lower chamber to popular election. The House version also proposed a Board of Public Works, appointed by the president. The houses eventually compromised and passed a bill to form a new government in the District of Columbia, effective June 1, 1871, essentially reflecting the House's amendments to the Senate's original version. The appointment, instead of popular election, of most district officers, it was hoped, would result in less partisanship and a more efficient, simplified government. With this renewed attempt to create workable governance in the district, and with Grant's plan to improve the city and put the poverty-stricken blacks to work, the support to move the capitol to St. Louis all but disappeared.

In March 1871, Grant appointed political allies to the new governmental positions in the District of Columbia. He appointed Henry D. Cooke, president of the First National Bank of Washington, as territorial governor,

In 1871, Frederick Douglass, a former slave, ran in the Republican primary to be the first delegate to Congress from the District of Columbia, but Chipman won the nomination. Black voters were the deciding factor when Chipman prevailed in the general election (National Archives).

believing Cooke's business background would be put to advantage in district fiscal affairs. As secretary, Grant appointed Chipman. The president also included the district's black leaders in the new government, appointing black statesman Frederick Douglass, along with two other blacks, to the upper chamber of the district legislature.

The hope of Congress and Grant that the new territorial government in the District of Columbia would be efficient and provide benefits beyond a more democratic government soon dissipated. And the source of mounting disillusionment was the powerful Board of Public Works, the commission appointed to implement Grant's vision of improving the city while putting the poor to work. Alexander Shepherd, a businessman and plumber, and former Union soldier, later known as "Boss" Shepherd, became the undisputed driving force on the five-member Board of Public Works. Tall, strong, and handsome, Shepherd was naturally likable and inspired the confidence of the president. His business ventures, however, had been aggressive and speculative.

With the vote for the elective offices in the new government approaching in April 1871, the district's Republican Central Committee gathered on March 29 to choose its candidate for delegate to the House of Representatives. Frederick Douglass chaired the committee and delivered the first speech. Chipman then took the floor and delivered his own speech. On the first ballot, Chipman received 43 votes, Douglass 27 votes, and others a total of 29 votes. The voting was conspicuously not along racial lines. Five black delegates voted for Chipman, while several of the white delegates voted for Douglass. Chipman's nomination apparent, all of the delegates threw their support behind him. Chipman resigned as secretary of the district and stood for election.[21]

In the general election, Chipman faced Democrat Richard T. Merrick, an attorney from a prominent Maryland family. The campaign was short — less than a month — but contentious. The Democrats sought to make race the divisive issue of the election. They accused Chipman and the Republicans of urging blacks from Maryland and Virginia to travel to the district on Election Day and vote. Congress was considering a bill to integrate the school system, and Merrick seized the opportunity to challenge Chipman to a debate on the issue. Chipman declined. Douglass used his influence and abilities to instruct the voters on the differences between the candidates — Merrick representing "the good old days of slavery," and Chipman "a new era in American civilization." "I say shame," wrote Douglass, "eternal shame on any colored voter who supports Richard T. Merrick, and withered be the black man's arm and blasted be the black man's head who casts a vote against General N.P. Chipman."[22]

On the Democrats' claims that the Republicans illegally imported black residents of Maryland and Virginia to vote in the district, Chipman issued a strong denial. Although the black population of the district came to the polls in droves, it was understandable, he explained, that a group denied its rights for so long would be zealous to vote when given the chance.[23]

The ballots were party tickets. The Democratic ticket included Merrick as the candidate for delegate to the House and several other Democrats running for other offices. Chipman led the similar Republican ticket. The Democratic ticket was white, and the Republican ticket was striped. The Democrats printed counterfeit Republican tickets and tried to deceive illiterate black voters into mistakenly voting for Merrick. Lord Stafford Northcote, a British statesman visiting Washington during the election, wrote in his diary: "Agents of either party stood at the windows of the polling-offices and tendered their respective tickets to the voters as they came up. As many of the voters (especially the coloured men) could not read, they took the ticket of their party colour without examination. The agents therefore had tickets of their opponent's colour with their own men's names printed on them, and tried to pass these off, but apparently without much success, as the opposite agent was always alive to the trick."[24]

The ploy to get the blacks to vote for Merrick was unsuccessful. Chipman won the election, getting 15,195 votes to Merrick's 11,104. According to Northcote, "[t]he election was carried entirely by the coloured voters, of whom there were about 10,000, as against 17,000 whites. The blacks voted for Chipman almost to a man."[25]

Once sworn in as the district's delegate, Chipman treated the position as work, not as an honorific title. He typically reported to his office each morning at nine and either received constituents with requests or met with members of the House until ten, when he attended hearings of the House's Committee of the District of Columbia. After committee hearings, he worked well into the evening on behalf of the district's interests.

During his first year in office, Chipman introduced 32 bills and presented 94 memorials on behalf of constituents. The private memorials sought all kinds of action from the House, such as pension claims, recompense for property destroyed by the government, and charters.

Much of Chipman's work went to encourage Congress to accept fiscal responsibility for the district. Congress' design in creating the district was to limit business interests and maximize governmental interests, which succeeded in minimizing the influence of business interests in the district but had the effect of providing little tax revenue. Chipman sought congressional funding for public schools, police, a new jail, sewers, streets, and bridges. In all, he obtained more than one million dollars worth of funding in his first year. He also began his endeavor to complete the Washington Monument, which stood ugly and unfinished in sight of the capitol.[26]

Chipman's speeches became the hallmark of his tenure as a House delegate. Full of historical perspective and convincing details mixed with principles of broad appeal and importance, the passionate speeches were reported in the local and national press. Historian Whyte called him "one of the best speakers in the party, a man outside the realm of petty feuds." From universal public education to federal responsibility for district infrastructure, presidential politics to local public finance, the plight of disabled veterans to the completion of the Washington Monument, Chipman lent his attention, research, scripting, and voice to the causes he believed in.[27]

This Currier and Ives print depicts the United States Capitol circa 1872 to 1874 while Chipman served as the District of Columbia's delegate to the House of Representatives (Library of Congress).

Concerning the right of the district's black population to public education, for example, Chipman urged: "These people cannot leave us nor would we have them. They are industrious, frugal, law-abiding, good citizens, but they came among us, many of them in a condition of illiteracy and poverty which had been enforced upon them by the nature of our laws, and being directly responsible for their condition as the general government is, it is plainly its duty to make provision for their education."[28]

Thomas Nast and the 1872 Presidential Campaign

As a delegate to the House, Chipman used what influence the position brought him not only to lobby Congress on behalf of the district but also to assist fellow Republicans politically. Always adept at speechmaking on behalf of his favorite candidates, Chipman found he could assist in other ways as an insider in the political establishment. In 1872, he worked closely with Grant and for Grant in the president's reelection campaign.

Chipman was not only politically attuned to Grant; he also admired Grant's strength of character. When Grant died in 1885, Chipman recorded:

"He was a devoted husband and father, loving and kind to his wife and children. I cannot conceive of a man truly great who has not these virtues." Chipman's most effective assistance to Grant during the election campaign came, not in speeches, though he delivered them in support of Grant both in Washington and in Missouri, but in his coordination with a political cartoonist on behalf of Grant.[29]

As growing numbers of Republicans became dissatisfied with Grant as a result of ineffective government and corruption among public officials, his reelection was not a foregone conclusion. Some in his own party opposed his insistence on maintaining a military presence in the South to enforce reconstruction. They also believed Grant had not done enough to reform civil service and prevent corruption. In January 1872, a call had gone out to convene a breakaway Liberal Republican convention to nominate an alternative to Grant. Horace Greeley, the editor of the influential *New York Tribune* emerged as the candidate of the Liberal Republicans and Democrats.

To help Grant, Chipman enlisted Thomas Nast, the political cartoonist for *Harper's Weekly*. Of Nast's influence during the Civil War, Lincoln said, "Thomas Nast has been our best recruiting sergeant. His emblematic cartoons have never failed to arouse enthusiasm and patriotism." Younger than Chipman, this German born but New York raised cartoonist deplored slavery and had a talent for portraying the important political and social issues of the Civil War. His cartoons urged northerners to support Lincoln and defeat the rebels. After the war, his popular-

Thomas Nast, considered the father of American political cartooning, influenced the Civil War and the 1872 presidential election with his cartoons. Chipman was Nast's contact in post-war Washington (Library of Congress).

ity swelled as his incisive cartoons helped root out corruption in New York. He created or popularized such lasting symbols as Uncle Sam, the Republican elephant, the Democratic donkey, and the modern rendering of Santa Claus, plump and jolly.

The Chipmans invited Nast to be their guest in Washington early in the presidential campaign. As Chipman dined with Grant one evening, Chipman confided to the president that Nast would soon accept the invitation. Grant replied, "I would very much like to see Mr. Nast again."[30]

In Nast's opinion, the politicians were cruel to Grant, expecting him to act on their every wish and getting angry with him when he did not. Nast arrived in the latter part of January and embarked on an aggressive social calendar, arranged by the Chipmans. When Grant heard Nast had arrived, he sent for the 31-year-old artist.

Nast wrote home to his wife about the presidential visit: "I had a very pleasant chat with him about everything in general, and I was very much pleased with the open way in which he spoke to me. I was with him about an hour. When we got through, he asked me to come and dine with him and his family at five P.M. I went to dine with Grant and his family at five and did not get away from the White House until nearly ten.... It is thought a great honor to be asked to dine with the President at his private table."[31]

Chipman threw Nast, in Nast's words, "a man's party for the big men of Washington to meet me, and I can tell you they came! The Vice-President came, judges from the Supreme Court, the Secretary of War, the Secretary of the Treasury, a great many senators, some members of the press — in fact, all that could come were here."[32]

The nation took an interest in Nast's presence in Washington. Back in New York, Nast's *Harper's Weekly* reported Nast's activities in its "Personals" section: "Mr. Nast, who was recently in Washington to look after our national interests, was obliged while there to undergo an amount of reception, lunch, dining, and that style of thing that well nigh shattered a constitution, by-laws, and rules of order previously deemed of adamantine strength. In an especial manner was he entertained by those superior beings who constitute the gov'ment."[33]

Several days after the party at the Chipmans' residence, Belle Chipman took Nast to make calls on women in the city. Nast thought it "strange" that the women were as interested in his work as were the men. He saw the president nearly every day and wrote home to his wife, "The power I have here frightens me. But you will keep watch on me, won't you? You will not let me use it in a bad cause." Before Nast returned to New York after a whirlwind two-week tour of Washington, Grant again invited Nast to dine with him at his private table, an honor that surprised even Chipman, who had worked so hard to orchestrate Nast's Washington experience and presence.[34]

Nast's biographer, Albert Bigelow Paine, recounted Nast's visit to Washington, examining the extreme flattery and celebration. Defending Nast's ethical position, Paine commented that "it was avowed that while Tommy Nast could not be bought with money, he could be influenced by adulation and fine dinners — and had left Washington, pledged to Grant and the Administration."[35]

Chipman, along with Grant and the entire Washington establishment, understood the power of Nast's pen. Perhaps more than any other time before or since, the political cartoon went well beyond the reflection of public opinion to the actual creation of public opinion. Nast had the power to help bring together the North in the struggle against the South and, in the postwar country. That power extended to influence on presidential elections. But despite this power and the understanding Chipman had of Nast's popularity and following, the relationship between Chipman and Nast was much more than a political alliance of convenience. When Nast later fell on hard times, Chipman organized an effort to raise funds for the struggling artist. Paine wrote that Chipman was "always a faithful friend of Nast."[36]

Nast's work during the campaign was effective, highlighting Greeley's embarrassing idiosyncrasies and inconsistencies. In a February 10 cartoon, Nast portrayed Greeley the editor presenting the nomination to Greeley the farmer. The caption, "Cincinnatus," was a play on the site of the upcoming Liberal Republican convention in Cincinnati. The caption also referred to the Roman general who left his farm to accept a commission as general. Though the attitude of the cartoon was mildly mocking, it was the harbinger of a fierce series of cartoons caricaturing Greeley and ridiculing him throughout the 1872 campaign.

Keeping a constant stream of correspondence, Chipman wrote to Nast in March, congratulating him: "Your last pictures are excellent. I fell in with the President this morning during his morning walk. He says you are not only a genius but one of the greatest wits in the country. He says your pictures are full of fine humor." Chipman continued: "Did you see what Greeley said of you the other day, editorially? Speaking of Harper's he spoke of you as the 'blackguard of the paper, paid to defame, etc. etc.'... I infer that Greeley gives up the Philadelphia Convention to Grant. So far as I can discover, the Cincinnati movement does not strengthen." Chipman's estimation of the strength of the Cincinnati movement, the Liberal Republicans, was inaccurate, but he was right about Grant prevailing in Philadelphia at the Republican convention. Chipman closed his letter to Nast: "I have very little gossip to send you."[37]

Nast continued to lampoon Greeley, depicting him with a pumpkin-like head, bespectacled and almost sightless. He made fun of Greeley's self-impor-

ROMISH POLITICS—ANY THING TO BEAT GRANT.

IRISH ROMAN CATHOLIC INVADER. "The Y. M. C. A. want the Bible in the public school, assuming that this is a Christian country. We want the Priest, the Brother, and the Sister in our public schools, not assuming, but endeavoring to effect, that this is a Catholic country."—St. Louis Western Watchman, July 13, 1872.

Thomas Nast's cartoon from the August 17, 1872, edition of *Harper's Weekly*, criticizing Greeley for conspiring with the "Irish Roman Catholic Invader" (Library of Congress).

tant pamphlet "What I Know About Farming," by including in Greeley's pocket various pamphlets such as "What I Know About Bailing Out," "What I Know About Eating My Own Words," and "What I Know About Everything." The most effective of Nast's cartoons featured Greeley handing over a defenseless black man to a Klansman who had just knifed a black mother and child and held the dagger hidden behind his back. Nast's intention was "to hit the enemy between the eyes and knock him down."[38]

While Grant's reelection was hotly contested, Chipman's reelection as the district's delegate to Congress was assured. He enjoyed the support of the most powerful political forces in Washington, from the president to the Republican leadership to the district's black leadership. Speeches made on Chipman's behalf reported the gains the district had made in congressional attention and funding. As a member of the Republican majority, Chipman could continue to obtain favorable treatment for the district.[39]

Chipman's own speeches concentrated on the presidential campaign and issues of national importance, as well as the attitudes of the presidential candidates toward the needs of the district. Greeley, pointed out Chipman, opposed improvements in the district, while Grant had proven his loyalty to the district by directing millions of dollars worth of funding to district interests. Chipman warned district citizens that Greeley preferred moving the capitol to St. Louis, or even New York.[40]

On Election Day, Chipman captured 12,793 votes to 7,155 for his opponent, C.H. Hines. Likewise, Grant prevailed over Greeley, and the district was not disappointed when Grant continued his policy of funding district improvements, despite the rising financial and political cost of doing so.[41]

Greeley's defeat was devastating. His wife died just before Election Day. Grief, disappointment, and recognition of his failure resulted in physical suffering and sickness. Within a month after the election he died.

Having opposed Greeley so vigorously and through so many means, Chipman was left empty by his political victories of that fall. Perhaps exhibiting a twinge of guilt, Chipman never again criticized Greeley by name but quoted him prominently and favorably in his later writings.[42]

9

The Unfinished Obelisk
(1872–1875)

While Grant enjoyed widespread support in the election of 1872, the tide of public opinion soon turned against him and the Republicans. Through Chipman's second congressional term, national support for Grant and the District of Columbia waned as the public and politicians recognized the out-of-control cost of the extensive improvements implemented by Boss Shepherd and the Board of Public Works. Cronyism and corruption diminished national interest in further district improvements and occasioned charges of graft against Grant and his administration.

Congress lost patience with the territorial government it had created for the district in 1871, and, in 1874, voted to disband it, effective in 1875. The organization of the government had been too cumbersome and expensive, without adequate checks against interests contrary to congressional and national desires. There was some interest in preserving a seat for a delegate from the district in the House of Representatives. But, finally, that proposal failed, and the seat was set to dissolve, along with the territorial form of government, upon Chipman's completion of his second term.

Although the die had been cast, Chipman still saw opportunities to draw lasting benefits to the district during his second term. But his inability to vote in Congress limited his influence. On the consequential and continuing issue of reconstruction, he had little to say. As a Union soldier and steadfast Republican, Chipman held views favorable to the North. His zealous prosecution of Captain Wirz sealed his reputation as an advocate for the view that the rebels should not be forgiven so easily. Yet, he was neither outspoken nor prominent with respect to the pressing national issues of the day, even though he continued to work behind the scenes in support of Grant's administration.

While he maintained a low profile on national issues, probably as a result of his lack of a vote, he became the champion the District of Columbia needed during the window of opportunity for development and growth in the nation's capital. Of the local issues, one, in particular, was of interest not only within the district but everywhere in the nation — finishing the obelisk to honor George Washington, the father of his country. It was an issue the North and South could agree on.

When Chipman took his seat as a delegate in the House of Representatives, the Washington Monument stood partially finished — untouched for more than 10 years. Only 174 feet of the planned 600 feet had been completed before funding ran out, political intrigue interfered, and the Civil War sapped both interest and further funding.[1]

Mark Twain provided a colorful and sarcastic visual perspective from the Capitol: "Still in the distance, but on this side of the water and close to its edge, the Monument to the Father of his Country towers out of the mud — sacred soil is the customary term. It has the aspect of a factory chimney with the top broken off. The skeleton of a decaying scaffolding lingers about its summit, and tradition says that the spirit of Washington often comes down and sits on those rafters to enjoy this tribute of respect which the nation has reared as the symbol of its unappeasable gratitude."[2]

Twain reflected the growing consensus and consternation of the citizenry when he scolded that, by the time the monument was finished, Washington would be known as the "Great-Great-Grandfather of his Country." He also commented on the irreverent scene around the neglected monument: "The memorial Chimney stands in a quiet pastoral locality that is full of reposeful expression. With a glass you can see the cow-sheds about its base, and the contented sheep nibbling pebbles in the desert solitudes that surround it, and the tired pigs dozing in the holy calm of its protecting shadow."[3]

The New York Herald, urging completion of the monument, called it "a disgrace to our people."[4]

The district faced many problems resulting from neglect and graft. Of these problems, the most obvious to any visitor to the nation's capital was the unfinished state of the Washington Monument. Appointed to chair the House's select committee on the Washington National Monument, Chipman undertook two tasks he believed were indispensable to garner support to complete the monument: he initiated a thorough review of the history of the efforts to build the monument and he obtained the help of the Army Corps of Engineers to study the existing structure and determine the feasibility and cost of continuing the work. Each of these two tasks turned out to be instrumental in Chipman's plan to see the monument completed. Although Chipman's initial goal was to finish the monument in time for the nation's centennial in 1876, the bill appropriating the needed funds was not signed into law until 1876 and work was not completed until 1885. Yet Chipman's tenacity and leadership on the issue in 1873 and 1874 eventually led to success.

Another improvement Chipman wished to bring to the District was women's suffrage. In 1872, Susan B. Anthony voted the Republican ticket in the presidential election by casting a ballot in Rochester, New York. The next year she was tried and convicted of illegal voting and fined $100. Anthony promptly refused to pay the fine and, in January 1874, went to Washington to present a petition to Congress asking that body to pay her fine "as an expression of the sense of this high tribunal that her conviction was unjust." Congress never acted on the petition, but Anthony's trial and the furor caused by Anthony's arrival in Washington gave the local suffragists the impetus to submit their own petition to Congress. Over the signature of Sara J. Spencer and 600 other local citizens, the petition called upon Congress to extend to women the right of suffrage in the district. As the district's delegate to the House, Chipman considered it an honor to present the petition to the House. The petition was dutifully referred to the Committee on the Judiciary because it was based on the argument that the recently adopted Fourteenth Amendment gave women the right to vote as a privilege of citizenship. But the committee took no action to give women the right to vote in the district.[5]

Federal Responsibility for the District

Federal funding for district projects such as the Washington Monument had long been a contentious issue. Although Congress had limited the indebtedness of the district to fund its own improvements, the Board of Public Works disregarded limits and justified its spending as necessary for the district under a comprehensive plan that Shepherd had created for civilizing the city. Shepherd expected that he could expend funds beyond the means and limited indebtedness of the district and that Congress would provide the rest. Chipman had neither the jurisdiction nor the political clout, and perhaps not the will, to resist Shepherd's excesses. Although this method of operation became apparent to Congress soon after Shepherd took office, Congress did nothing to staunch the flow of funds until, in 1874, the district was saddled with suffocating debt.

In 1871, when the territorial government took power, the district had a public debt of about $3 million. According to a minority report of a special joint committee formed to restructure district governance, "In four years only, of Executive government, the debt has been increased $20 [million] with proportionately far less to show for it than had the preceding original debt of three millions. And of this increase, $4 [million] only, had been authorized by the [district legislature], or by the people."[6]

Looking back on the failed experiment of a partially elected legislature with an appointed executive, a senator lamented: "The attempt to charge to the account of popular suffrage, acts of persons whom suffrage could not reach, is an absurdity.... It is urged that the proposed form of government is more simple. In one sense that is true. A few only exercise power. Despotisms are always simple, and always ruinous, of liberty."[7]

Despite the serious fiscal mismanagement, Shepherd's comprehensive plan resulted in public improvements on a grand scale, with a modernized sewer system, water services, and paved streets. This "new Washington" brought in investments from outside interests and inspired pride in district residents. Reviled by many during his term of office, Shepherd's memory is revered by those who recognize his role in modernizing Washington. Formerly despised, Washington was gaining respectability.

Social and economic problems, however, were devastating to many. The schools, in particular, suffered from lack of funding. Well-to-do white parents could avoid the issue by sending their children to private schools, but public schools were cramped, with an average class enrollment of 59 pupils, and teachers sometimes went unpaid. Chipman proposed to Congress the sale of 2.5 million acres of public land to fund the district's schools. Congress responded with only a part of a square on Virginia Avenue in Washington, formerly a stable, worth only $1,000. With the abysmal fiscal situation, efforts to improve the schools were fruitless.[8]

Many members of Congress desired to hold the people of the district liable for the debt created by the activities of the Board of Public Works. Chipman, described by a historian on this issue as "a very industrious, able and honorable gentlemen," labored to make it clear to Congress that the people of the district did not elect the Board of Public Works and had no authority over that body and, therefore, did not create the exigency. The people could not possibly shoulder the enormous debt.[9]

Chipman saw the problem principally as a misapprehension of the relationship between the District of Columbia and the federal government. He also saw his role as delegate of the District of Columbia to educate the voting members of Congress on their collective responsibility toward the district, which was fundamentally different from the responsibility of Congress toward the states. Chipman put to work his legal skills and his growing penchant for placing contemporary events in proper historical perspective, which he would also do later that year to convince Congress of its patriotic and moral responsibility concerning the Washington Monument. On February 28,

1874, Chipman delivered a speech in the House of Representatives, presenting his view of the duty of the nation to its capital, which became a benchmark for relations between the District of Columbia and the federal government.[10]

"The difficulty," began Chipman, "which I have found in tracing the relations of the District of Columbia to the General Government, and the embarrassment I have experienced in ascertaining important facts upon that subject, have induced me to relieve others of the labor which I have been forced to undertake by presenting a succinct history of these relations...." "It occurred to me," he continued, "that the great public interest now being felt upon this subject would warrant a careful examination into it, and that I might be able to render the House some service in collating the essential facts."

Chipman's review of the history of the national capital prepared his congressional audience for the heavy burden he believed Congress was obligated to bear. In the early years of the nation, "Congress was practically on wheels." In 1783, Congress determined that it should have a permanent seat where no state exercised control. The next year, it created a commission to lay out a city on the Delaware River. Because there was no satisfactory location on that river, the commissioners did not undertake their duties. As the debate continued over a location for the federal city, it became clear that the city should not be close to any of the large, commercial cities and therefore fall within its sphere of influence. Neither should the federal city become, itself, a commercial city but, instead, should be primarily the seat of government under the exclusive control of Congress. After further prolonged and intense debate and research, including James Madison's treatment of the subject in the *Federalist*, an act was passed in 1790 to create the federal city on the banks of the Potomac River. The president appointed three commissioners to obtain land for the city, "the only child of the Union," and to construct suitable buildings for the public offices of the government by December 1800.[11]

The establishment of a city over which no state would be sovereign was, itself, evidence that Congress intended to maintain exclusive control over and retain sovereign responsibility for the city. There was other evidence, however, of the intention to create a city that was not fiscally self-sustaining. "There was involved in the very idea of building up a great political and noncommercial city, with the view of accommodating the necessities of the Government, " asserted Chipman, "the implied pledge that Government would take upon itself the burden of public improvements in that city."[12]

The very layout of the city was proof that the city was not intended for commercial activity. By September 1791, the government had determined to call the federal city Washington, in a federal district to be called the "Territory of Columbia." Major Pierre L'Enfant made the first plans for the layout of the city. In 1874, when Chipman delivered his speech on the relationship between the District of Columbia and the federal government, his audience was well acquainted with that plan because they lived and legislated in that city envisioned eight decades earlier. Noted Chipman, referring to the city plan: "The evidences of the intention of the Government to make this a great city at Government expense are everywhere apparent. Standing at the site of the Capitol building as the center, we have this immense area divided by wide streets crossing each other at right angles, while radiating to every point of the compass, and in remote parts of the city crossing diagonally the rectangular streets, are broad, magnificent avenues, with many reserved sites for public buildings, and seventeen large reservations for parks, or for Government use, dotting the plan in all parts of the city." "No one looking at the plan," observed Chipman, "would conclude that convenience and economy for transacting business, which are the first considerations in laying out commercial cities, for a moment entered into the minds of the founders of this great city."[13]

Washington's purpose and layout foreordained that it would be impossible to build and maintain the city at purely local expense. Chipman highlighted the wide streets in Washington to prove this point. Streets occupied 25 percent of the area in Paris and 35 percent in Vienna. In New York, streets occupied 26 percent of the city, similar to Paris. In Washington, however, the streets occupied 54 percent of the city. Chipman explained:

> From this ... it will be seen that Paris, thought by many to be the most beautiful city of Europe, notwithstanding its grand boulevards, and its Champs Elysée, has less than one-half the street area of Washington City. The greater part of the business streets in Paris are, for the convenience of business, made narrow, while their avenues and boulevards are broad and beautiful; but here there is not a street less than double the width of Broadway, New York. [¶] That Government ever could have designed to tax property in this city for the entire improvement of these streets and avenues is to the last degree absurd.[14]

Consistent with the history and layout of the city, Congress, initially, took upon itself the burden of providing for public improvements. Some of the funds for the improvements were raised by selling lots within the district. This source, however, was limited. President Thomas Jefferson warned that the government should resist the temptation to sell too much of the land to satisfy public debts.[15]

As the burden of overseeing the district grew, the need to delegate civic governance became apparent. In 1803, Congress gave the city a charter, with a mayor appointed by the president. Although Congress continued to fund the construction of federal buildings by selling lots, it dedicated none of that money to improve the streets, sewers, and sidewalks between 1807 and 1823. Instead, the municipal government taxed the private property, in Chipman's words, "almost to confiscation in the effort to make the city what its founders designed it should be...." The district also borrowed money from the Dutch government. In 1835, with the government in arrears on the Dutch debt, Congress pitched in to prevent foreclosure. The dismal condition of the city continued, however, because of the lack of funds to build and maintain the streets.[16]

For this, Chipman chastised Congress:

> We are set down as a miserable community of paupers and beggars, hanging on the skirts of Congress for sustenance; whereas the truth is the United States for the past seventy years have kept this people down in a condition of vassalage, squeezing the last possible penny out of them to carry on the very work which the founders of the capital had pledged their faith should be done by the United States.
>
> The United States have stood by and have seen their capital become a by-word and scoffing throughout the civilized world. They have seen the shafts of scorn and contempt and satire pointed toward it without making a single creditable effort to avert them.
>
> Not only this, but they have themselves largely contributed to the condition of things which, until within a few years, made us a just object of contempt.[17]

Chipman pointed out to the members of the House a fact that every one of them already knew — the Capitol building, though magnificent, was located in a barnyard-like environment. "It only lacks a horse-block and hitching-rack to make it perfectly primitive and rural." Chipman used this appeal to national pride, or, rather, national embarrassment, to lead into his argument that money expended on the district was not an outlay with only local benefit but an investment with truly national advantage. "This is the only spot common to the whole people on the face of our vast empire, where the humblest citizen can come and claim he is in the midst of his own, and where he feels he has a personal pecuniary interest in everything he beholds."[18]

Having made his points primarily with respect to the broad and space-consuming streets of the district, Chipman expanded his argument to include the incidents of every city of significance — police, water, lighting, sanitation, fire protection, and common schools. Although the police department was adequately funded, with the help of Congress, Chipman maintained that every other department needed crucial leadership and funding from Congress. He gave extended treatment to the public schools. The city had, through taxes, developed a public school system and more wealthy residents sent their children to private schools, but school capacity was insufficient, excluding more than one-fourth of the district's children from educational opportunities. A large proportion of the district's residents arrived during the Civil War, many of them black. Chipman explained that blacks came to the district because, in essence, they were "invited by the laws of Congress which first gave them freedom, and next the ballot, and where they have felt peculiarly under the protection of the Government." In Chipman's opinion, they had just as much claim on the government for a free education for their children as any: "Education here should be free as air, and the District government will never discriminate against any one class, but it will continue to demand of Congress some assistance in this direction." Acknowledging Congress' contribution of $1,000 from the sale of the stable lot, Chipman informed the members of the House that the district in the prior 14 years had expended on other priorities more than $2 million from its taxation of district residents.[19]

Speaking on behalf of the citizens of the district, Chipman reassured the members of the House that they did not "seek to drive a hard bargain with the United States, and would not even ask reimbursement if we had a business interest, manufactures, trade, commerce, or revenues, to which we could look in the immediate or remote future for reimbursement." Chipman pleaded for the members of Congress to create a well-defined policy toward the district and gave his opinion, alluding to the extravagances of the Board of Public Works, that "a more inexpensive form of local government can be devised than the present one." Yet he maintained that district citizens were entitled to a representative form of government.[20]

Having fully developed and supported his arguments, Chipman quoted Grant's most recent annual message to Congress in which Grant praised the public improvements being made in the district and encouraged the federal government to "'bear its fair share of the expense of these improvements.'" With that, Chipman closed: "I commit the subject to your earnest, intelligent and patriotic consideration."[21]

Washington Monument Society

Chipman believed that the district could not be esteemed among the capitals of the world until it completed the Washington Monument. The unfinished obelisk stood as a symbol of the unfulfilled promise of a prominent federal city.

Opposite: The Washington Monument stood unfinished at 174 feet for many years. As delegate to Congress from the District of Columbia, Chipman led the effort to finish the monument, which eventually reached 555 feet (Library of Congress).

In 1783, the Continental Congress had adopted a resolution to erect an equestrian statue of George Washington. Still basking in the recent victory of the War of Independence, the people desired to honor their great revolutionary leader who was, as yet, unknown as a great president. With this simple resolution, Congress began a 100-year story of apathy, contention, intrigue, failure, and, finally, unity and success in erecting a fitting monument to honor the national icon.

When Washington died in 1799, a national outpouring of love for Washington prompted Congress to resolve to build the monument in Washington and to inter his remains there. The next year, the House of Representatives created a select committee to provide for both the equestrian statue and a marble monument. Although attempts were made, no funds were appropriated. And the national sentiment faded. In 1833, Chief Justice John Marshall and other private citizens organized the Washington National Monument Society to solicit private funds to build the monument, and architect Robert Mills won the competition in 1836 to design it. His design included a circular, colonnaded building resembling a Greek temple and an obelisk shaft with a total height of 600 feet. It took another 11 years until the society had collected enough funds, $87,000, to begin construction. Congress granted the site of the monument, and, on July 4, 1848, President James K. Polk and numerous other politicians and dignitaries attended the groundbreaking. Participants included James Buchanan, Millard Fillmore, Abraham Lincoln, and Andrew Johnson, all then-future presidents.[22]

Work began first on the obelisk. Within six years, it was 170 feet tall, but the society was out of funds, so it turned to Congress. Although a select House committee recommended appropriating $200,000 to the society, a contest arose to control the society.

As a way to obtain widespread support for the monument, the society asked states, foreign governments, and others to donate memorial stones. The Vatican sent a stone with the inscription, "Rome to America." Anti-immigrant and, specifically, anti–Catholic sentiment increased in the 1840s and found a home in the Know-Nothing Party. On March 6, 1854, a gang of Know-Nothings surrounded the shack where a guard was stationed to watch the "Pope's Stone," as it became known. They wrapped a rope around the shack, preventing the guard from getting out, and stole the stone. It was never recovered, and the society believed the gang broke it up and dumped it in the Potomac River. The next year, Know-Nothings gained control of the society through a rigged election. The society added 4 feet to the obelisk, but, in 1856, the Know-Nothing Party collapsed and work stopped on the monument at 174 feet.[23]

The society's futility in obtaining funding, lack of congressional interest, and the Civil War combined to stall construction of the obelisk. The Union used the area around the monument to drill troops during the early part of the war. Later, it became a pasture for animals destined to feed the troops. These conditions led to the disdain with which the citizenry, including Mark Twain, viewed the ugly stump.

The intended design of the monument also became fodder for public derision. With the pantheon and shaft, it would resemble "a pumpkin with a stick stuck in it," editorialized Horace Greeley. This mockery aroused distrust and contempt in the minds of those who may have otherwise contributed. Instead, the monument was essentially a permanent stump.[24]

House Select Committee

During the difficult postwar years, North and South could scarcely agree on anything. The approaching centennial of the Declaration of Independence, however, provided an opportunity for patriotic opinion both north and south of Washington. Still, opposition to further work on the monument persisted. Some opposed use of public funds to complete what was essentially a private project, funded thus far by private contributions. Others questioned the stability of the foundation in the marshy land near the Potomac River. To resolve these issues and test the resolve of Congress to get involved in the funding and construction of the Washington Monument, the House formed a select committee on January 27, 1873, with Chipman as its chairman, to prepare a report by February 22, less than four weeks hence.[25]

Chipman went right to work with the short timeline. The most important and time-consuming task was to get an expert's analysis of the existing foundation. Chipman referred the issue to the Army Corps of Engineers, and Lieutenant William L. Marshall, a bright, young West Point graduate, received the assignment to evaluate the foundation. Chipman asked Marshall to address three issues: the security of the foundation, the probable cost of finishing the obelisk, and the probable cost of creating an inexpensive terrace. Marshall had only four days to examine the site and, in making his report, warned that the inspection was necessarily "hasty and superficial." He noted that an engineer had analyzed the foundation in 1859, fourteen years earlier, and had reported on its condition. Marshall found no material change had occurred since the 1859 examination and, therefore, referred the committee to that report. Beyond that, he criticized the use of blue gneiss as masonry in the foundation because it had turned to rubble, a condition that opponents of the monument would latch onto later as their reason for opposing funding. Marshall recommended that the most economically and physically feasible

Chipman's congressional desk and chair. He purchased the desk and chair when Congress replaced them after Chipman's first term. He later gave them to the California Court of Appeal, Third Appellate District, where they remain (California Court of Appeal, Third Appellate District).

route would be to limit the monument to the obelisk and a paved terrace. Without plans, though, he could not venture a guess as to the cost of such a project.[26]

    Chipman and the rest of the committee submitted their report to the House on time, even though the tight schedule did not allow for a full examination of the foundation and good estimate of the cost of finishing the monument. The report addressed criticisms concerning the site selected for the monument. Referring back to the original selection of the site, Chipman noted the view of the Potomac River, the relative elevation of the site, and ease of transporting materials on the nearby river. More importantly, the site overlooked Mount Vernon, Washington's home and final resting place and the selection of the site by Washington, himself, as a place for a monument commemorating the American Revolution.[27]

Given the difficulty concerning the foundation and expense associated with the monument, Chipman's report recommended that the pantheon be scrapped and the obelisk built as a standalone memorial: "The completion of the shaft may be accomplished without reference to this elaborate pantheon, and it is recommended that the completion of the obelisk alone should be undertaken, leaving the matter of constructing the pantheon to be determined in the future if it should ever become necessary. This rich and massive shaft, though simple and plain, would be a noble monument, worthy the sublime character which it is designed to testify."[28]

Although the committee report did not result in an appropriation to finish the monument, it served two important purposes: first, it refocused attention on finishing the monument and, second, it set the stage for eliminating the pantheon from the project.

The 1873 committee report also reflected an important aspect of Chipman's character, seen for the first time in his writing here but substantially borne out in his later writings and speeches. Chipman commented, in the report, on the respect and honor due our national heroes. This is a view he held concerning Lincoln and Grant, not just Washington. "No people can truly appreciate the principles of free government," he wrote, "without cherishing with something like religious fervor the memory of those men who are conspicuous from time to time in preserving those principles."[29]

As he prepared to give his written report to Congress, Chipman delivered a speech on the floor of the House, seeking support for the proposed appropriation — "a very eloquent plea," reported a capitol correspondent. The speech recounted what would be found in the select committee report. Chipman was obviously worried about public sentiment. "It is usually much easier, and generally more acceptable to the public," he lamented, "to satirize any work of art than to praise it." He assailed Greeley — though without naming him — for deriding the design, lamenting that the critic "unconsciously aroused not only a feeling of distrust in the minds of the public as to the plan of the monument, but he created a sentiment of absolute contempt for it, and it has been this sort of flippant criticism which has done more than all other things to deaden into insensibility the patriotism of the public which was expressing itself from every quarter of the country by liberal donations at the time the monument was begun." Acknowledging that the criticism about the design had some merit, Chipman proposed elimination of the pantheon. He pleaded that the obelisk was the only feature that could not be changed.[30]

The speech included an episode of humor, most likely unintended. Chipman read a description of the original monument design, more then 1,200 words of technical narrative and dimensional explanations that took at least 10 minutes to recite. At the end of this mind-numbing exercise, Chipman exulted: "Any one capable of forming a picture of this description in his mind must admit that the design is of unparalleled beauty."[31]

Chipman's speech may have been comprehensive, but it lacked in persuasiveness. Congress failed to enact the proposed legislation but extended the charge of the select committee. Finishing the Washington Monument with public funds was not on the fast track but still under consideration.

The select committee had worked quickly to report to Congress, but, without a more convincing report on the stability of the foundation and a better estimate of how much money it would take to complete the structure, members of Congress were reticent to act. Congress adjourned without taking action. At the beginning of its next session, however, the House reappointed the select committee to continue its work. Chipman again solicited the help of the Army Corps of Engineers, this time specifically seeking answers to questions such as how much it would cost to complete the obelisk without the pantheon and whether it could be completed in time for the national centennial. With more time — three months — to further study the existing structure, Marshall was more confident in his conclusions. He determined that the foundation could safely support a 437-foot obelisk. Chipman prepared a new select committee report and submitted it to the House on May 1, 1874, along with a proposed joint resolution committing Congress to fund the society's completion of the monument.

Washington Monument Speech

Chipman took to the floor of the House on June 4, 1874, to give a half-hour speech in favor of allocating funds for the completion of the monument. Much depended on his ability to sell the idea to the members of Congress. His speech the year before had been long on detail but short on persuasive reasoning. The House had promptly filed it away in the appendix of the *Congressional Globe* and moved on to other business. The tide was turning in 1874. More support surfaced in Congress and in general, but more opposition also emerged. Funding was problematic. Therefore, many members of Congress felt no continuing responsibility to see the project completed or, worse, opposed the idea of making any improvements in Washington.

Chipman began his remarks by painting the scene in Washington 74 years earlier as Congress received the news of Washington's death. Tobias Lear,

Washington's private secretary, notified President John Adams from nearby Mount Vernon. "His last scene," Lear wrote, "corresponded with the whole tenor of his life; not a groan nor a complaint escaped him in extreme distress. With perfect resignation, and with full possession of his reason, he closed his well-spent life." The sad news reached Congress along with a message from Adams. The Senate responded to the president and urged Americans to "consecrate the memory of the heroic general, the patriotic statesman, and the virtuous sage." A resolution prepared by General Henry Lee and offered in the House of Representatives by John Marshall coined the enduring portrayal of Washington, "first in war, first in peace, and first in the hearts of his countrymen."[32]

On the same day this resolution was passed, another resolution to erect a marble statue to the memory of Washington received unanimous consent. As the congressional session proceeded through 1800, further discussion ensued and, eventually, dissension arose over the specifics of constructing a memorial to Washington. The disagreement crested when the House considered a bill to appropriate $200,000 toward the memorial. Representative John Rutledge expressed frustration over the inability of Congress to reach agreement: "Now, when we propose to carry [plans] into effect, objections are stated to every measure offered; objections that rise eternally in our horizon, which, whenever we pursue, fly from our reach, and which, always moving in a circle, we can never overtake."[33]

Chipman reviewed the scattered efforts, or lack of effort, from 1800 to 1848, when the Washington Monument Society laid the cornerstone, using private funds for the work. When the private funds ran out in 1854, the society asked Congress for $200,000. Although Congress appropriated the funds, the Know-Nothings took over the society, and Congress repealed its appropriation. After the demise of the Know-Nothing Party, the society continued in its attempts to secure private funding but soon came to the conclusion that, if the monument was to be completed, it would take public funding to do so. "This brings us face to fact with our duty," Chipman urged. Referring to the report of the select committee, from which he wisely did not read all of the technical details, he said: "Every question as to cost, stability of the shaft, and appearance when completed is answered in the report."[34]

Because of the continued opposition to the design of the monument, Chipman argued against backtracking. If the monument had not already reached an advanced stage, at least in the construction of the obelisk, it might have been feasible to redesign and start over. But subscribers had dedicated a quarter of a million dollars toward the present design and tearing the monument down would dishonor their sacrifice. "[T]here is something in this simple, majestic obelisk to my mind eminently proper as commemorative of the character of Washington...."[35]

In closing, Chipman appealed to the patriotic sentiment of the members of the House. He chastised them for neglecting the memory of Washington. Finally, he resorted to hyperbole and warning: "Complete it ere your centennial day arrives, or let no American citizen look toward heaven on that glad morn and thank God that this is a land of liberty and that we are free people. Complete it, or look not back to a noble ancestry; but confess that your nation is in its decadence, and that its days are already numbered."[36]

When Chipman finished his speech, Representative John B. Storm, a Democrat from Pennsylvania, immediately rose to speak on behalf of Chipman's call for an appropriation. He complimented Chipman for his "very exhaustive and full speech." He lamented that the failure to complete the monument "is a subject of regret on the part of every one who visits the national capital."[37]

But the response was not universally complimentary.

Representative Jasper D. Ward, a Republican from Illinois and a member of Chipman's select committee, followed up Chipman's speech and Storm's support with a harangue against "that shaft." He attacked the design, both its aesthetic aspects and its stability. He claimed that any common person on the street believes the monument was "located in a very bad place." "I have listened to the eloquent and energetic gentleman [Chipman] who has the management of this matter with great pleasure speaking in laudation of it, but I have never had any gentleman speak to me on the streets with regard to it who did not regret that such a shaft as that was ever to be erected, who did not think in its conception, in its plan, in its whole design, it did not seem to be a proper thing for the American people to attempt to erect." He argued that the foundation was insufficient for further building and predicted that it might blow over in the first storm. He concluded that not another cent should be expended on the monument because he did not "believe it to be either safe or proper."[38]

Chipman probably knew beforehand, through their dealings on the select committee, that Ward would state his opposition to the legislation. And Chipman was ready. Ward had said he doubted that people in Illinois were prone to support the funding proposal, and he hesitated to pay with tax dollars for a project that the citizenry had failed to support voluntarily. As to the feelings of people in Illinois, Chipman quoted an editorial from an Illinois newspaper, from an editor with whom Ward was well acquainted, that had argued in favor of completing the monument with an appropriation from Congress, even if the work was "in bad taste" in its inception. Representative James B. Sener, a Republican from Virginia, added some insights into Ward's motivation that may have been known to the other members of the House but perhaps would have been lost to later generations if not stated on the record.

Ward, Sener posited, stated his opinions on every subject "with great force." Sener speculated, without naming Ward, that there were some who wanted to move the national capital to the west and therefore did not wish to spend any money on public works in Washington. This sentiment, though never a successful movement, was ever a burden on Chipman's ability to obtain funding for the Washington Monument and to obtain congressional help with any district improvements.[39]

As it turned out, Chipman's term ended and he was already in California before Congress took the long-awaited action. On July 4, 1876, the 100th anniversary of the signing of the Declaration of Independence, when Chipman had hoped to have the monument completed, Senator John Sherman, moved to appropriate $200,000 to fund construction of the obelisk. The Senate, in a patriotic paroxysm, approved the resolution, passing it on to the House. Although the Senate believed the House would cut the appropriation in half, the House joined in the fervor of the day and accepted the resolution in full, as sectional and party differences vanished for a harmonious, if brief, national celebration. After the Senate and House passed the bill unanimously, Grant signed it into law on August 2.

The Army Corps of Engineers further studied the foundation and decided to reinforce it before finishing the obelisk. Although other designs were considered, the original obelisk design, without the pantheon, was approved. Construction began again in 1879, and the monument was completed in 1885, thirty-seven years after laying of the cornerstone.

Retirement from Congress

Throughout his tenure in Congress and, specifically, in his speech concerning the relationship between the federal government and the District of Columbia, Chipman encouraged Congress to accept its burden to support the district. Congress responded by agreeing to pay half the cost of maintaining the capital city. As for governance, however, Congress determined to take away representative government, perhaps under the misapprehension that representative government had led to the colossal debt, despite the fact that the debt was incurred almost exclusively by appointed, not elected, officials. In sweeping legislation to set the district on a sound fiscal setting for the future, Congress, in 1874, just three years after the creation of the territorial form of government, abolished the district's governorship, legislature, and, most understandably, the Board of Public Works. Instead, the district would be governed by three commissioners appointed by the president. This legislation had the effect of totally disenfranchising the district's residents, just six

Chipman sat for a portrait by Mathew Brady during the time he held office as a delegate to the House of Representatives representing the District of Columbia (Library of Congress).

years after blacks first voted and some whites had expressed the desire to lose their own suffrage rights rather than share them with black citizens. Unwilling to give up his loyalty to Shepherd, Grant nominated him as one of the new commissioners, prompting Nast to publish his first political cartoon critical of Grant. The Senate refused to confirm Shepherd, thus ending his hold on the visually reinvigorated, but fiscally strapped district.

The 1874 legislation also abolished the District of Columbia's non-voting seat in Congress. In his farewell speech in 1875, Chipman made it clear to Congress why its territorial form of government experiment had failed:

I have laid our burden at your feet, and I declare, not defiantly, but earnestly, that we cannot take it up unless you assist us....

For four years I have striven to impress upon you the needs of this District. And my only hope now is, that between the despotism set up here, by the last session, and the anarchy to which we seem fast drifting, Congress will soon wake up to the fact in this capital, here at the Nation's center, where we should have a model government, where, by common consent and pride, a generous policy should govern, is the most vacillating, uncertain, ignorant and unpatriotic course pursued.

During the four years, since I have been upon this floor, I have not uttered one word of partisan appeal, for while sent here upon nomination of one of the great parties of the country, I have felt it was to serve interests purely local, on behalf of which there should be no party disputes.

But it is a disappointing reflection that that party with which most of my constituents are in sympathy, however much it may have done to beautify this city, has destroyed the only government we had, and has not given us a better one....

While in spasms of good feeling, [Congress] has appropriated generously, it has wholly overlooked the greater duty of providing here a wise, efficient and model government....

There is grave responsibility somewhere; and I hope that there may yet be patriotism and national pride enough to perform it.

While you are agonizing over states, with machinery to operate themselves, I beg of you, do not forget the heart of the Nation; which cannot live without your consent. Do not longer drag this "child of the Union" at the heels of Neglect.

Do not forget that this entire community, as large as some of your states, in population, is existing practically under a despotism, which might, if it would, oppress this people to a point that would bring lasting disgrace upon every one of you, and tarnish the fair name of American liberty.

There is not, I believe, within the range of Christian Nations, a spot as badly governed as this District, where Congress has exclusive jurisdiction. Taking the District of Columbia as an example of the wisdom of Congress, this nation would not exist twenty-four hours, if it were not for the reserved rights of the several States, which secures for them good government.[40]

Commenting on this farewell speech, a historian of this tempestuous period noted:

There is an inspiring frankness and evident fairness about these closing paragraphs of Mr. Chipman's last prepared speech in the House, that makes it easier to understand the high esteem in which he was held during his service in the difficult and delicate position of a voteless spokesman for the District, in the Federal Congress.

From Mr. Chipman's remarks the serious truths are forced upon the close student of that period; that popular government, local self-government, was sacrificed for material gain, for partizan advantage.[41]

10
Sierra Flume and Lumber Company (1875–1878)

Chipman left his mark on Washington after the war. As prosecutor in the Andersonville Prison trial, he gained fame in the postwar nation. He then turned his attention to his new home, the District of Columbia, representing its people in Congress. His skill in arguing for the interests of the district eventually led to the completion of the Washington Monument. But the work pace of the city and the stress of politics took a toll on his health and happiness. As he filled his second term as the district's congressional delegate, he recognized the need, and perhaps the desire, for a change.

In March 1875, Chipman, having completed his congressional service, resolved to go to California to regain his health. In his writings, he mentioned his poor health, not specifying any particular ailment, but, once in California, he soon found himself in a land that fascinated him and among a people he found enterprising and refreshing. Traveling northeast of Sacramento in the Sierra Nevadas, he discovered an expanse of untouched timber. Even if he did not travel to California with permanent change in mind, a month of rest, mixed with a clear mind, awakened his penchant for the grand. He had some experience in timber investing. That, along with his organizational training and abilities, inspired him to organize mentally a grand scheme for developing the Sierra's timber resources.

It baffled Chipman that others had not already thought of the full extent of the opportunities in California timber or, if they had, that they had not acted. He wrote: "Here was an apparent field for a magnificent lumber project on a scale unparalleled; an opportunity to acquire and work out a forest of timber of great extent and incredible wealth. Lands yielding three thousand to five thousand feet of lumber to the acre had all been eagerly bought in the pine regions of the north-west, and were being held on speculation; and yet here stood thousands of acres that would yield forty thousand to sixty thousand feet per acre, and no one would take them as a gift and pay taxes on them."[1]

Northern California

Childless after a decade of marriage, Chipman and Belle had welcomed Chipman's preteen niece, Isabel Dawson, into their family as they relocated to California. Isabel's parents, Luther G. Dawson and Helen Mar Chipman, Chipman's younger sister, were married in Washington, Iowa, in 1867. Isabel, their only child, was born the next year in Mankato, Minnesota. When Chipman was serving in Congress, the Dawson's moved to the District of Columbia, where Luther found employment as a clerk of the police court. But Helen died in the mid–1870s, leaving Luther a single father. The Chipmans were willing and able to give Isabel the life that Luther wanted her to have, so Luther consented to the adoption by the Chipmans. Isabel, like her adopted mother, was known as "Belle." She remained close to Chipman and Belle until their deaths more than 40 years later. The Chipmans maintained contact with Luther Dawson, who also emigrated to California, finding work as a land agent in Oakland.

After his visit to California, Chipman returned to Washington D.C. with the singular purpose of selling his law practice, packing up his residence, and moving west to become a citizen of California. While Chipman's earlier visit to California had been by train, the Chipman family boarded a ship and traveled around Cape Horn to California with all their possessions. They settled in Red Bluff, a town favorably located along the Sacramento River, which drains the watershed of the northern Sierras. Red Bluff was first settled in 1849, and became the seat of Tehama County in 1856. Its location on the Sacramento River at the north end of the Sacramento Valley facilitated a rapid rise as an important commercial center. The Chipmans moved into an appropriately dignified home in town, with a large garden, and quickly became leading citizens.[2]

The newcomers endeared themselves to their new neighbors in Red Bluff, even if some of those neighbors did not have the same culture and refinement the Chipmans had, with their circulation among some of the East's elite.

An avid hunter and trout fisherman when he could find the time, Chipman and his friends from San Francisco joined some of the locals in a bear hunt. Old Uncle Joe, their guide, was well known for his bear hunting prowess, and had numerous scars from the activity. He called the Chipman party the "big bugs from Frisco — fellows with biled shirts." Unknown to Chipman and the others, Old Uncle Joe had killed a bear in a tree, at dusk, before they arrived, but the bear did not fall out of the tree. He pointed out the bear to the Chipman party but did not tell them it was already dead. All evening, the "big bugs" bragged about how good they were at shooting and how they would bag the bear in the morning. They stayed up all night guarding the bear. At dawn, they pumped 50 rounds into the bear before Old Uncle Joe mentioned to them that it was already dead. The "big bugs" felt plenty sheepish about the whole affair and agreed among themselves not to talk about it. But Old Uncle Joe never tired of telling the story about how the "big bugs from Frisco" sat up all night guarding a dead bear.[3]

Later in his life in California, Chipman had another run-in with the Wild West. While traveling by train from Red Bluff to Sacramento, as he frequently did, he lost his pants. The *Grass Valley Union* reported: "General Chipman, the dignified lawyer of Red Bluff had his pantaloons stolen from his sleeping berth by some of the Sacramento thieves. When he reached that city early Tuesday morning, he had to remain in bed until the porter obtained the necessary outfit to make the General presentable to the public eye. To say that he was mad over the affair expresses it but mildly."[4]

Although Chipman had some timber investments in the North, he needed a large amount of additional funding. A lumber company of the magnitude he envisioned would require significant capital, and such substantial amounts of money were likely to be found only in the major financial centers, like San Francisco, where the silver bonanza of the Comstock Lode had enriched the society initially financed by the earlier Gold Rush. Chipman gathered the results of his careful, though hurried, research and reconnaissance and went to San Francisco to place before the wealthy capitalists of that city his vision of a lumber enterprise. There, he found Alvinza Hayward, who was convinced Chipman had a workable plan. Hayward met considerable success mining the Mother Lode with his own hands. He then parlayed an investment of $24,000 into a return of $22 million in the Nevada Comstock Lode. At home both in the financial district of San Francisco and the mining camps of the Sierras, Hayward knew the mountains and had the money to develop their resources. Together, Chipman and Hayward obtained additional backing from Edward and John C. Coleman of San Francisco's Merchants Exchange Bank.[5]

Chipman and Hayward personally inspected the timber of the area around Big Meadows, present-day Lake Almanor, on a hunting and fishing trip. Soon after the trip, they filed claim location notices for 80,000 acres of timber land in that area. The checkerboard manner in which they claimed the land rendered it impractical for anyone else to claim the interspersed unclaimed locations. Therefore, their claim of 80,000 acres effectively gave them control of about 180,000 acres of timber.[6]

V-Flumes

While it was relatively simple to hire men to go into the mountains and cut the lumber, it was difficult and costly to transport the lumber out of the mountains to rivers and railroads. From Nevada came a recent innovation in transportation of lumber — the V-flume. The miners in Nevada needed wood for support structures within the silver mines. Although wood was scarce in the immediate area, there were plentiful timber resources on the eastern slope of the Sierras. A long trough, filled with water from mountain streams, could be used to float the lumber to the lower elevations. A square-box flume, however, was prone to jams. An enterprising timber man came up with the idea of a V-shaped flume because it would tend to clear itself of jams. If a log became wedged in the flume, subsequent water and logs would force the jammed log up to the wider part of the trough. Additionally, a V-flume took less lumber to build and less water to operate than a square-box flume.[7]

In the early 1870s, C.F. Ellsworth brought the V-flume to the northern Sierras. When he began the enormous project of constructing the flume from the mountains to the river, some dubbed the project "Ellsworth's Folly." Each mile of flume required 135,000 board feet of lumber, making Ellsworth his own best customer during those years of construction.

A history of the northern California lumber industry provided insight into the use and maintenance of the flumes: "At various points along the flume, cabins were built for flume tenders, 'lumber herders,' who patrolled the flume, keeping it in repair and clearing any jams that might get started. Lumber was flumed 'loose,' plank by plank. However, the more valuable grades might be clamped together in rafts or 'bundles' for the flume passage, and sometimes were sent down as the top layer on a raft of common lumber. When lumber was being flumed at night, the lumber herder hung a coal-oil can from a rope across the flume. As long as the can kept rattling, the lumber was coming down all right. If it stopped rattling, the herder started patrolling up-flume to find out what was wrong. Since the flume often was a hundred feet in the air and the walk-way planks were slick with spray, a lumber herder had to have a certain disregard for his own safety."[8]

Creative entrepreneurs found other uses for the flumes. Packed in snow, venison and trout could be shipped to valley eateries. If a worker was injured in the mountains, he could be transported to the valley for medical care in a flume boat. Others used the flumes for personal transportation, but only at great risk. One man, desiring to attend a Fourth of July celebration in Red Bluff, decided to ride the flume. Rounding a sharp curve, he was killed instantly by a sliver from the flume protruding into his path.[9]

When Ellsworth's business, the Empire Lumber Company, finished the major flume from the mountains to Sesma, near Red Bluff on the Sacramento River, it brought lumber down from the mountains at such a reduced cost that the company quickly undercut the prices of competitors. Sadly, Ellsworth was not around to see the vindication of his venture. While overseeing the final stages of construction, he fell from the flume and eventually died of his injuries.[10]

Other companies joined Empire in building flumes from the mountains to the valley. Blue Ridge Flume and Lumber Company flumed lumber to Red Bluff, and Butte Flume and Lumber Company operated with Chico as its flume terminus. Despite the benefit of the flumes, these lumber companies, to varying degrees, failed to thrive because of mismanagement and external financial pressures. This was the condition of the lumber industry in the northern Sierras when Chipman and Hayward incorporated the Sierra Flume and Lumber Company in November 1875.[11]

Chipman immediately recognized the V-flume's importance to his grand scheme. He observed: "Nature rarely stows away her treasure where the wants of man cannot reach them; and the V-flume was the key to unlock those treasures; for where water will run, the V-flume will carry lumber." Sierra's V-flumes, built from a few feet off the ground to more than 100 feet high, with sophisticated trestle work, cost $2 million. Together with the water, for which Sierra owned the rights to the runoff streams from Mount Lassen and surrounding mountains, the V-flumes promised to carry as much lumber out of the mountains as Sierra could sell.[12]

Opening for Business

As Sierra prepared to open for business in the spring of 1876, the other three lumber companies evaluated their chances against the behemoth wedging itself into their competitive market. In all, the other three companies controlled about 25,000 acres of land, compared to the 180,000 acres controlled by Sierra. Empire succumbed to pressures independent of Sierra's potential competition, and Chipman's company acquired its assets. Blue Ridge and Butte dared not even to compete with Sierra. After swift negotiations, Chipman acquired the other two companies, before powerful dealers and operators in San Francisco had a chance to intervene.[13]

Although the acquisition of the other lumber companies did not greatly increase the amount of land Sierra controlled, Sierra obtained many of the accoutrements of an established lumber company which it did not expect to obtain except through future construction and development. The acquisitions gave Sierra five saw mills, cattle, trucks, yards, and an additional 100 miles of V-flumes. Instead of operating from one valley terminus at Vina, Sierra began operations from Chico, Sesma, and Red Bluff.[14]

Such total domination of the north state lumber industry could have merited alarm in those who relied on the availability and price of lumber. But these concerns were allayed by the reputation Chipman brought to California from his service in the Civil War and at the seat of national government. One publication confidently declared that Norton Parker Chipman was a man of honor and would not countenance unfair exploitation of the dominant position.[15]

Sierra began operations in 1876 without a serious competitor and within a year became the largest and most complex lumber operation in the world.[16]

Chipman perceived several shortcomings in the acquired companies. The Chico flume terminated four miles from the railroad connection. The Red Bluff flume terminated at the river but lumber had to be floated 14 miles downriver to its railroad connection. The woodworking machinery at each terminus was insufficient to handle the amount of lumber that could be transported down the flumes. With an infusion of Hayward capital, Chipman went right to work on capital improvements. This influx of capital, alone, contributed to the economic well-being of the north valley towns. Red Bluff had suffered through an economic downturn, but soon new homes were started and old ones improved. Farmers whose profit was strained by the necessity of shipping produce to faraway markets could sell locally to the new lumber industry personnel. The locals hoped that this boon would be permanent, unlike the many short-lived mining booms in northern California over the prior quarter century. Sierra, itself, employed as many as 500 people in its operations.[17]

Chipman implemented every innovation he could find to enhance the lumber business. As Sierra hit its stride in 1877, it cut about 50 million feet of lumber, up from 30 million feet the prior year. Ten saw mills operated at full capacity. One hundred and sixty miles of flumes brought the lumber down from the mountains. Three hundred oxen and seventy-five horses pulled loads of lumber to and from the flumes and to the river and the railroad. Two hundred miles of telegraph line kept the entire operation in close communication with every other unit and with Chipman, the manager of day-to-day operations. Sierra's was the largest private communications network of its time in California, and possibly the nation.[18]

Chipman described the benefits of the innovations he found so important to Sierra's success: "A builder finds his work at a stand-still for want of a stick of timber; he goes to the office at Chico; his want is telegraphed to the mill; the log is cut, hauled and sawed, and by night his stick comes booming into the yard." This innovative business model was well ahead of its time.[19]

Chipman brought advances to the timber industry by many means. He published the first timber industry employee manual, durably bound and small enough for every key employee to keep in his pocket.

The policies spelled out in the manual reflected good business sense:

"It is suggested that during the long days when logging is best trees should be taken from the most distant and difficult places, reserving the most favorable logging for short days or bad weather."

"It is more important to make good lumber, even and of saleable sizes, than to cut a great deal of a poor quality."

General common sense:

"It is not economy to work an ox until he is broken down."

The safety of Sierra's employees:

"Employees of the company will not be permitted to ride in any of the flumes, except to make repairs or in case of emergency where the business of the company requires someone to go quickly to the valley."

And preservation of the forest resources:

"Superintendents will use every precaution to preserve the forest from waste and destruction."

"The danger of loss from fire increases yearly as the tops of fallen trees and the accumulation of dry branches and debris increases. Superintendents will give this subject special attention. Upon the occurrence of a fire at any point within a radius of two miles of any of the mills, the superintendent will at once cause it to be extinguished."[20]

Chipman proudly described the "history of a piece of lumber" in Sierra's enterprise:

> The tree is felled by what are called the fallers, who use saws and not axes; great care and skill are needed to lay the tree where it should go, to avoid being broken or split in the fall. Most of these trees have to be wedged over, for they will stand erect after being cut clean off. The tree is then cut into logs of proper lengths. They go down chutes, are snaked on the ground down steep mountain sides, or are loaded on to logging trucks and drawn to the tramways.
>
> There is many a man who can engineer a railroad line or run a steamship across the Atlantic, who would cut a sorry figure in engineering one of these big trucks and its load, drawn by six or seven yoke of cattle. "Ob. Fields," the champion driver, will handle fourteen head and one of these mountain ships, and take them through places where some of us would stall a light wagon. He comes and goes with his enormous loads, and unless you see him, you won't

know he is around. He has a way of using his goad, with its sharp point, on all the oxen at the same instant, and his look will bring an ox down to his best pull, as surely as an engineer can bring his engine by opening the throttle-valve.

The log thus gets to the mill; is sawed to the best advantage; the lumber is piled openly for rapid seasoning; is run through the flume in a month; is again piled openly at the valley yard; and then is ready for market in about two months; it is sold in the rough, or worked at their factories into various useful forms. Few persons can imagine the variety of labor, the skill involved, and the many really interesting employments that are embraced in this business; but it is all hard work from first to last, and with all its fascinations no one may engage in it unless he makes up his mind to renounce the world, the flesh, and the devil, if he wants to succeed as a saw-mill man.[21]

His management of Sierra required Chipman to utilize many of the talents he developed in years of public and private service. His legal training allowed him to work through the legal complexities of starting up such a large venture and to negotiate effectively to acquire assets and whole companies. His political skills in lobbying for the good of the District of Columbia helped him to focus on a substantial undertaking and convince others, especially Hayward, to join him. His experience of evaluating so meticulously the money expended on the Washington Monument and forecasting what it would take to complete the monument prepared him to handle the financial concerns of a large corporation. It would seem that Chipman's whole life had dovetailed into this California opportunity. He assumed the heavy responsibilities with relish, determined that he not only would become very wealthy, but that he would also vastly improve the economic condition of northern California.

Steep Rise and Precipitous Fall

Validating the public's faith in Chipman's moral code, Sierra did not show the detriments of a monopoly. The retail price of lumber in San Francisco dropped from 1876 to 1877, even as demand rose. Sugar pine, Sierra's main product, cost 60 to 80 dollars per thousand board feet in 1876. That price went down to between 30 and 40 dollars per thousand board feet. Before Sierra ramped up its vast enterprise, lumber was available only sparingly. By selling in much larger quantities, Sierra passed along the economies of scale.[22]

New markets for the lumber emerged. Railroad construction in places as far away as Arizona and New Mexico created demand for northern California pine for ties, bridges, stations, fences, and fuel. For the first time, lumber became a stable commodity in northern California, with stable prices. Beyond San Francisco, Sierra exported lumber to such faraway places as Japan,

China, Chile, Peru, Australia, and New York. The prices obtained in those ports covered the costs of production, shipping, and commissions, and still left Sierra a profit.[23]

Chipman attempted to foresee every possible contingency in operating Sierra, and by many accounts he succeeded in every aspect of his planning and execution, except for his timing. In 1873, an economic panic hit the East Coast of the United States. A major investment banking concern in the East failed. The New York Stock Exchange closed for ten days. Financial institutions stopped extending credit. Banks failed. Factories closed. And thousands of workers lost their jobs. Many of the railroads, overbuilt in the period after the war, went out of business. The panic and resulting depression spread westward. The price of silver slumped, devastating the San Francisco markets where many of the silver barons had taken their wealth. The Bank of California failed in 1875, leading to bankruptcies of those concerns that needed credit to stay afloat. While the Comstock Lode delivered its best year in 1877, it slumped badly after that year and by 1880 had permanently failed.

As Sierra picked up steam in its pursuit to become the supplier of all the lumber needed in northern California with extra to export, the market for the lumber collapsed as the 1877 season hit its stride. Unsold lumber piled up — 30 million board feet in Sierra's Red Bluff and Chico yards. Accounts receivable were overdue with no prospect of collection. In its rapid emergence, Sierra had spent $11.5 million and had already borrowed another $600,000.[24]

By July 1878, the hope of reviving the company was gone. Joseph Cone, the leading merchant in Red Bluff, acquired the assets of the company and began paying off local debts. A dispatch from Red Bluff appeared in San Francisco's *Alta California*: "The employees of the various mills are arriving on stage and by foot. There are no demonstrations as all feel sure they will get their wages." This tipped off Sierra's creditors, who immediately moved in and put Sierra into bankruptcy. Cone may have succeeded in paying off as much as $250,000 in debts to local merchants and bondholders before the San Francisco creditors figured out what he was doing. Although Chipman was not directly involved in this scheme, it had the fortuitous effect of preserving his pristine and prominent reputation in the northern California region, even if the big-city creditors were none too pleased.[25]

As the company struggled to reorganize in bankruptcy, one of the mountain mills and the Chico factory were destroyed in fires. The new company, Sierra Lumber Company, began operations in November 1878, but only at a much reduced capacity and, to some extent, to preserve the ability to sell off properties and wait for better economic conditions. Chipman agreed to lend his expertise to the new company, but only for a few months.[26]

Writing shortly after the failure, he said: "The high hopes that filled the projectors were cruelly blasted, and an untoward fate overcame the scheme. 'Hard times,' the relentless destroyer of fortunes and enterprises, drew its fatal coils around this young Laocoon of the forests."[27]

Seeing his dream disintegrate required Chipman to rethink his future. After the collapse of Sierra, Chipman met his commitment to stay with the new company for a few months to assist in reorganization. He and his family wrapped up their affairs.

Chipman departed for Oregon and the Washington Territory to seek new business opportunities and, perhaps, to lick his wounds. Shortly, he returned to Tehama County, firm in his belief that the natural resources of the region and the prosperous community were the most favorable for his family. They determined to identify themselves permanently with the people of Red Bluff. Already known and respected in town, Chipman formed a law partnership with Charles A. Garter, who later served as the United States Attorney in San Francisco, and practiced law downtown.[28]

11
Greater California
(1878–1918)

A history of Tehama County published in 1880, recounted Chipman's life to that point and his contributions to the county and concluded with a note about Belle, stating that Chipman's "wife has been his constant companion ever since [their marriage], and by her many virtues has contributed very much to whatever success has attended him. Wherever they have lived their home has been a hospitable retreat for their many friends, and a delightful resort for young and old. [¶] Such homes cannot fail to have a good influence, and we welcome this one to those already in our county."[1]

The Chipman family spent many peaceful years in Red Bluff, living the life of a well-to-do family out in the country. In 1880, when young Belle was 12 years old, the Chipmans added another daughter to the family, adopting Alice as a newborn. Alice was born in California, but the records do not provide any further information on her background before she was adopted.

A mild climate, with no snow but plenty of rain in the winter and warm, dry summers was well-suited for comfortable living and profitable fruit-growing. But the pull of public service began to lure Chipman to the bigger cities, starting with his years as a leader of the State Board of Trade, continuing with his employment as a commissioner of the California Supreme Court in San Francisco, and culminating with his 16 years as presiding justice of the California Court of Appeal, Third Appellate District, in Sacramento.

After 20 years in Red Bluff, with many long absences to fulfill duties around the state, especially in San Francisco, the Chipmans moved to Sacramento, where they lived until Belle's death and Chipman's retirement from the Court of Appeal.

Promoting California

The mid–1870s were a turning point for Red Bluff. From a village, stage-stop environment emerged a more sophisticated, though still rustic, town. Gains in trade, agriculture and the timber industry provided money for handsome dwellings and substantial buildings. Centennial Hall, built in 1876, and named for the nation's centennial, provided a large meeting place. But the bane of old-town life struck in 1880, when a fire broke out in a dilapidated shack and spread to the surrounding, more modern buildings. Before it could be suppressed, the fire destroyed Centennial Hall, the new livery stables, a hotel, and other adjoining buildings. The flames were so hot they scorched the buildings across Main Street, nearly 100 feet away. The only thing that saved the rest of the town was that there was not a wisp of wind blowing.[2]

In another fire, about the same time period, the Chipmans lost their beautiful home in town. Chipman managed to save from the fire his large painting, *Fort Sumter After the Bombardment*, by his friend Emanuel Leutze, of *Washington Crossing the Delaware* fame. He also rescued his collection of correspondence with Thomas Nast. But the rest of his art and treasures were lost. *Harper's Weekly* reported the Chipmans' fire in the "Personal" section, along with Charles Dickens' tour of New York, Walt Whitman's lectures in Boston, and Mark Twain's financially successful reading tour.[3]

The fire gave Chipman the impetus to participate in what he perceived as the future of California — growing fruit. He moved to a farm in Antelope Valley, just outside Red Bluff and, while maintaining his law practice, managed his own small-scale fruit-growing operation.

His big-business and leveraging days behind him, Chipman devoted himself again to public service, working to promote California. Fruit production became his passion. He wrote and lectured extensively, trying to encourage farmers who grew wheat to produce fruit instead. These magnanimous efforts made him a popular figure in the West. After he moved to Sacramento in 1905, he maintained ownership of his 700 acres in Tehama County, with a manager to run the operation, until 1916, when he finally sold off the lucrative business.[4]

Much of Chipman's work in promoting California agriculture and industry were channeled through the State Board of Trade. One contemporary stated, concerning Chipman, that "no man has written more or with better effect or given more of his time and energies to advertise to the world the attractions of California," and attributed to Chipman the dictum that "the climate of California is the State's most valuable asset." Chipman regularly quoted Horace Greeley, who said, "Fruit growing is destined to be the ultimate glory of California."[5]

The State Board of Trade, of which Chipman was one of the founders, was organized in San Francisco in 1887, as an association of a few public-spirited gentlemen who wished to promote the interests of the state. To give the organization more permanency, the Board was incorporated in 1890, with the mission to promote immigration to the state, publish and circulate information concerning the growth and products of the state, and "generally to advance the material interests of the state by any appropriate means." Counties and individuals joined the Board, but no state aid was needed or accepted. As president of the Board from 1895 to 1906, Chipman directed the multifaceted, but entirely voluntary work, traveling both within the state and outside, publishing, speaking, organizing, and helping others to do the same, all to accomplish the mission of the Board.[6]

Chipman envisioned a Greater California: "The Greater California to which my mind now turns is not the California of to-day, but it is the California which I see before me, looming up in the not distant future; and it is her present intrinsic elements of greatness and her situation on the map of the world which justify the horoscope I would cast of that future." He wrote these motivational and prophetic words in 1899.[7]

An article Chipman wrote for the San Francisco *Morning Call*, in 1893, was typical of his advocacy in favor of fruit trees over wheat. He argued:

> Let our wheat-grower remember that what is the product of all lands and climes. Wherever man can live wheat will grow. Not so of the orange, the lemon, the fig, the prune, the olive, the raisin grape, the almond, the apricot, or even the pear or the peach — all distinctively California fruits.... [¶] What is it that gives value to California land? It is not richness of soil alone, for Kansas and the great Northwest have the fattest land in the world. It is not in the profitableness of our cereal crops, for our grain farmers will testify that they are not making money. What then is it? It is the adaptability of climate and soil to the production of the most profitable fruits of the earth.

As evidence of Chipman's labors and advocacy, shipments of fruit out of the state more than doubled from 1890 to 1895, and he expected that it would double again over the next five years.[8]

As president of the Board, Chipman became famous for his reports on California agriculture, and he gradually expanded his audience from local, to statewide, to all parts of the nation. His reports detailed the progress California was making in realizing its destiny as the agriculture capital of the nation. "All his papers have been characterized by fairness, frankness and entire impartiality," wrote the *Los Angeles Times*. The newspaper called Chipman "a man of large experience in affairs, of excellent executive ability, agreeable and pleasing of manner and public spirited to a degree beyond the point of personal interest."[9]

Chipman was also a strong supporter of fairs — local fairs to share the most recent agricultural innovations and world fairs to promote California's interests. In this promotion of agricultural fairs, Chipman followed the example of his hero, Abraham Lincoln, who famously touted agricultural fairs in his Wisconsin state fair speech of 1859. Chipman gave the annual address at the California State Fair in 1886. His wide-ranging speech predictably covered the question of whether wheat farmers should convert their lands to fruit production, but it also touched on such diverse topics as the labor market, population distribution, irrigation and water resources, the industrial revolution and its draw on the young, transportation, and, finally, prohibition. While denying that he was a "shouting evangelist, nor yet, I fear, a good Christian," he decried the unrestricted liquor traffic and the "practical abolition of the Sabbath as a day of rest and worship" as twin corrupters. In 1896, he traveled to Atlanta to lend the resources and prestige of the Board to California's world fair exhibit.[10]

Politically, Chipman was reliably Republican. He campaigned regularly for the Republican candidates up and down the state, using his good name, national renown, and speaking skills for the benefit of his fellow party members. Until 1890, he made no attempt to run for political office. But that year he allowed the Humboldt County Republican delegation to present his name for the governor's race at the state convention. His platform, not atypical of his time, included protectionism and tariffs. Despite strong support among the northern counties, it was not enough, as Henry Harrison Markham secured the nomination and later the governorship. Some of his friends also encouraged Chipman to run for a seat in the House of Representatives. He flatly turned them down, preferring to stay in California.[11]

Supreme Court Commissioner

As California became more populous, the judiciary, with its two-tier system of trial courts and one appellate court, strained to bear the load. The Supreme Court, the only appellate court in the state, began to fall behind in its work. Repeated attempts to amend the state constitution to provide for intermediate courts failed, so the Legislature came up with its own, albeit temporary, solution — Supreme Court commissioners.

In 1850, when California became a state, less than 100,000 people resided within its borders. The constitution provided for a Supreme Court, consisting of a chief justice and two associate justices, each elected to a six-year term by popular vote. This arrangement amounted to one justice per 33,333 residents. By 1860, the population of the state was approaching 400,000. An amendment to the constitution increased the court membership to five justices and lengthened their terms to ten years, still by popular election. And in 1879, when the population exceeded 800,000, the people adopted a new constitution under which the Supreme Court consisted of the chief justice and six associate justices holding 12-year terms in office, as it stands today. However, unlike today's system of confirmation elections, in which a justice runs unopposed in a yes or no vote to keep the seat for another 12 years, the Supreme Court justices faced partisan elections. The 1879 constitution also required the Supreme Court to decide the cases on its docket in writing, with the grounds for the decision stated, further increasing the workload of the court.[12]

In 1885, the population having grown to about 1 million, the Supreme Court could no longer keep pace with the number of appeals from the trial courts. But the electorate showed no willingness to amend the constitution again to deal with the growing problem. So the Legislature acted. It authorized the Supreme Court to appoint Supreme Court commissioners, to act for short terms, at first four years, later reduced to two years, as employees chosen by the court. These commissioners performed the same work as the justices of the Supreme Court and for the same pay. The only difference was that their decisions required the approval of the justices. In an analysis of the state judicial system, which he wrote in 1907, Chipman observed, "These Commissioners were selected with reference to their learning of the law, and their duties were in all respects similar to those of the Justices of the court, except that before their decisions became operative they were to receive the approval of [the] Justices.... Such distinguished jurists as Niles Searls, Jackson Temple, Ralph Harrison, and Isaac Belcher served as Commissioners at different times. Notwithstanding this additional assistance given the court the cases on appeal continued to increase more rapidly than they could be disposed of. The situation had become so grievous a burden to litigants, and decisions were so long delayed, that still further relief was demanded."[13]

In April 1897, the Supreme Court appointed Chipman as one of five Supreme Court commissioners, a position he held with a salary of $6,000 per year until 1905, when the position was abolished. In most respects, the new work was ideal for Chipman. It allowed him to use his legal education and 37 years of legal experience, as well as his well-honed analytical and writing skills. He worked closely with the elite in California's legal and political circles. And, as a commissioner, there was no need to run for office. The drawbacks, however, were that, first, it required him to close his law practice and, second, the Supreme Court conducted its business in San Francisco, 200 miles from his beloved Red Bluff and fruit trees. Because the State Board of Trade was a private organization, Chipman's appointment as a commissioner did not necessitate giving up the presidency. Chipman stopped practicing law, but he did not move to San Francisco. Instead, for eight years, he and his family stayed in San Francisco when his presence was needed there, occupying a temporary residence, and returned to Red Bluff whenever possible.

The work of the Supreme Court required Chipman to span broad areas of law in his opinion writing — property law, family law, mining disputes, agricultural litigation, criminal law, constitutional law, and many other legal subjects. From the profound to the mundane, the justices and commissioners of the Supreme Court were required to decide every appeal brought to them, having no discretion to refuse to hear a case. Chipman, for example, authored an opinion holding that a common carrier, such as a railroad, owed the utmost care to its passengers and was liable for injury sustained to those passengers. In another case, he concluded that a cow thief was improperly convicted because the only evidence of his thievery came from an accomplice whose testimony was unreliable. He showed no partiality, ruling against the powerful railroads when the law was not in their favor and allowing a libel action to go forward against the Times-Mirror Company, the publisher of the *Los Angeles Times*.[14]

Court of Appeal

Even with the help of five commissioners, the Supreme Court could not keep up with the caseload coming from a growing population. In 1900, the population hit 1.5 million, a 15-fold population increase in the first 50 years of the state's existence, resulting in a residents-per-justice or -commissioner ratio of 150,000. This resulted in an oppressive caseload for the court, with the average case delayed two to three years. The public's concern with the Supreme Court's inability to render decisions at a pace that came close to matching the number of new appeals filed in the court finally pushed the electorate into action. A 1904 constitutional amendment created a Court of Appeal with three districts — the First District in San Francisco, the Second District in Los Angeles, and the Third District in Sacramento. Each district would have a presiding justice and two associate justices to be appointed by the governor in 1905 and then subjected to contested, partisan election in 1906. "The jurisdiction theretofore vested in the Supreme Court," wrote Chipman, "was divided between the Supreme Court and the District Courts of Appeal, each of the latter having the same jurisdiction. In the creation of the courts some novel features were introduced, in some respects unlike any other system in other states. Strictly speaking these new courts are not intermediate courts in the sense that an appeal lies from them to the Supreme Court, for such is not

Chipman at his desk in his state Capitol chambers of the Court of Appeal. In the background are lithographs of Ulysses S. Grant and Abraham Lincoln and an Emanuel Leutze painting, *Fort Sumter After the Bombardment*, all of which are still on display at the California Court of Appeal, Third Appellate District (California State Library).

the case. Final jurisdiction, so far as it extends, is given to the District Courts of Appeal in the same terms as it is vested in the Supreme Court. But the losing party may petition the Supreme Court for a hearing of the case in that court, much the same as rehearings ... which [is] far from the absolute right of appeal."[15]

Governor George Pardee, a Republican, appointed Chipman as the first presiding justice of the Third District of the new Court of Appeal on April 10, 1905. Pardee, a physician who made house calls even while serving as governor, had been a compromise candidate among the factions of the Republican Party. He received the party's nomination in 1902 by avoiding identification with either the powerful railroad lobby or the reform-minded party members. He served only one term for the same reason, failing to satisfy any of his Republican constituents. In his appointments to the Court of Appeal, nine positions in all, Pardee took the opportunity to give the court instant credibility, appointing men of legal and ethical distinction to the $7,000-per-year positions. The three presiding justices had all served with the Supreme

Court. Chipman and Wheaton Gray, presiding justice of the Second District, had each served eight years as a Supreme Court commissioner. Ralph C. Harrison, presiding justice of the First District, had been, for 12 years, an associate justice of the Supreme Court. The appointed associate justices in the districts were also well known. In the Third District, Pardee appointed Abraham J. Buckles, a Solano County judge who had received the Congressional Medal of Honor for his service in the Civil War, and Charles E. McLaughlin, a Democrat and Plumas County judge. Of the nine justices appointed to the newly formed Court of Appeal, in its three districts, Chipman was the oldest, 71 years old, yet he served the longest, by far, of those initial appointees.[16]

In writing about Pardee's initial appointments to the Court of Appeal, Chipman acknowledged that "conventional rules of propriety" dictated that he should not "say much of the personnel" selected. But he ventured, "The Governor, in setting the new courts in motion, presumptively at least, was guided by considerations that seemed to commend themselves to the public judgment. He selected the five Commissioners who had served for several years with the Supreme Court, and the remaining Justices were chosen from citizens of high standing and long experience as judges of the Superior Courts. The new courts, therefore, were launched with every promise of effective organization and of speedy and good work. How far the promise has been fulfilled is for others to judge."[17]

From the outset, Chipman approached his appointment to the Third District Court of Appeal differently from his service as a Supreme Court commissioner. Because of the added administrative duties that the role of presiding justice would bring and the caseload that would necessitate his almost constant attendance, he moved his family to Sacramento, buying a home on the corner of 15th and I Streets, just one block from the new governor's mansion. For 30 years, Tehama County had been the Chipmans' home. They raised their daughters there, and returned to their farm at every opportunity, even though Chipman's duties with the State Board of Trade or the Supreme Court often drew them away. Before Chipman and Belle moved to Sacramento, however, the younger Belle married James Finnell and Alice married Chester Smith, leaving the older Chipmans alone.

Established in Sacramento, Chipman participated fully in the social, cultural, and religious life of the capital city. He and Belle enjoyed the numerous parties thrown by the leading families of the city, and Belle was involved in the women's organizations. They attended St. Paul's Episcopal Church, just a block from their home, on the corner of 15th and J Streets. In his will, Chipman left a bequest of $2,500 to the Sacramento diocese, in Belle's name, to help fund an endowment to support the bishop. On Memorial Day, the

Fourth of July, and Veteran's Day, Chipman was to be found speaking on Lincoln, the Civil War, and other patriotic themes at picnics and other celebrations or riding in parades with other notables, often as grand marshal. It was during his first year in Sacramento, on George Washington's birthday, that Chipman was the honored guest and featured speaker of the Cherry Tree Club, delivering his famous address on Lincoln.[18]

In 1906, Chipman put his name before the voters of the Third District. It had been 33 years since he faced the popular vote. He did not relish the prospect, but he was determined to continue his service as presiding justice. The Republican Party nominated him, and he ran against Joseph W. Hughes, a Democrat and long-time Sacramento Superior Court judge. Before the election, however, he did what many thought unthinkable. At the Republican convention, held in Santa Cruz, he threw his support behind James Gillett for governor, opposing Pardee, who had appointed him to the bench. Pardee was unpopular with the trade groups and the railroads, and Chipman's position reflected that sentiment. The *Sacramento Bee* reported that Chipman had "dragged the ermine," the mink in its white-coat phase, "of the judiciary in the muck and mire at the Santa Cruz convention when he turned down Governor George C. Pardee and supported Gillett for Governor."[19]

On Election Day, Hughes captured a large majority of the vote in Sacramento. A two-to-one margin in the county favored this darling of the local community and of the *Sacramento Bee*. However, although the vote in Sacramento was tabulated and reported in the papers the next day, the results from many of the outlying areas of the Third District had not yet been reported. The *Bee* gleefully reported that Hughes had "received a handsome vote." Reflecting the returns up until 3 P.M. on Wednesday, the day after the November 6 election, the *Bee*, under a picture of Hughes, informed its readership that Hughes was leading with a margin that "will be hard for Chipman to overcome."[20]

On Thursday, under a subheading stating, "Hughes Probably Elected," the *Bee*, though not willing to call the election, reported, "It is generally believed that Judge J.W. Hughes has defeated Justice N.P. Chipman for Presiding Justice of the Appellate Court. Judge Hughes received a very large plurality in Sacramento County, which it is believed Chipman cannot overcome." The article noted that Chipman beat Hughes by a mere 93 votes in Chipman's own Tehama County. "He figured on a big vote in Tehama, but his own people did not stand by him." Gloating that the Republican Party had "practically conceded" Chipman's defeat, the article cited Hughes as believing "from the advice he had received," possibly from the *Bee*, that he had been elected.[21]

By Friday morning, the indications were that Hughes' lead was insurmountable. For a year and a half, Chipman had labored to get the new appellate court on its feet, uprooting his family from Red Bluff and identifying himself with the citizens of Sacramento. Not only would a defeat mean the loss of a job, but most likely the end of his willingness to return to a career that required the approval of the voters. Not even his own party seemed to appreciate him. The Republican ticket won generally the statewide races, with Gillett elected governor. In the race for the two associate justice seats on the Third District, the two Republicans won, Elijah C. Hart, who would become Chipman's closest friend over the last 18 years of his life, and Albert G. Burnett.

But on Friday, three days after the election, the leaders of the state Republican Party conceded Chipman's defeat. Of the 35 counties in the Third District, 23 had reported 100 percent of the election returns, and Chipman still trailed by about 600 votes. Only some of the least populated counties had failed to report their returns. The front page of the *Bee*, over pictures of Hughes and Chipman, trumpeted, "Republican Managers Say Chipman Has Met With Defeat." Also on the front page, the Friday evening edition carried a message to the editor from Hughes: "Sir: Won't you tell the people that to-day, in all my vocabulary, I can find three words only. They are: 'God bless Sacramento.'"[22]

It has been said that sometimes the facts get in the way of a good story. That seems to have happened to the *Bee*. Although the *Bee* never called the election in Hughes' favor, its fawning over him was evident, ironic considering Chipman's later close friendship with C.K. McClatchy, the *Bee's* editor. About the time the Friday edition of the newspaper hit the streets, the results from most of the remaining counties landed in Sacramento, giving Chipman the advantage he needed to retain his seat as presiding justice of the Third District. Loath to congratulate Chipman, the *Bee*, on the front page of its Saturday edition, used the headline, "Hughes is a Cheerful Loser." "Superior [Court] Judge J.W. Hughes," reported the *Bee*, "has conceded the election of N.P. Chipman as Presiding Justice of the Appellate Court. The fight was a very close one, and the result of the election was in doubt until last night, when returns were received from several of the counties in the District that had been slow in reporting, which insured Chipman's success. All the counties have not yet been heard from but Chipman's plurality will not be more than 700 or 800, which is exceedingly small in a District where more than 100,000 votes were cast."[23]

Containing but one further mention of Chipman, in noting that all three elected justices were Republicans, the *Bee* article predictably turned its attention to Hughes: "Although defeated, Judge Hughes is proud of the run he made. The magnificent plurality of 3531 that he got in Sacramento County shows how well he is thought of by the people who know him best. He also ran very strong in every county where he has ever tried a case or where he is personally known. [¶] Judge Hughes is a very good loser, and has gracefully accepted his defeat. In speaking of the result of his fight to a Bee reporter this morning, he said: [¶] 'It is true I have been beaten by a small plurality. Although I was not elected, I am very proud of the run I made....."[24]

Once all of the votes were counted, Chipman managed a plurality to beat out Hughes by two percentage points. Chipman found his greatest support in the northern and more rural counties of the district, those that were the most remote and, hence, the last to report their results. Of the three pre-

The California state Capitol courtroom of the California Supreme Court and the Court of Appeal, Third Appellate District, during Chipman's tenure as presiding justice (California State Library).

A view from the north of the California State Capitol, as it appeared about the time Chipman moved to California in 1875. Chipman's court and his chambers were located in the eastern portion of the Capitol, which was removed when the annex was added in 1952 (California State Library).

siding justices appointed by Governor Pardee in 1905, only Chipman retained his seat on the bench after the 1906 elections. In all, five of the original nine justices of the Court of Appeal districts either did not run or lost the contested election.[25]

To stagger the terms so that a seat on the Third District would be up for election every four years, the legislature required the justices to draw lots for the four-year, eight-year, and twelve-year terms. Chipman drew the twelve-year term, meaning that he would not have to run again until 1918.[26]

After the election, Chipman went back to work, though with two new associate justices. The Third District's courtroom and chambers occupied a portion of the first floor of the state Capitol. In an apse, a rounded extension of the Capitol building, on the east side of the Capitol, looking out over the beautiful grounds of Capitol Park, the court sat as a three-judge panel on all of its cases. With their backs to the rounded exterior wall, the three judges heard the arguments of counsel in a courtroom wider than it was deep and interrupted by two columns reaching up to the 20-foot ceiling. Chipman's chambers, as well as those of the other two justices, were also on the first floor, along with the state library. In Chipman's chambers, he prominently displayed a lithograph of Lincoln, as well as one of Grant which Grant had autographed for Chipman. He also displayed his original of Leutze's *Fort Sumter After the Bombardment*, a painting of large proportions, five feet tall and seven feet wide, with the ornamental frame.

Justice Hart served as associate justice with Chipman for 15 years and became an admirer of his older colleague. Hart marveled at how tirelessly Chipman labored, not just in his court duties, but also in his continued efforts to promote California agriculture and industry to the world. Remembering Chipman, Hart told a reporter: "His was a charming personality. [¶] While he was a man of undaunted courage — a man who would not be swerved from

Fort Sumter After the Bombardment, **painted by Emanuel Leutze of *Washington Crossing the Delaware* fame. Chipman brought this large painting (5 feet by 7 feet) to California from Washington, D.C. It depicts Fort Sumter, South Carolina, after Union forces bombarded it in April 1863, after it had fallen into the hands of the Confederacy (Sarah Clift).**

his conviction of right by the clamorings of the mob — still his nature was always gentle and gracious. He possessed a big broad mind and devoted it to the achievement of big things. He had none of the ego which so often handicaps a man who has the capacity through learning, experience and determination to solve stupendous problems." Hart found Chipman's modesty remarkable, given his well-known achievements in life. "He loved his friends," recalled Hart, "but he never nourished resentments against his enemies, if any he had." That modesty was apparent to all after Chipman's death. Even though he had gathered his papers, from the Civil War on, into 14 volumes to give to his daughters, he recommended that they be offered to the California State Library, but only kept there if the library deemed them worthy.[27]

Chipman served as the first presiding justice of the California Court of Appeal, from 1905 to 1921 (California Court of Appeal, Third Appellate District).

A distinguishing characteristic of Chipman on the bench, even his "pole star," as Hart called it, was that he never lost his temper. He listened patiently and attentively to all, no matter the merit of the argument. But that is not to say he did not assert himself when the circumstances called for it, especially in defense of the court and his fellow jurists.

Such was the case when a Stockton attorney accused the court of corruption. A.H. Carpenter, a veteran attorney, represented many litigants not only in the trial courts but also in the Supreme Court and Court of Appeal. In one case, Carpenter represented three men accused of stealing a pig. One of those men, in the hope that he would be dealt with more leniently, turned state's evidence and, as a result, it came to light that Carpenter suborned perjury. The attorney was convicted and served a short term in jail. Thereafter, he sought vengeance on the sheriff and the district attorney, suing them for slander. Carpenter lost at trial and, when he appealed to the Third District, the judgment against Carpenter was affirmed. This so enraged Carpenter that he drafted a petition calling for the impeachment of Presiding Justice Chipman and Associate Justices Hart and Burnett.[28]

Carpenter presented the petition to the speaker of the state Assembly, A.H. Hewitt. The petition was promptly referred to the judiciary committee for investigation. The three judges jointly filed a letter with the committee, conceding that, if the charges were true, they "should be broken of their office as quickly as legal machinery can be made to do so." But they denied any wrongdoing and urged the committee to act quickly to determine the truth of the allegations. The judges reminded the committee that the records on which Carpenter's appeals were decided were available for perusal and evaluation and that the Supreme Court had denied Carpenter's petitions to review the cases. From trial court to Supreme Court, 11 judges had agreed on the outcome of the cases.[29]

As presiding justice, Chipman took upon himself the responsibility to defend the court and his fellow justices. At the hearing of the judiciary committee, Carpenter presented his case, trying to convince the legislators that it was only by corrupt judging that his conviction for subornation of perjury and his nine-month jail term were allowed to stand. Chipman left his work in his chambers on the first floor of the capitol to attend the judiciary committee hearing on the second floor. Rather than argue for the correctness of his court's decision on appeal, which he felt spoke for itself, Chipman simply denied the charge that he or his colleagues were corrupt in their decision. At the close of evidence, the judiciary committee concluded that Carpenter's charges were unfounded and recommended that the full Assembly take no further action toward impeachment. The matter was dropped.[30]

Chipman's reelection in 1918, at the age of 84, didn't entail nearly as much drama in the vote count as the 1906 election. He won handily, even though the new 12-year term would end when he was 96 years old. On Election Day, however, two major world events were unfolding: the end of World War I and the worldwide influenza pandemic. News of the end of hostilities in Austria and Hungary, followed by the flight of the Kaiser out of Germany and a German revolution, overshadowed the statewide elections in California. The joy engendered by the success of the allies, however, was, itself, overshadowed for many by the fear of contracting influenza. The United States was in the midst of the pandemic, which affected more than one quarter of Americans and killed more than half a million. Officials worried that citizens would stay away from the polls, so a campaign was launched encouraging them to "Wear Your Mask and Bring Your Little Pencil." No one well enough to be up and about should stay away from the polls, the campaign advised. Assuring that there was no danger "if you wear your mask," officials decided not to allow anyone into a voting booth without wearing a gauze mask.[31]

12
Last Years (1919–1924)

Eighty-four years old and with a twelve-year term ahead of him, Chipman was set to work through his old age. But, instead of marking the beginning of a new era in his judicial career, his reelection marked the beginning of the end of that career. Old age and its trials were soon to beset the octogenarian, starting with the loss of Belle.

On February 6, 1919, just three months after Chipman's reelection, Belle Chipman passed away. Her death came six days after their 54th wedding anniversary. From their Civil War wedding in St. Louis, through ten years in Washington, D.C., and on to California, where they lived in Red Bluff and Sacramento, with long visits to San Francisco, the Chipmans raised their daughters, traveled internationally, associated with presidential families, and built a successful life together. In the sad days after her death, her body was cremated and the ashes sent to St. Louis to be interred in the Robert Holmes family plot. Now alone, Chipman suffered, his physical ailments becoming, first, hindering and, finally, debilitating.

Later in 1919, Chipman was diagnosed with an enlarged prostate, which had gone untreated long enough that it resulted in permanent damage to his bladder. Soon after he underwent surgery to remove his prostate in September, glaucoma clouded his vision in his left eye. Treatment was unsuccessful and, in November, the doctors removed the eye. After a long period of hospitalization in San Francisco, which apparently was continuous from August to December, Chipman was released, but he was required to stay in San Francisco because of ongoing treatment. Constant infections and poor eyesight made it impossible to work.[1]

Chipman lived with his widowed daughter, Alice, on Bush Street in San Francisco. Still unable to work, Chipman held on to the hope that his physical condition would improve enough for him to return to Sacramento. He felt guilty that his absence from the court caused his colleagues to work harder, though they claimed not to mind and to be concerned only with his welfare. His role as presiding justice was filled by other judges on temporary assignments. Through 1920, Chipman did not rally. Instead, the infections continued and the sight in his remaining eye deteriorated. In early 1921, Chipman finally faced the inevitable and wrote to Governor William D. Stephens that he would resign as of the end of April 1921. Accepting the resignation, Stephens thanked Chipman for his "wonderful service to the people of our state, and to the nation...."[2]

Chipman received no pension for his 16 years as presiding justice of the California Court of Appeal, Third Appellate District. His only income from the time he retired to his death was his Civil War pension of $72 per month. He was fortunate to have money left over from the sale of his acreage in Tehama County and his residence in Sacramento to pay for treatment and nursing care in his home.[3]

Unable to move about because of his deteriorating health, Chipman withdrew from most aspects of public life, though he still enjoyed letters and visitors. He dictated letters to his nurse and signed them himself. In 1921, his condition improved sufficiently to allow him to visit his daughter Belle in Chico for several months.

On Chipman's 89th birthday, the *Recorder*, the local business and legal newspaper, ran an article on Chipman's life. It told the remarkable story of a man, born in Ohio and raised in Iowa, who volunteered for Civil War service and, by the end of the war, found himself in Washington, working with Lincoln and Stanton. The article memorialized Chipman's service in Washington, D.C., and his adoption of California as his new home, where he "did much to make California and its manifold attractions known to the world." "Surely such a career of service is worthy of more than passing notice. When a man has given upwards of sixty years of an active life to the service of his country and his state it merits recognition, not alone by the members of the profession he dignified, but by the people whom he served." The *Recorder* offered its "cheerful greeting and heartfelt recognition" to the old general. The nurse, Elise Anderson, read the article to Chipman and noted on the page of the scrapbook in which the article was placed, "He was almost overwhelmed by this."[4]

The condition of Chipman's right eye, also caused by glaucoma, required its removal, and so he was left completely blind. Douglas MacArthur would later say, "Old soldiers never die; they just fade away." That seemed to be Chipman's lot. But as his 90th birthday approached, Chipman slipped away, dying in San Francisco on February 1, 1924.[5]

Having lived such a long, full life, Chipman outlived most of his friends

Chipman, after his retirement from the Court of Appeal. Although he retired because of failing health, especially deteriorating eyesight, Chipman remained popular as one who fought in the Civil War and knew Abraham Lincoln. Here, he is seen in a parade, with a reporter and the reporter's son (California State Library).

and all of his heroes. No one in Washington remembered Chipman. In the ephemeral world of national politics, where popularity and power can change in a matter of months, weeks, or even days, an absence of almost 50 years turned Chipman into, at best, the answer to any one of several trivia questions, such as who prosecuted the commandant of the Andersonville Prison or who served as the only delegate to Congress from the District of Columbia.

But Chipman was not forgotten in California. Funeral services, attended by many of the government and social leaders of the day, were held at Grace Cathedral of the Episcopal Church on California Street in San Francisco. His pallbearers included colleagues from the court, friends from Red Bluff, and C.K. McClatchy, editor of the *Sacramento Bee*. Chipman's body was interred at Cypress Lawn Cemetery, south of San Francisco, despite his wish that he be cremated and his ashes deposited with Belle's in the Robert Holmes family plot in St. Louis.[6]

Justice Hart eulogized Chipman as "ever unselfishly devoted to service — service to his country and to his fellow man. There are few men of whom it can be truly said, as thus it may be of the late soldier, statesman, judge and lawyer, that his field of activities in this life was as boundless as it was varied, and all directed to the accomplishment of good for his God and his country."[7]

Epilogue

At the modern-day Andersonville National Historic Site in Georgia, a beautiful and serene scene is punctuated by thousands of grave markers, lined up across the landscape, in stark contrast to the ugly, agonizing scene at the close of the Civil War. More than 12,000 bodies of Union soldiers are buried there, with about 500 of the graves marked "Unknown." Today, Andersonville stands as a symbol of the sacrifice of Americans captured in times of war. The National Prisoner of War Museum, opened in the Andersonville National Historic Site, tells the story of American prisoners of war from the American Revolution to the present. Each Memorial Day, the graves are decorated with small U.S. flags.

The Andersonville trial is the event for which Chipman is most known today. In 1957, on a live television program called "Climax!," Charlton Heston played Chipman in an episode called "The Trial of Captain Wirz." On Broadway in 1959 and 1960, George C. Scott starred as Chipman in "The Andersonville Trial"—a role for which Scott was nominated for a Tony Award. William Shatner played Chipman in the 1970 made-for-television movie "The Andersonville Trial." The movie was nominated for five Emmy Awards and won three, including Outstanding Single Program.

Although Chipman was not among the most famous Americans of the late 19th century and early 20th century, he had the uncanny fortune to be where history was being made. He enjoyed the trust and company of the country's greatest figures, and he was there when some of the greatest events of his day transpired. A study of his life is a study of his era.

Chipman played a supporting role in preserving the Union, honoring the dead, establishing a national seat of government, building an economy, and creating a judicial legacy. He witnessed and participated in turning points with reverberations through today. While this may be expected of a prominent participant, such as Lincoln, Chipman was just a seemingly ordinary individual who, time after time, found himself in remarkable situations.

American historian and biographer David McCullough reminds students of history that "nothing ever had to happen the way it happened. Any great past event could have gone off in any number of different directions for any number of different reasons."[1]

The absence of any one of many events or personalities during the Civil War could have caused a very different result. Chief among these were events such as the unifying and motivating Gettysburg Address and the promulgation of the Emancipation Proclamation and personalities such as Grant, Lee, and Lincoln.

While it is fruitless and perhaps frivolous to assert that without any particular person, such as Chipman, the course of history would have changed in a specific way, it is not beyond reason to conclude that some apparently minor contributions were actually much more important than they seem, more significant than we remember them. Especially when one considers turning points in history, small contributions gain in prominence because who is to say which of many minor circumstances tipped the balance?

Grant rose to prominence after his victory at Fort Donelson. When Grant was promoted to lieutenant general, Sherman told him: "You are now Washington's legitimate successor." Lincoln had finally found a general who was willing to fight. But it was not his gallantry alone that won the day. Chipman's regiment, the Second Iowa, untested in battle, charged on the Confederate position, even while some of its members, including Chipman, were gunned down. It was this kind of courage that won the battle and earned Grant the praise of the country and the respect of Lincoln.[2]

Sheridan's legendary run through the Shenandoah Valley was a key to the Union's victory over the Confederacy. But he may not have succeeded there without intelligence concerning the location and strength of Confederate forces. Chipman's ride from Washington, through Snicker's Gap, to Sheridan's advanced position prompted Sheridan to pull back in the face of peril and thereby preserve his strength for a later day.

Chipman confronted timeless quandaries, such as the meaning of "patriotism" and the determination to take a stand as a country and be willing to fight for that purpose. In his 1863 speech to his Iowan hometown, in the midst of the Civil War, Chipman expounded on an issue that his country has faced in every war, and one which has often divided the country. It was a speech that could have been given at any time in American history.

> Let me tell you that it is not the bayonets alone that end wars, nor the lack of their vigorous use that prolongs them, but that very much rests with the public sentiment at home. If all that force known in politics as "outside pressure,"

which is used and misused to govern our nation, could be brought to embrace the rebellion, the enemy might be pressed into submission by it alone. You who remain at home are responsible for your words, as are soldiers for their bullets. You have more right to talk against the president or government than have they to shoot in that direction. Everything said and done detrimental to the common cause is unpatriotic and just as far is he not a patriot as he indulges in this abuse of the powers that be. There is a class of men whom for want of a milder term I call growlers. They are loyal I think and really wish our government to succeed, but they have no very high ideas of the interests involved in this struggle and catch no brighter glimpse of the coming glory of America than they can get in looking back into the past, when all was peace and quiet in the country, when freedom and slavery walked hand in hand, truth and error slept side by side and no one seemed to question that they were born of the same parents. These are men who have never felt one genuine patriotic thrill in their lives, under their incrustations of self, a way down deep in their hearts as can be. They are not patriots. They are loyal but have not that noblest passion which characterizes the citizen. This is what I mean and be assured there is a difference between loyalty and patriotism. They always take the worst view of everything.[3]

The definition of patriotism and the role of the United States in war are questions that continue to vex Americans and divide the country. In the future, the American people will face the same questions.

Also divisive is the issue raised by the Andersonville trial concerning the proper use of military tribunals, questions that persist. With enemy combatants detained at Guantanamo Bay and other locations, Americans have debated what rights these detainees have in American institutions or whether they have any rights at all. Even the United States Supreme Court has grappled with these issues, which have their genesis in the birth of the nation, the trial of Benedict Arnold, and the Andersonville trial.

Chipman's efforts on behalf of the District of Columbia, his assertion that in creating this federal city the government necessarily took upon itself the responsibility for its success, are continuing themes. For almost 100 years, Chipman remained the only delegate who had represented the district in Congress. Since 1971, the District of Columbia has again been represented by a non-voting delegate to the House of Representatives: Walter E. Fauntroy and Eleanor Holmes Norton. Efforts continue to gain the district a vote in the House.

The Washington Monument dominates much of the D.C. landscape. It attracts more than 800,000 visitors every year and fittingly honors the father of our country.

Chipman's efforts on behalf of California also continue to be significant. When he served as president of the State Board of Trade, the California economy was still in its infancy. In modern California, fruits and wine are major industries and as of 2006 the state's economy made up about 13 percent of the United States' gross domestic product.

The Third Appellate District of the California Court of Appeal preserves the memory of its first presiding justice. Chipman's portraits of Lincoln and Grant adorn the chambers of Presiding Justice Arthur Scotland, the court's eleventh presiding justice. Next door, Chipman's congressional desk and chair occupy the corner of Justice Richard Sims' chambers. Chipman's Leutze painting, *Fort Sumter After the Bombardment*, hangs in the hall. Situated in the seat of California government, the court's eleven justices, sitting in panels of three, carry on the work that Chipman began, deciding cases involving everything from criminal law to election challenges.[4]

Zeal, honor, and loyalty guided and sometimes tugged Chipman through his life. He admired Lincoln's wisdom and compassion, though he did not always share the full compassion. He learned from Stanton that unbending posture may be necessary in wartime, but he never adopted Stanton's more mercurial tendencies. He recognized the great, yet quiet, leadership capabilities of Grant and proved himself a loyal friend of Grant, even as Chipman fought in Congress for the interests of the District of Columbia. In the end, Chipman, a product of his day and his circumstances, made his own indelible mark.

Appendix:
Abraham Lincoln

*Address of Hon. N.P. Chipman, Presiding
Justice of the District Court of Appeal.
At a Banquet given by the Cherry Tree Club
of Sacramento, February 22, 1906.*

Mr. President and Gentlemen:—As I am informed, the Cherry Tree Club meets once each year to commemorate the birthday of the Father of his Country. Your club is composed almost entirely of young men, most of whom were born since the close of the Civil War, and few, if any, of you were old enough at that time to have any personal recollection of the events that marked the most tragic period in the history of the Republic. I am asked to portray the character of the man who was not only the central figure in that Titanic struggle, but whose memory is, and will ever be, enshrined in the hearts of all liberty-loving people throughout the habitable globe. May I not hope that you will bear with me if I shall attempt more than a brief passing tribute to the character of this remarkable man[.] May I not be indulged in an endeavor to quicken in your minds the meaning of that great epoch in our history, while bringing to your atten-

tion some of the conspicuous characteristics of the man about whom I am to speak, and some of the events connected with which he will always be the one prominent personality[.]

In devotion to his country; in breadth of statesmanship; in exalted character; in blameless private life, the name of Abraham Lincoln will grow brighter with the ages — the synonym of true greatness — the harbinger of the period to which we all look, of peace on earth, good will to man. "In his early days he struck his roots deep down into the common soil of the earth, and in his latest years his head towered and shone among the stars!"

Some one has said that the American people are peculiarly fortunate in the coincidence that they may celebrate the birthday, in the same month, of two of the most illustrious men in all the world. It was eminently appropriate, therefore, that in assembling to honor the memory

203

of George Washington your thoughts should also turn to the man who preserved to us the Nation so nobly established by the Fathers of the Revolution.

It is a question whether we get the true perspective of historical personages through the opinions of contemporaneous observers. In some respects we probably do not. It is in the fullness of time that the true value of great public service and distinguishing traits of personal character can be rightly and adequately estimated.

And yet there is a certain indefinable sympathy and feeling of brotherhood existing among contemporaries that arouse in them a keener appreciation of what has been accomplished by one of their number than is possible to kindle in the hearts of posterity for the deeds of their remote ancestors.

I am trying to convey this meaning: That it is not possible, for example, to portray the life and services of George Washington at this distance, so as to reach a personal, sympathetic chord such as is awakened in our hearts when contemplating the life and services of Abraham Lincoln, whose tragic martyrdom touches the tenderest feelings of our natures, and for whose services and sacrifices we experience a sense of personal indebtedness and sympathy.

The appropriateness of connecting the name of Lincoln with that of Washington is attested by the fact that we have come to associate these two persons, each in his time, as the two most distinguished leaders in the two great epochs of American history.

I had thought of comparing the lives and achievements of these two colossal characters as perhaps a satisfactory method of performing my task. But a little reflection convinced me that this would be most incongruous and inadequate.

The personal characteristics of these two men were wholly unlike; the condi-

tions confronting them were entirely dissimilar; the responsibilities assumed by Washington, though great, were infinitely less weighty, less complex, and, in their consequences to mankind, less portentous than those cast upon the shoulders of Lincoln.

May I ask you then to give me your attention while I shall endeavor to place before you Lincoln the man and Lincoln the President as he appeared to me.

With the history of his birth, early life, and subsequent career as a lawyer, attending to the petty controversies among his neighbors, I need not speak. There was nothing in this period to mark him as distinguished above a thousand other plodding lawyers by whom he was surrounded. He had been in the Legislature, he had been in Congress, and while we now, looking back, may see in him then some of those characteristics that distinguished him in after life, they were not so pronounced as to lead his most intimate friends to predict for him a career in any sense conspicuous.

And yet in all those years his sturdy common sense; his matchless honesty and probity of character; his sympathy with the people and his vigorous mental capacity, were gradually preparing him for his great work, and as gradually centering public confidence upon him as the type of American leadership in the great antislavery struggle then developing.

Prior to his famous debate with Stephen A. Douglas, Mr. Lincoln's reputation was scarcely more than local, but that intellectual combat focalized the Nation's thought upon him and his nomination at Chicago was both logical as well as a natural expression of his party's wisdom and foresight. I was a spectator of that splendid and inspiring scene, when it seemed as if the pent-up protests and accumulated remonstrances of long years against Southern aggression and arrogance broke forth in unrestrained and unrestrainable manifestations, and rang out in one great burst of defiance — at once a clarion note prophetic of war, and the death knell of human slavery in America. It was a scene of wild rejoicing, and unfaltering consecration to an exalted purpose. The Annunciation of the Nation's Savior was proclaimed at that hour. The Solid South repudiated the Messiah, but the Loyal North made him President and crowned him with immortality.

It is now accepted history that the election of Mr. Lincoln was made the pretext of withdrawal from the Union by the Southern States, and rebellion in arms followed in hot haste. The interval between his election and inauguration was an interval of war-like preparations by the South; of larceny of the munitions of war, and rape of the fortresses of the Union.

All the arts of the wicked one were used to instill into the minds of the officers of the army who owed their titles and distinction to the Nation's generosity, the fatal poison of love of the State before love of the Nation; and that other and most destructive fallacy — the right of a State to withdraw from the Union. So powerful were these seductive influences that even that Prince of Chivalric Honor — that man of spotless integrity and high promise, Robert E. Lee, stripped from his shoulders the insignia of office in the Union army and drew his sword against his country.

Washington City swarmed with traitors; the halls of Congress rang out with treasonable utterances; the very fountain of loyalty was polluted.

Into this fetid atmosphere, amid these depressing surroundings; into this awful shadow of rebellion hanging over the Nation's Capital, this modest son of the Republic came upon a mission that was to cost him his life; that was to drench our land in fratricidal blood; but that was to witness a Nation new born.

When he arrived in Washington Mr. Lincoln was as far from appreciating the strength and value of his personality as were those around him of realizing fully the momentous importance of the events he was to control or of understanding how great was the man who was to lead us to victory.

The oath of office was administered in front of the Capitol by Chief Justice Taney, who had in effect declared it to be the judgment of the Supreme Court of the United States that negro slaves had no rights which a white man was bound to respect. And singularly enough the man who was soon to strike the shackles from these same bondsmen, in his Inaugural Address declared it to be the Republican doctrine, entrenched in the Constitution, that a slave who escapes from a slave State into a free State is not thereby made free, but became so only when voluntarily taken into free territory. Upon the question of the right of a State to secede his argument was clear, luminous and unanswerable. He declared that "no State could lawfully get out of the Union," as he expressed it, and that he would do all in his power to enforce the laws. He added: "I trust this will not be regarded as a menace, but only as the declared purpose of the Union that it will constitutionally defend and maintain itself. In doing this there need be no bloodshed or violence, and there shall be none unless it is forced upon the national authority." We now know that at that moment plans were being perfected by rebel conspirators to seize the forts, arsenals and other Government property. Lincoln's plea for peace, designed to placate the South, had little effect upon her people, but it turned upon the rebel leaders the responsibility of beginning hostilities. Lincoln's voice was sharp and penetrating, with a plaintive intonation, and his almost pathetic plea must have deeply moved the throng who hung upon his matchless address. The concluding paragraph will ever stand as one of the most remarkable perorations ever uttered by man. He said: "I am loath to close. We are not enemies, but friends.

We must not be enemies. Though passions may have strained, it must not break our bonds of affection. The mystic cords of memory, stretching from every battlefield and patriot grave to every living heart and hearthstone all over this broad land, will yet swell the chorus of the Union, when again touched, as surely they will be, by the better angels of our nature."

Alas! As an appeal with a promise of immediate fulfillment it fell on many unresponsive ears. As prophecy it now reads to us as a vision of light from on high, though its realization came after long years and long after the close of the most sanguinary strife in modern history.

I can[no]t hope that your indulgence will permit me to even sketch all the strenuous and crowded years through which he passed and the relation he bore to the momentous events that filled the pages of our Civil War. I shall only here and there notice them and then only to convey some idea of the man Lincoln, through some of the more striking features of his Administration. With characteristic magnanimity and against the advice of many friends he called to his Cabinet four men — Seward, Chase, Bates and Cameron — who had been candidates for the Presidency when Lincoln was chosen. He refused to believe at such a time that men worthy to serve as his advisers would be unfaithful to their trust and seek self-aggrandizement. He said to his friends: "Let us forget ourselves and joins hands, like brothers, to save the Republic. If we succeed there will be glory enough for all."

Lincoln was inaugurated March 4, 1861, and on March 9th the Rebel Congress, having previously assembled at Montgomery, Alabama, passed a Bill for the organization of an army. Commissioners were sent to Washington to negotiate a treaty with the Government. The President would not see them, but sent them a copy of his Inaugural Address. They remained until in April, Mr. Lincoln meanwhile giving no sign, and were then informed by Mr. Seward that they could have no recognition from the Government of the United States. Mr. Lincoln was determined that the overt act for which everybody was waiting, and about which everybody was talking, should come from the Rebels. It came when the resolve was taken to provision Major Anderson's gallant company at Fort Sumter. General Beauregard opened fire on April 12th, and war was declared by the South, and on April 15th the President called for 75,000 troops. The North was aflame. Party ties for the time disappeared — but one sentiment prevailed — that for the preservation of the Union. Congress was called to assemble at the Capital on July 4, 1861. As showing the spirit of the North, Ohio, whose quota was 13,000, within one week after the call was issued, offered the services of 70,000 patriots to Governor Denison; and to the call generally more than 500,000 had sprung to arms.

Jefferson Davis in his message to the Confederate Congress had by an artful and insidious argument urged the right of secession for which the South were bound to fight if necessary. In his message to the American Congress, which assembled July 4th, Mr. Lincoln, after recounting the events of the past two months showing that the Rebels had forced the issue of war or dissolution of the Union, pointed out with great clearness and force the impending consequences of this issue. He said: "It presents to the whole family of man the question whether a Constitutional Republic or Democracy — a Government of the people by the same people — can or cannot maintain its territorial integrity against domestic foes. It presents the question whether discontented individuals, too few in numbers to control administration according to organic law in any case, can always, upon the pretenses made in this case, or any other pretenses, or arbitrarily, without any pretense, break up their Government, and thus practically put an end to free Government upon the earth. It forces us to ask, 'Is there in all Republics this inherent and fatal weakness? Must a Government, of necessity, be too strong for the liberties of its own people, or too weak to maintain its own existence?'"

There was no mistaking now the stupendous issue. It meant not only the possibility of free government in America but whether it ever could exist anywhere upon the earth. It meant that the heresy of the right to secede, which Mr. Calhoun and his school had long taught, should once and for all time be fought out at the cannon's mouth. Behind it of course stood the spectre of human slavery, but the great moving cause was the asserted right of a State to withdraw from the Union. As this was the crucial issue, and should not be permitted to be clouded by pretense of other grounds for rebellion, I must be permitted to quote another brief paragraph from Mr. Lincoln's unanswerable argument. "The sophism," he said, "is that any State of the Union may consistently with the National Constitution, and therefore lawfully and peacefully, withdraw from the Union without consent of the Union or any other State. The little disguise, that the supposed right is to be exercised only for just cause, themselves to be the judges of its justice, is too thin to merit notice. With rebellion thus sugar-coated they have been drugging the public mind of their section for more than thirty years, and until at length they have brought many good men to a willingness to take up arms against the Government the day after some assemblage of men has enacted the farcical pretense of taking their State out of the Union, who would have, could have, been brought to no such thing the day before."

In the following November occurred the affair of the British packet-ship Trent. Mason and Slidell, two rebel envoys, took passage, one for England and the other for France, on the Trent, their purpose being to induce those great Powers to recognize the Confederacy as a Nation. Captain Wilkes of the man-of-war San Jacinto, overhauled the Trent, brought her to by a shot across her bow, and took off the two envoys and carried them to Boston, where they were lodged in Fort Warren.

This event created pronounced approving enthusiasm throughout the North; it was looked upon as a defiant reply to the attitude of the English and the French Governments towards our Government. The demand of the British Government that the envoys should be surrendered because they had been taken from under the British flag and against the protests of the Commander of the Trent, only inflamed the popular indignation. Confronted with the danger of war with England at this critical moment, that recognition of the Confederacy might follow, resulting possibly in the permanent division of the States and dissolution of the Union, the people, nevertheless, stood firm and declared that the envoys should never be given up. Congress passed a vote of thanks to Captain Wilkes; the Secretaries of War and Navy approved his act. Secretary Seward at first also opposed any concessions to the British Government. And now shown out one of Mr. Lincoln's strong traits of character. From the first he doubted the lawfulness of the seizure, and the more he reflected the stronger became his conviction that these emissaries must be given up. Amid the popular clamor for their retention he stood thoughtful, anxious, but with calm determination to act with due regard for international law and for the highest interests of our country. A weak man would have drifted with the strong current of opinion though it might lead to war with England. But Mr. Lincoln was not a weak man. His reply to his Cabinet and to the people was: "Once we fought Great Britain for doing just what Captain Wilkes has done. If Great Britain protests against this act and demands their release, we must adhere to our principles of 1812. We must give up these prisoners. Besides, one war at a time." It is difficult at this distance from the war period to realize what courage and steadfastness were required to stem the popular tide at this important juncture. Some idea of the strain put upon Mr. Lincoln's character may come to you when I repeat the declaration of Senator John P. Hale of New Hampshire. "If," said he, "this Administration will not listen to the voice of the people, they will find themselves engulfed in a fire that will consume them like stubble; they will [be] helpless before a power that will hurl them from their places." The sober judgment of time has fully vindicated the wisdom of Lincoln's action at this perilous crisis.

No phase of the Civil War like that of the slavery question brought out more clearly the strength of Mr. Lincoln's character or showed in stronger light the dominant thought in his mind which was the preservation of the Union.

The popular clamor was insistent and strong for the immediate and unconditional abolition of slavery. General Fremont in August, 1861, undertook to cut the Gordian knot with the backing of his sword in Missouri. He issued a proclamation of confiscation of rebel property, including the liberation of slaves. Unwilling to rebuke Fremont, Mr. Lincoln, in his kindly and conciliatory way, so characteristic of him, wrote a letter asking General Fremont to modify his order and pointing out the difficulty he was having in the border States to maintain a loyal spirit. But Fremont was obdurate and refused, believing, which was true, that the popular feeling of the North was behind him. Mr. Lincoln was, in September, 1861, compelled to modify Fremont's proclamation and make it conform to the Act of Congress and the rules of war. Later, in May, 1862, he was compelled to revoke General Hunter's proclamation of emancipation in the States of Georgia, Florida

and South Carolina, and in doing so proclaimed "that neither General Hunter nor any other Commander has been authorized by the Government of the United States to make proclamations declaring slaves of any State free." And to settle the matter he declared that he "reserved to himself the right to determine whether it should become a necessity indispensable to the maintenance of the Government to exercise the supposed power of proclaiming emancipation of the slaves."

Mr. Lincoln's anxiety and embarrassment were greatly increased by the attitude of General McClellan on this subject, which brought out the suggestion from the impatient people that McClellan was more anxious about the rights of the slave-holders than for the prosecution of the war. Mr. Lincoln was brutally criticised by political enemies in the North for going too fast in the direction of the destruction of slavery, and on the other hand by his ardent and indiscreet friends for his slowness in the same direction.

In the summer of 1862 Mr. Greeley published an open letter to the President in the New York Tribune which gave expression to the prevalent feeling at the North for immediate emancipation. Mr. Lincoln seized upon the opportunity to reply through the same medium. This letter is a fine example of Mr. Lincoln's lucidity of expression as it also is of the frankness and simplicity of his character. I hope you will bear with me while I read a paragraph or two from this remarkable document.

"As to the policy 'I seem to be pursuing,' as you say, I have not meant to leave anyone in doubt. I would save the Union. I would save it in the shortest way under the Constitution. * * * If there be those who would not save the Union unless they could at the same time save slavery, I do not agree with them.

"If there be those who would not save the Union unless they could at the same time destroy slavery, I do not agree with them. My paramount object is to save the Union, and not either to save or destroy slavery.

"If I could save the Union without freeing any slaves, I would do it; if I could do it by freeing all of the slaves, I would do it; and if I could do it by freeing some and leaving others alone, I would also do that.

"What I do about slavery and the colored race, I do because I believe it helps to save the Union; and what I forbear, I forbear because I do not believe it would help to save the Union. * * * I have here stated my purpose according to my views of official duty, and I intend no modification of my oft-expressed personal wish that all men everywhere could be free."

General Lee had achieved some notable successes and flushed with victory, crossed the Potomac into Maryland. Lincoln was profoundly stirred. No border State had as yet been invaded and Maryland was loyal. He had been contemplating Emancipation early in 1862, but hesitated to proclaim it. This last movement of the Rebel army settled the matter, and he resolved if Lee was driven back the Proclamation should issue. Lee's army was driven back into Virginia. South Mountain and Antietam were fought on the 14th and 17th of September, 1862. The Rebels were routed, broken in pieces, and Maryland and Pennsylvania were saved. On the 22nd of September Mr. Lincoln issued his proclamation, which, at the period of probation, January 1, 1863, was to strike the shackles from millions of slaves, and which ultimately left not a single bondsman on American soil. Henceforward the war assumed a new aspect. It had thus far been waged to save the Union with or without slavery. Now it was a war for the re-establishment of the Union — the Union without slavery.

In the West, Belmont, Fort Donelson, Shiloh, and Pea Ridge brought some ray of hope to the heart of the President, but he was being sorely tried by the vacillation, timidity and open insubordination

of McClellan, and by the failures of the Generals who succeeded to the command of the splendid Army of the Potomac. There are no more pathetic pages in American history than those recounting the struggles of the President to maintain relations of mutual amity and confidence between himself and McClellan. If I could trespass upon your patience by reading from Mr. Lincoln's correspondence at this period, in his effort to induce McClellan to press the advantage he had, you would see shining out the strong points in Lincoln's character, and how with tearful reluctance he was finally forced to retire McClellan from further military duty. These were gloomy, depressing days for Lincoln, but amid all discouragements he never once faltered in his faith that ultimate victory would crown our arms.

The year 1863 brought great anxiety to Lincoln and at times he almost lost hope. Through many portions of the North secret societies were forming in aid of the rebellious South. General Burnside had issued his famous order giving notice that all persons within his lines, including the State of Ohio, who should be guilty of acts designed to assist the enemy, would be arrested as traitors and spies, tried, and, if convicted, be put to death.

Vallandingham, a prominent politician of that State, immediately denounced General Burnside's order and called upon the people to resist. He was arrested, tried, convicted, by Military Commission, and sentenced to imprisonment in Fort Warren. The President changed the penalty to expulsion through the Union lines into the Rebel States. The Democrats demanded his return and nominated him as their candidate for Governor. To the deputation that visited Washington, Mr. Lincoln said: "Your own attitude encourages desertion, resistance to the draft, and the like, because it teaches those who incline to desert and to escape the draft, to believe it is your purpose to protect them," and he added: "Must I shoot a simple-minded soldier boy who deserts while I must not touch a hair of the wily agitator who induced him to desert? I think that, in such a case, to silence the agitator and save the boy is not only Constitutional, but withal a great mercy." Vallandingham was defeated at the polls by a Republican majority of over 100,000.

Depressing as were the early days of 1863 with defeat after defeat to our arms in the East, the clouds rolled by in July, when on our Natal day the glorious Fourth was made memorable and more glorious by the victories of Grant at Vicksburg and Meade at Gettysburg.

Among the many trying experiences of the President none were more vexatious than the jealousies and bickerings among the officers of the army — especially the Army of the Potomac. Even while Grant was successful in pushing his operations on the Mississippi there were constant efforts to have him superseded. The reply of Lincoln in this particular case is one of the many evidences of his characteristic manner of answering malcontents.

The trial and conviction of Fitz John Porter, one of General McClellan's favorites, for his failure to support General Pope, who was being driven towards Washington by Jackson, Longstreet and Lee, was one of the tragic episodes illustrating the gangrene of jealousy and insubordination that was disintegrating one of the finest armies ever assembled.

When the President placed General Hooker in command he wrote this gallant officer a most remarkable letter. I cannot read it all to you, but I must read a paragraph. He said: "I much fear that the spirit which you have aided to infuse into the army, or criticising their commander and withholding confidence from him, will now turn upon you. I shall assist you as far as I can to put it down. Neither you nor Napoleon, if he were alive again, could get any good out of an army while such a spirit prevails in it. And now, beware of rashness." Knowing fighting Joe

Hooker as he did, he repeated: "Beware of rashness, but, with energy and sleepless vigilance, go forward and give us victories." The answer Hooker gave at last was Chancellorville, with its appalling story of disaster.

On May 6th a dispatch came from General Hooker's Chief of Staff stating that the army had safely recrossed the Rappahannock. The message was read aloud to Lincoln, who with his eyes streaming with tears, cried out: "My God! My God! what will the country say? What will the country say?" Within an hour and in a pouring rain he and General Halleck were on their way to the army by Acquia Creek.

Is it strange that he was uplifted by the great victories of the succeeding July, or that he later found cause for discouragement at the continued failures of that year to achieve decisive results in the East and at the increasing spirit of discontent among the peace-at-any-price patriots and the non-combatants of the loyal North?

On July 18, 1864, the President issued a call for 500,000 men. At that time the draft was in force and he was a candidate for re-election. He was besought by his Republican friends to postpone the order in view of the strong resistance to the draft. He was told that he was sacrificing every hope of success at the polls by enforcing this drastic measure for more troops. His reply was: "What is the Presidency worth to me, if I have no country?" and no persuasion could drive him from his firm resolution.

The days were dark to Lincoln in the year 1864. Campaign slanders were rife as usual, and among them that Mr. Lincoln would, if defeated at the polls, devote the remainder of his term to ruin the Government. Mr. Lincoln rarely replied to such charges, but this touched a very tender and sensitive spot. In a speech to some serenaders he took the opportunity to meet these charges: "I am struggling to maintain the Government, not to overthrow it," he said. "I am struggling especially to prevent others from overthrowing it. Whoever shall be Constitutionally elected in November shall be duly installed as President on the Fourth of March. * * * In the interval I shall do my utmost that whoever is to hold the helm for the next voyage shall start with the best possible chance to save the ship." Referring to the possible choice of some one unfriendly to continuing the war, he said: "If they should deliberately resolve to have immediate peace, even at the loss of their country and their liberty, I have not the power or the right to resist them." It was during these dark days on August 26th that he wrote: "This morning, as for some days past, it seems exceedingly probable that this Administration will not be reelected. Then it will be my duty to so cooperate with the President-elect as to save the Union between the election and the inauguration, as he will have secured his election on such ground that he cannot possibly save it afterwards." He folded this paper so that it could not be read and requested each member of the Cabinet to sign his name on the reverse side.

In the end Mr. Lincoln's gloomy forebodings were wholly dissipated. The Republicans elected 212 Presidential Electors and the Democrats with McClellan as their champion, and a platform declaring the war to be a failure, received but 21.

Mr. Lincoln refused to receive the news as evidence of his personal triumph. He was absolutely dispassionate and impersonal in his political relationships and in his official action. This trait in his character can find but few parallels in history. An instance occurred upon the death of Chief Justice Taney, October 12, 1864. Mr. Chase's friends at once named him for the succession. Those of you who have read the history of those days will recall that Mr. Lincoln had little personal reason for favoring Mr. Chase, who was known to have intrigued to prevent his

nomination and secure it to himself; who was known to have spoken contemptuously of Mr. Lincoln and who sustained a sort of condescending and patronizing attitude towards his chief. Mr. Lincoln had strong reasons for favoring Montgomery Blair. But he put aside every other consideration and appointed Mr. Chase, believing that he was the best man for this great office.

When Congress assembled in December, 1864, the doom of the Confederacy seemed certain. Victorious Grant had been called to the leadership of all the armies of the Union, and had fought his way through the wilderness amid frightful slaughter and was beleaguering Petersburg, with the capture of Richmond almost assured in the near future. Sherman had marched gaily through the heart of the South. Thomas had broken Hood's army, which Sherman left in his rear. The notorious destroyer, the Alabama, had been sunk by the Kearsarge. The Shenandoah, the last of the Rebel privateers, sailed into Liverpool, and was turned over by the British to Federal officials. Lieutenant Cushing had, by a matchless and daring stroke of gallantry, destroyed the Rebel ram Albermarle. Fort Fisher and Wilmington had fallen and Farragut had bottled up Mobile Bay to blockade runners. With this hopeful outlook Mr. Lincoln was nevertheless besieged by wellmeaning people in the North to enter upon some sort of negotiations with the leader of the Rebellion. His message to Congress in December is a masterful reply to those who entertained a hope of settlement by a cessation of hostilities except upon the terms demanded by the leader of the Rebellion. In his message, Mr. Lincoln said: "He," (referring to Jefferson Davis, whom he never mentioned by name, I believe, in any State paper), "would accept nothing short of severance of the Union — precisely what we will not and cannot give. His declarations to this effect are explicit and oft-repeated. He does not at-

tempt to deceive us. He affords no excuse
to deceive ourselves. He cannot voluntarily reaccept the Union; we cannot voluntarily yield it. Between him and us the
issue is distinct, simple and inflexible. It
is an issue which can only be tried by war,
and decided by victory."

Notwithstanding these strong convic-
tions, Mr. Lincoln yielded to the persuasion of the peacemakers and consented to
send Mr. Seward to meet the Confederate
Commissioners, Messrs. Stephens, Camp-
bell and Hunter, on January 31, 1865. Mr.
Davis had appointed them "with a view to
secure peace between the two countries,"
as he expressed it. Mr. Lincoln refused to
act until the last two words were stricken
from the instructions. Mr. Lincoln's
memorandum to Mr. Seward embraced
three indispensable conditions:

First — The restoration of the National
authority throughout all the States. Second — No backward step on the slavery
questions. Third — No cessation of hostilities short of an end of the war and the
disbanding of all forces hostile to the
Government. Mr. Lincoln became uneasy
at being represented in so important a
matter by any person, and he decided to
go himself. Then followed the famous
Hampton Roads Conference. Although
historic, it came to nothing, as he expected. But it brought out many interesting incidents. One of these illustrates Mr.
Lincoln's ready wit. Mr. Lincoln took the
position that he could not enter into any
agreement with "parties in arms against
the Government." Mr. Hunter, one of the
Commissioners, to the contrary cited pre-
cedents "of this character between Charles
I of England and the people in arms
against him." Mr. Lincoln replied: "I do
not profess to be posted in history. On all
such matters I will turn you over to Seward. All I distinctly recollect about the
case of Charles I is, that he lost his head."

The fourth of March was approaching
when for the second time he was to address the people who had freely chosen

him as their leader. The black pall of war
that had hovered over the country for four
years was rapidly passing away. The fury
of the Rebellion was fast subsiding into
hopeless regrets and heartburnings.

Mr. Lincoln's inaugural address was a
short but most graphic statement of the
then situation of our country as compared
with its condition in 1861, at his first inaugural. One of Mr. Lincoln's biographers
has truthfully said that this speech has
taken its place among the most famous of
all written or spoken compositions in the
English language. In parts it has been
compared with the lofty portions of the
Old Testament. In it we find exhibited the
deep religious spirit that pervaded the soul
of Lincoln. I quote the closing passage:
"Fondly do we hope, fervently do we pray,
that this mighty scourge of war may
speedily pass away. Yet, if God wills that
it continue until all the wealth piled up
by the bondsman's two hundred and fifty
years of unrequited toil shall be sunk, and
until every drop of blood drawn by the
lash shall be paid by another drawn by the
sword, as was said three thousand years
ago, so still must it be said, 'the judgments
of the Lord are true and righteous altogether.'" Then follows the oft-quoted
passage as exhibiting the great heart of
Lincoln: "With malice toward none, with
charity for all, with firmness in the right,
as God gives us to see the right, let us
strive on to finish the work we are in; to
bind up the Nation's wounds; to care for
him who shall have borne the battle, and
for his widow, and his orphan — to do all
which may achieve and cherish a just and
lasting peace among ourselves, and with all
Nations."

The Proclamation of Freedom embraced only slaves held in States in rebellion; it did not determine universal freedom of the slaves throughout the Union.
This was accomplished by the thirteenth
amendment. When proposed in 1864, the
House of Representatives refused to pass
the joint resolution by two-thirds major-

ity. Mr. Lincoln insisted that the party platform on which he was to stand should declare in no uncertain terms for emancipation, and so it did. On reassembling in December, the House reconsidered the matter, and, with the aid of Democratic votes, to the credit of that party be it said, the resolution was passed. One after another of the States not then in rebellion adopted the amendment, but Mr. Lincoln died before enough States had acted to pass the amendment. At the conclusion of the vote in the House of Representatives, there arose an irrepressible outburst of triumphant applause. Speaker Colfax vainly struggled to resume the regular order of business, but the House adjourned "in honor of this immortal and sublime event."

It was decreed that from the day of the second inauguration Mr. Lincoln was to be given less than five weeks to live. But he was to have the satisfaction of witnessing the crowning glory of his Administration — the overthrow of rebellion, the reestablishment of the Union, and the extirpation of slavery forever from our fair land. His last days were filled with anxious thoughts and with a full comprehension that the termination of the war would bring with it new and profoundly complex and difficult problems of government. He was now about to enter upon the great work he foresaw in closing his second inaugural address — "To finish the work we are in, to bind up the Nation's wounds, to care for him who shall have borne the battle, and for his widow and his orphans, to do all which may achieve and cherish a just and lasting peace among ourselves and with all Nations."

He was now about to realize the prophecy of his first inaugural address when he said: "The mystic chords of memory, stretching from every living heart and hearthstone all over this broad land, will yet swell the chorus of the Union, when again touched, as surely they will be, by the better angels of our natures."

God be praised! Although Mr. Lincoln did not live to see it, the day has come when the better angels of the natures of all the American people have led them to swell the chorus of the Union.

Mr. Lincoln, throughout all the rebellion, seemed to bear upon his own shoulders and in his own heart, all the woes of his people. I was on duty in the War Department from the winter of 1862-3, and passed and repassed the Executive Mansion almost daily to the close of the war. It was my privilege to perform some services directly under his eye and by his personal instruction. I saw him many, many times after victories and after defeats; when important legislation was passing the crucible of opposition in Congress; when political cabals were forming to defeat his re-election; when passionate patriots were urging him to push the war with greater vigor; when conservative halfhearted Republicans were begging him to desist; when well meaning but erratic friends were urging him to compromise on any terms; when a great opposition party in the North were resolving in National Convention that the war was a failure; when riots and revolts threatened to stop further enlistments; when the Knights of the Golden Circle and other secret treasonable organizations were seeking to undermine loyal sentiment and intimidate loyal men in loyal States; when a policy of reprisals was inaugurated in Rebel prisons to starve Union soldiers to death; when the long list of the dead and the dying and the wounded Union soldiers was laid before him from a hundred battlefields, — and, yet, amid it all, he stood the one determined, hopeful, courageous figure; never doubting, never flinching, never hesitating, but suffering as no man can know how it is to suffer.

I stood by his side at Gettysburg when he delivered that marvelously beautiful tribute to the noble dead who lay at his feet. I saw him when with clear and almost angelic voice he turned his care-furrowed face towards the sky and uttered those immortal lines, speaking as one inspired, and as though in the very presence of the throne of God!

Let me repeat to you the golden words as they fell from the lips of Lincoln on that solemn occasion:

"Fourscore and seven years ago our fathers brought forth on this continent a new Nation, conceived in liberty, and dedicated to the proposition that all men are created equal. Now we are engaged in a great Civil War, testing whether that nation, or any nation so conceived and so dedicated, can long endure. We are met on a great battlefield of that war. We have come to dedicate a portion of that field as a final resting place for those who here gave their lives that that Nation might live. It is altogether fitting and proper that we should do this. But, in a larger sense, we cannot dedicate, we cannot consecrate, we cannot hallow this ground. The brave men, living and dead, who struggled here, have consecrated it, far above our poor power to add or detract. The world will little note nor long remember what we say here, but it can never forget what they did here. It is for us, the living, rather to be dedicated here to the unfinished work which they who fought here have thus far so nobly advanced. It is rather for us to be here dedicated to the great task remaining before us; that from these honored dead we take increased devotion to that cause for which they gave the last full measure of devotion; that we here highly resolve that these dead shall not have died in vain; that this Nation, under God, shall have a new birth of freedom; and that government of the people, by the people, for the people, shall not perish from the earth."

Here, everywhere, and always, he seemed to me to be personifying the intense and awful strain of one standing for a Nation and vicariously bearing its burdens.

I saw him, too, when the Rebel hosts had laid down their arms; when the glad tidings of peace were upon every tongue; and all the land was filled with rejoicings; but even yet peace had not come to him.

The great problems of reconstruction, the labor of building up a stricken and devastated country, of bringing two great warring regions into harmonious relations of peace and unity; of restoring the Union in the hearts of all the people; all these questions, this labor, were before him. For the moment he was overjoyed, for the moment his mind and soul relaxed, but only for a moment.

Unlike him in almost every other respect, in this one characteristic of unbending and unceasing devotion to the restoration of the Union, absorbed and possessed by the awful reality of war and its consequences, I never knew but two men like him; one was his faithful and greatest Lieutenant, Edwin M. Stanton, Secretary of War; and the other was Joseph Holt, Judge Advocate-General of the Army.

It was a dreadful hour when the assassin struck down this hero of heroes. The blow was given in the name of the rebellion, but it was a blow that even rebellion disowned and repudiated, for it was a blow portentous of evil to the South.

I am endeavoring, my young friends, to bring before you something like an adequate picture of the man Lincoln as I saw him and knew him. I cannot go further into incidents in his life, so full of dramatic interest; with these indeed you are familiar, for our histories are filled with them.

The conspicuous and dominant traits of his character and mind as I would analyze them, were: Sagacity, Firmness, Modesty, Patience, Magnanimity, Courage, Charity and Loyalty.

Lincoln was a sagacious man; his wisdom was broad, penetrating, almost infallibly discriminating. It embraced with it also what we call in animals instinct, in men intuition, inspiration. He made mistakes in men, though seldom, but rarely in policies. His messages, correspondence, State papers and speeches, show a wonderful mental acuteness and discernment.

Firm as the granite hills where once his judgment was fully satisfied and his sense of duty fully awakened, no man was ever more considerate of the opinions of others or more eager to obtain light from the counsels of those in whom he had confidence.

His patience and forbearance under great trial were so pronounced and so conspicuous that he was often the victim of persecution and even vilification by those who mistook these sublime traits for pusillanimity. A striking illustration is found in his generous treatment of McClellan in the face of gross disrespect shown by him of the President; and, in his almost paternal kindness towards Horace Greeley, under circumstances that would have warranted the severest measures towards the one and the absolute withdrawal of all confidence from the other.

He was as modest as he was magnanimous — indeed, these two qualities lie in close companionship. An arrogant and vain man cannot well be magnanimous. The natural kindness and gentleness of Lincoln's heart brought him into close sympathy with the people; kept him from building up a wall between him and them, and fostered and developed these two qualities of modesty and magnanimity into prominent characteristics.

Of his courage — that high moral development that distinguishes a man from a lion — he gave the highest evidence. He showed it in his emancipation of Southern slaves and putting hostile arms in their hands and making them soldiers of the Union; he showed it in sustaining officers against public clamor for their removal; and in removing officers whom the public demanded should be retained; he showed it in daring to differ with Congress in the reconstruction of Louisiana

and Arkansas, when sturdy Ben Wade and hot-headed Henry Winter Davis, both in Congress, appealed to the country in a manifesto that denounced the President as guilty of dictatorial usurpation; in a hundred ways he displayed this striking characteristic of high moral courage.

His charity was as broad as the human race. It was the charity of the Apostle Paul — "that envieth not; that vaunteth not itself; is not puffed up; thinketh no evil; beareth all things; believeth all things; endureth all things." This striking feature of his character is seen in the concluding paragraph of his second inaugural address, March 4, 1865, which I have read to you, where he speaks "with malice towards none, with charity for all."

But the crowning glory of this man's character, viewing him only in his relation to the great work before him, was his deep, intense and all-pervading sentiment of loyalty to the Union. The one great purpose that possessed his soul was the desire to preserve the Union. This was manifest always and everywhere. It ran like a golden thread through all his policies, through all his messages, through all his addresses, through all his sincere but futile efforts to effect a peace by compromise. It was the one thought paramount to all others. So profound was this feeling that even as late as in August, 1862, and while he was pressed to issue his proclamation of emancipation, and only one month before he actually did promulgate it, he would, had it been necessary, have restored the Union with its Constitutional protection over slavery.

The possible success of Rebellion and the dissolution of the Union were to him the knell of Republican Government throughout the earth. Rather than this he would see African slavery fight its way to freedom by the sure though prolonged processes of moral evolution, and the march of progressive ideas that must in time have wrought out the problem of universal manumission.

This is Lincoln as he was manifested to me, and as I still see him — a grand and noble man. Since the coming of the Savior of mankind the human race has been blessed by no other so great a benefactor.

There can be no doubt, there never will arise a doubt in the ages to come, that ABRAHAM LINCOLN was the most heroic, the most exalted character in American history.

Chapter Notes

Prologue

1. *Sacramento Bee*, February 22, 1906.
2. *Ibid.*; Chipman, Cherry Tree speech.
3. *Sacramento Bee*, February 22, 1906.
4. Chipman, Cherry Tree speech.
5. Chipman, Cherry Tree speech.
6. *Sacramento Bee*, February 23, 1906.

Chapter 1

1. Obituary of Norman Chipman, Chipman Collection, vol. l; N.N. Hill, Jr., comp., *History of Licking County, Ohio*, 591.

2. Leigh H. Irvine, *History of the New California*, vol. 2; *History of Union County* 2:26, 196–197.

3. There is some confusion concerning Chipman's year of birth. Various sources state Chipman's birth year as 1834, 1835, 1836, 1837, or 1839. Union County, Ohio, where Milford Center is located, did not start recording birth records until 1867, after Chipman's birth. He appears in the censuses of 1860 (Iowa), 1870 (District of Columbia), 1880 (California), 1910 (California), and 1920 (California). In the 1860 census for Washington, Iowa, taken in July, he was still a member of his father's household and his age is recorded as 26. This reflects a birth year of 1834. This information may have been provided by his parents, since he was living in their household. The 1870 census, taken in July when he was head of his household in the District of Columbia, reports his age as 36. Again, this reflects a birth year of 1834. This data was probably reported to the census taker by Chipman or his wife. The 1870 census records Mary Isabel Chipman's age as 26. In 1880, in Tehama County, California, however, Chip-man's age is recorded as 43, instead of 46. His wife's age is reported as 32, instead of 36. In 1910, in Sacramento, Chipman's age is recorded as 72 and his wife's age as 62. The 1920 census, taken again in Sacramento, states Chipman's age as 83. Therefore, the censuses taken in the earlier part of his life reflect a birth year of 1834, while subsequent censuses reflect a birth year of 1837 or 1838. Except for lapses in recollection, there is no ready explanation for the differences. Because the data in the earliest census, 1860, may have been reported by Chipman's parents and because the first two censuses agree and are closer in time to his birth, the 1834 birth year is the most defensible and will be used in this work. Further supporting 1834 as his birth year is the official military record, which reported him as 27 years old when he volunteered in May 1861. His official United States Congress biography also indicates 1834 as his birth year.

That Chipman, himself, was confused about his year of birth is evident from his military records. In 1911, he applied for a pension that was based on his current age. After the Bureau of Pensions noted that he had reported 1836 or 1837, variously, on prior applications, it conducted a review. It concluded: "It is true that in a prior declaration filed April 1, 1907, claimant stated date of birth as March 7, 1837, but prior to adjudication of said claim he filed the identity circular in which he gave date of birth as March 7, 1836 and he was not called upon to explain the discrepancy. The report from the War Department indicates that he was born in 1834, and as applicant is the Presiding Justice, Court of Appeal[], Third Appellate District, Sacramento, California, occupying an honorable and responsible position, it does not seem possible that he would try to make his age greater than it really is, or that an explanation is required from him in regard to it. With his application is an accompanying letter filed June 7, 1911, in which he reiterates that he has passed his 75th birthday, and this should be sufficient." (Military service records of Chipman, National Archives.)

4. *History of Union County,* 2:194.

5. *Ibid.,* 2:162–163, 192–193.

6. *Ibid.,* 2:183–184.

7. Irvine, *History of the New California,* vol. II.

8. Marcus L. Hansen, "Official Encouragement of Immigration to Iowa," *Iowa Journal of History and Politics* 14, no. 2 (April 1921).

9. John B. Newhall, *A Glimpse of Iowa in 1846,* 14.

10. Bruce E. Mahan and Ruth A. Gallaher, *Stories of Iowa for Boys and Girls,* ch. 32; Henry Sabin and Edwin L. Sabin, *The Making of Iowa,* ch. 25.

11. Hubert L. Moeller and Hugh C. Mueller, *Our Iowa Its Beginning and Growth.*

12. Newhall, *Glimpse of Iowa,* 35–36; Obituary of Norman Chipman, Chipman Collection, vol. 1.

13. *History of Washington County, Iowa,* 557–558; Irvine, *History of the New California,* vol. II.

14. *History of Henry County, Iowa,* 430–432, italics in original; "Story of the 'Old Mill,'" *Mt. Pleasant News,* November 11, 1972.

15. "Story of the 'Old Mill.'"

16. Chipman, 1863 Political Speech, Chipman Collection, vol. 3. In a compilation of speeches preserved in the California State Library's Chipman Collection, Chipman included this speech under the title "1862 Political Speech." It is evident from the events recounted in the speech, however, that it was given in the summer of 1863. Chipman probably failed to recollect the date accurately years later when he put together the collection of speeches.

17. Obituary of Norman Chipman, Chipman Collection, vol. 1.

18. *Portrait and Biographical Album — Washington County, Iowa* (1887) 296.

19. *Dred Scott v. Sanford,* 60 U.S. 393 (1857).

20. *Ibid.*

21. *Ibid.*; Chipman, Cherry Tree speech.

22. O.A. Garretson, "Traveling on the Underground Railroad in Iowa," *Iowa Journal of History and Politics,* no. 22 (July 1924).

23. *Ibid.*

24. Chipman, Cherry Tree speech.

25. Abraham Lincoln, "Address before the Wisconsin State Agricultural Society, Milwaukee, Wisconsin," in *Collected Works of Abraham Lincoln,* 3:472–473.

26. *Ibid.,* 3:476, 478–480 (italics in original).

27. Chipman to Justice E.C. Hart, Chipman Collection.

28. Moeller and Mueller, *Our Iowa: Its Beginnings and Growth.*

29. Chipman, Cherry Tree speech.

30. *Ibid.*

Chapter 2

1. Chipman, Cherry Tree speech.

2. Chipman, 1863 Political Speech.

3. Chipman, Cherry Tree speech.

4. Abraham Lincoln, "First Inaugural Address," in *Collected Works of Abraham Lincoln,* 4:264.

5. *Ibid.* 4:264–266, 271 (italics in original); Chipman, Cherry Tree speech.

6. Lincoln, "First Inaugural Address," in *Collected Works of Abraham Lincoln,* 4:271; Chipman, Cherry Tree speech.

7. Chipman, Cherry Tree speech.

8. *History of Washington County,* 450.

9. *Ibid.*

10. Moeller and Mueller, *Our Iowa Its Beginning and Growth.*

11. Benjamin Gue, *History of Iowa: From the Earliest Times to the Beginning of the Twentieth Century,* vol. 2, ch. 9; *Roster and Record of Iowa Soldiers in the War of the Rebellion Together with Historical Sketches of Volunteer Organizations 1861–1866,* vol. 1; A.A. Stuart, *Iowa Colonels and Regiments: being a History of Iowa Regiments in the War of the Rebellion,* 35–37.

12. Iowa State Historical Society, "The Army of the South-West, and the First Campaign in Arkansas," *Annals of Iowa* (April 1868).

13. Chipman, Cherry Tree speech.

14. *Ibid.*

15. William E. Gienapp, "Abraham Lincoln and the Border States," *Journal of the Abraham Lincoln Association,* vol. 13 (1992) 29.

16. Chipman, Cherry Tree speech.

17. Gue, *History of Iowa,* vol. 2, ch. 9; *Record of Iowa Soldiers,* vol. 1; *History of the New California,* vol. 2.

18. *Collected Works of Abraham Lincoln,* 4: 562–563; Stuart, *Iowa Colonels,* 37–38.

19. Chipman, 1863 Political Speech.

20. Galusha Anderson, *The Story of a Border City During the Civil War,* 187–189.

21. Gue, *History of Iowa,* vol. 2, ch. 9; Chipman, 1863 Political Speech; William F. Switzler, ed., *History of Boone County, Missouri,* 50.

22. Military service records of Chipman, National Archives (abbreviations corrected); Stephen E. Ambrose, *Halleck: Lincoln's Chief of Staff,* 12, 17–18; Iowa State Historical Society, *Annals of Iowa; Collected Works of Abraham Lincoln,* 6:40–41 [stating brigadier general not entitled by law to a major on his staff].

23. Military service records of Chipman, National Archives.

24. Gue, *History of Iowa,* vol. 2, ch. 9; *Record of Iowa Soldiers,* vol. 1.

25. Anderson, *Story of a Border City,* 244.

26. Ulysses S. Grant, *Personal Memoirs of U.S. Grant,* 1:124–128.

27. *Ibid.*
28. *Ibid.*, 1:129–138.
29. *Ibid.*
30. *Ibid.*
31. *Ibid.*; Gue, *History of Iowa*, vol. 2, ch. 9; Lew Wallace, "The Capture of Fort Donelson," *The Century* (December 1884) vol. 29.
32. Gue, *History of Iowa*, vol. 2, ch. 9.
33. *Ibid.*; *Record of Iowa Soldiers*; Grant, *Personal Memoirs*, 1:129–138.
34. Grant, *Personal Memoirs*, 1:129–138.
35. Horace Porter, *Campaigning with Grant*, 381.
36. Grant, *Personal Memoirs*, 1:129–138.
37. *Ibid.*
38. Gue, *History of Iowa*, vol. 2, ch. 9; "The Second Iowa at Fort Donelson," *The Vinton Eagle* (Vinton, IA), December 19, 1884; O.R., Ser. I, Vol. 52 (part I), p. 8; Stuart, *Iowa Colonels*, 165.
39. "Second Iowa at Fort Donelson," *The Vinton Eagle*.
40. *Record of Iowa Soldiers*; military service records of Chipman, National Archives; O.R., Ser. I, Vol. 7, p. 230.
41. Daniel W. Brown of Pueblo, Colorado, to Chipman, October 21, 1921, Chipman Collection, vol. 11.
42. O.R., Ser. I, Vol. 7, p. 229 & Vol. 52 (part I), p. 10.
43. O.R., Ser. I, Vol. 52 (part I), pp. 8–9; Vol. 7, pp. 229–230.
44. *Record of Iowa Soldiers*; O.R., Ser. I, Vol. 7, p. 230; Stuart, *Iowa Colonels*, 165.
45. Gue, *History of Iowa*, vol. 2, ch. 9.
46. *Ibid.*; "Second Iowa at Fort Donelson," *The Vinton Eagle*.
47. Gue, *History of Iowa*, vol. 2, ch. 9; Grant, *Personal Memoirs*, 1:129–145; "Second Iowa at Fort Donelson," *The Vinton Eagle*.

Chapter 3

1. John Y. Simon, ed., *The Papers of Ulysses S. Grant*, 4:260–261.
2. Military service records of Chipman, National Archives.
3. *Ibid.*
4. Lurton Dunham Ingersoll, *Iowa and the Rebellion*, 33–51.
5. *Ibid.*; military service records of Chipman, National Archives.
6. Stuart, *Iowa Colonels*, 44.
7. Samuel R. Curtis to Chipman, March 30, 1862, Chipman Collection, vol. 1.
8. Jacob Dolson Cox, *Military Reminiscences of the Civil War*, 158; military pension records of Chipman, National Archives.
9. Stuart, *Iowa Colonels*, 44–45.

10. David G. Surdam, "Traders or Traitors: Northern Cotton Trading During the Civil War," *Business and Economic History* (Winter 1999) 301, 305.
11. Samuel R. Curtis to Abraham Lincoln, November 9, 1862, Abraham Lincoln Papers, Library of Congress.
12. *Ibid.*
13. *Tehama County, California*, 106.
14. Abraham Lincoln to Samuel R. Curtis, November 6, 1862, State Historical Society of Iowa.
15. Samuel R. Curtis to Abraham Lincoln, November 9, 1862, Abraham Lincoln Papers, Library of Congress.
16. Samuel R. Curtis to Abraham Lincoln, October 4, 1983, Abraham Lincoln Papers, Library of Congress.
17. Chipman, Cherry Tree speech.
18. *Collected Works of Abraham Lincoln*, 5:388–389, italics in original; Chipman, Cherry Tree speech.
19. *Collected Works of Abraham Lincoln*, 5:336–337.
20. Chipman, Cherry Tree speech.
21. Chipman, 1863 Political Speech.
22. *Ibid.*
23. Stuart, *Iowa Colonels*, 45.
24. Anderson, *Story of a Border City*, 276–278.
25. *Ibid.*, 278–280.
26. *Ibid.*, 280.
27. O.R., Ser. I, Vol. 34 (part II), pp. 375–76; Stuart, *Iowa Colonels*, 4.
28. Samuel R. Curtis to Abraham Lincoln, November 9, 1862, Abraham Lincoln Papers, Library of Congress.
29. Benjamin Gratz Brown to Abraham Lincoln, November 25, 1862; Benjamin Gratz Brown to John G. Nicolay, November 25, 1862, Abraham Lincoln Papers, Library of Congress.
30. Anderson, *Story of a Border City*, 273–274; Howard L. Conard, ed., *Encyclopedia of the History of Missouri*, 3:571–572; 5:524; Irvine, *History of the New California*, vol. 2; James Peckham, *General Nathaniel Lyon and Missouri in 1861*, 38. Robert Holmes contributed $100 to the Union cause in St. Louis in 1861.
31. L.P. Brockett and Mary C. Vaughan, *Woman's Work in the Civil War: A Record of Heroism, Patriotism and Patience*, 630.
32. *Ibid.*, 630–631.
33. *Ibid.*, 631–632.
34. *Ibid.*, 631–632, 635.
35. Abraham Lincoln to John M. Schofield, May 27, 1863, Abraham Lincoln Papers, Library of Congress.
36. *Collected Works of Abraham Lincoln*, 6:8; Samuel R. Curtis to Abraham Lincoln, December 20, 1862, Papers of Abraham Lincoln, Library of Congress.
37. O.R. Ser. 1, vol. 22 (part I), ch. 34, p. 852.

38. Hamilton R. Gamble to Abraham Lincoln, December 5, 1862; Abraham Lincoln to Samuel R. Curtis [telegram], December 10, 1862, Abraham Lincoln Papers, Library of Congress.

39. Abraham Lincoln to Samuel R. Curtis, January 5, 1863, Abraham Lincoln Papers, Library of Congress.

40. Samuel R. Curtis to Abraham Lincoln, December 28, 1862, Abraham Lincoln Papers, Library of Congress.

41. Samuel B. McPheeters, December 19, 1862, clipping; Samuel B. McPheeters to Edward Bates, December 23, 1862, Abraham Lincoln Papers, Library of Congress.

42. Franklin A. Dick to Montgomery Blair, December 19, 1862; Archibald Gamble to Edward Bates, December 22, 1862; Samuel B. McPheeters to Edward Bates, December 23, 1862; Apolline A. Blair to Montgomery Blair, December 29, 1862, Abraham Lincoln Papers, Library of Congress.

43. Samuel R. Curtis to Abraham Lincoln, December 29, 1862; Abraham Lincoln to Samuel R. Curtis, January 2, 1863, Abraham Lincoln Papers, Library of Congress.

44. Abraham Lincoln to Samuel R. Curtis, January 2, 1863, Abraham Lincoln Papers, Library of Congress.

45. Samuel R. Curtis to Abraham Lincoln, April 3, 1863; Oliver D. Filley to Abraham Lincoln, November 9, 1863; Abraham Lincoln to Oliver D. Filley, December 22, 1863, Abraham Lincoln Papers, Library of Congress.

46. Abraham Lincoln to Samuel R. Curtis, January 5, 1863, Abraham Lincoln Papers, Library of Congress.

47. Anderson, *Story of a Border City*, 282–283.

48. Richard McAllister to Abraham Lincoln, July 13, 1863, Abraham Lincoln Papers, Library of Congress.

49. *Collected Works of Abraham Lincoln*, 6: 345.

50. *Ibid.*, 6:344.

51. Richard McAllister to Abraham Lincoln, July 13, 1863, Abraham Lincoln Papers, Library of Congress.

Chapter 4

1. Chipman, "Some Personal Recollections," *Sacramento Bee*, February 12, 1909.

2. *Ibid.*

3. Anthony Trollope, *North America*, 305–306, 315.

4. Trollope, *North America*, 313.

5. Trollope, *North America*, 314–315.

6. Charles Dickens, *American Notes for General Circulation*, 146.

7. *Ibid.*, 143.

8. Jay Monaghan, *Civil War on the Western Border*, 292.

9. Samuel R. Curtis to Abraham Lincoln, June 5, 1863, Abraham Lincoln Papers, Library of Congress.

10. Richard McAllister to Abraham Lincoln, July 13, 1863, Abraham Lincoln Papers, Library of Congress.

11. *Collected Works of Abraham Lincoln*, 6: 253.

12. Chipman, Cherry Tree speech.

13. *Ibid.*

14. Chipman, 1863 political speech.

15. *Ibid.*

16. *Ibid.*

17. *Ibid.*

18. *Ibid.*

19. *Ibid.*

20. *Ibid.*

21. *Ibid.*

22. Samuel J. Kirkwood, "Organizing and Arming Volunteer Companies," in *Annals of Iowa*, vol. 19, 3d ser., 625–627; Frank W. Eichelberger, "Governor Kirkwood and the Skunk River War," in *Annals of Iowa*, vol. 19, 3d ser., 627–630.

23. *Tehama County, California*, 106.

24. Chipman, "Some Personal Recollections."

25. *Ibid.*

26. Grant, *Personal Memoirs*, 2:492.

27. *Ibid.*

28. Edwin M. Stanton to Abraham Lincoln, Wednesday, November 18, 1863 (telegram concerning Burnside's army); Edwin M. Stanton to Abraham Lincoln, Thursday, November 19, 1863 (telegram reporting military developments in Tennessee); Edwin M. Stanton to Abraham Lincoln, Tuesday, November 17, 1863, Abraham Lincoln Papers, Library of Congress; Chipman to Mr. Johnston, Cal. Court of Appeal, Third Appellate District [the letter is undated, but from internal references appears to be from 1922 —16 years after the Cherry Tree speech].

29. Garry Wills, *Lincoln at Gettysburg*, 20–22; Chipman, "Some Personal Recollections."

30. Wills, *Lincoln at Gettysburg*, 23–24; Chipman, "Some Personal Recollections."

31. Chipman, "Some Personal Recollections" [quoting the text of the invitation].

32. *Ibid.* [responding to a request by C.K. McClatchy].

33. Chipman, "Some Personal Recollections"; Wills, *Lincoln at Gettysburg*, 26, 30.

34. Chipman, "Some Personal Recollections."

35. *Ibid.*

36. This is the text of a copy of the Gettysburg Address written in Lincoln's own hand. Wills, *Lincoln at Gettysburg*, 263.

37. Chipman, "Some Personal Recollections."

38. Harold Holzer, "The Gettysburg Myth Revisited," in *The Lincoln Forum: Abraham Lincoln, Gettysburg and the Civil War*, John Y. Simon,

Harold Holzer, William D. Pederson, ed., 34; Chipman to Mr. Johnston, undated, Cal. Court of Appeal, Third App. Dist.

39. Chipman to Mr. Johnston, undated, Cal. Court of Appeal, Third App. Dist.; Chipman, "Some Personal Recollections."

40. Chipman, Cherry Tree speech.

41. Chipman, "Some Personal Recollections"; Holzer, "The Gettysburg Myth Revisited," 41–42, quoting Ward Hill Lamon; *Recollections of Abraham Lincoln, 1847–1865,* 174–75.

42. Chipman, "Some Personal Recollections."

43. *Ibid.*

Chapter 5

1. Chipman, "Some Personal Recollections."

2. *Collected Works of Abraham Lincoln,* 7:78–79.

3. *Tehama County, California,* 106.

4. O.R., Ser. I, Vol. 34 (part II), pp. 273–275, 282, 290, 301, 313–314, 323.

5. O.R., Ser. I, Vol. 34 (part II), p. 313.

6. Chipman to John Nicolay, January 28, 1864, Abraham Lincoln Papers, Library of Congress.

7. O.R., Ser. I, Vol. 34 (part II), pp. 375–76.

8. P.J. Staudenraus, ed., *Mr. Lincoln's Washington; selections from the writings of Noah Brooks, Civil War correspondent,* 11, 275–277.

9. *Ibid.,* 277–278.

10. J.W. Clous, Judge Advocate General's Department, *The Army of the United States, Historical Sketches of Staff and Line with Portraits of Generals-in-Chief,* 33–37.

11. Chipman, Cherry Tree Speech.

12. Chipman, "Some Personal Recollections."

13. Grant, *Personal Memoirs,* 313.

14. Chipman, "Some Personal Recollections."

15. *Ibid.*

16. Chipman, *The Tragedy of Andersonville,* 438–473.

17. O.R., Ser. II, Vol. 4, p. 721.

18. Chipman, *Tragedy of Andersonville,* 458.

19. *Ibid.,* 461.

20. *Ibid.,* 438–441.

21. *Ibid.,* 441–445.

22. *Ibid.,* 445–447.

23. *Ibid.,* 448.

24. *Ibid.,* 448, 465.

25. *Ibid.,* 449, 453–454.

26. *Ibid.,* 463.

27. *Ibid.,* 449, 463.

28. Grant, *Personal Memoirs,* 386.

29. O.R., Ser. I, Vol. 37, pp. 234–35.

30. John G. Nicolay, *A Short Life of Abraham Lincoln,* 403.

31. Margaret Leech, *Reveille in Washington,* 420.

32. *Ibid.,* 422–23.

33. Chipman, "Some Personal Recollections."

Chapter 6

1. O.R., Ser. I, Vol. 37 (part II), p. 318.

2. *Ibid.,* 343–344.

3. John McCausland, "The Burning of Chambersburg, Penn.," *New Orleans Picayune,* August 2, 1906.

4. O.R., Ser. I, Vol. 43 (part I), pp. 40–42.

5. James J. Williamson, *History of Mosby's Command,* 207–210.

6. O.R., Ser I, Vol. 43 (part I), pp. 42–43.

7. Chipman, "Some Personal Recollections."

8. *Ibid.*

9. O.R., Ser. I, Vol. 43 (part I), p. 779.

10. Chipman, 1864 Political Speech in Washington, Iowa, Chipman Collection, vol. 3.

11. Williamson, *Mosby's Command,* 211, fn. 10.

12. O.R., Ser I, Vol. 43 (part I), pp. 43.

13. *Ibid.,* 858–859, 870–871, 877–878, 880–881, 906–908, 917, 932–933, 940, 953–954.

14. *Ibid.,* 858–859, 940.

15. *Ibid.,* 870; *Collected Works of Abraham Lincoln,* 7:511.

16. O.R., Ser I, Vol. 43 (part I), pp. 871, 880–881.

17. *Ibid.,* 906–908.

18. Nicolay, *Short Life of Abraham Lincoln,* 403–404.

19. *Ibid.,* 470.

20. Grant, *Personal Memoirs,* 2:331.

21. Military pension records of Chipman, National Archives; J.C. Bates, *History of the Bench and Bar of California,* 259.

22. Benjamin P. Thomas and Harold M. Hyman, *Stanton: The Life and Times of Lincoln's Secretary of War,* 349–352.

23. Chipman, "Some Personal Recollections."

24. Staudenraus, ed., *Mr. Lincoln's Washington,* 441–442.

25. James M. Hudnut to Chipman, June 8, 1921, Chipman Collection, vol. 11.

26. Chipman, Cherry Tree Speech.

27. James M. Hudnut to Chipman, June 8, 1921, Chipman Collection, vol. 11.

28. *Ibid.*; Alice Woods, "S.F. Man, Lincoln Escort, Tells of Martyr: Gen. Chipman, at 89, Gives 'Close Up' of Liberator," *The San Francisco Call,* Chipman Collection, vol. 16.

29. Chipman, Cherry Tree speech.

30. *Sacramento Bee,* February 1, 1924.

Chapter 7

1. Chipman, *Tragedy of Andersonville,* 18, 51, 64, 69, 375.

2. *Ibid.,* 82.

3. Walt Whitman, "Memoranda," 50, in *Two*

Rivulets including *Democratic Vistas, Centennial Songs, and Passage to India.*

4. *Ibid.*

5. Chipman, *Tragedy of Andersonville,* 27–28.

6. *Ibid.*, 31, 387; see also John Stibbs, "Andersonville and the Trial of Henry Wirz," *Iowa Journal of History and Politics.*

7. "From Washington," *New York Times,* August 21, 1865.

8. See, e.g., "The Rebel Assassins," *New York Times,* August 22, 1865; "Trial of Capt. Wirz," *New York Times,* August 29, 1865; "Trial of Capt. Wirz," *New York Times,* September 23, 1865; "Trial of Capt. Wirz," *New York Times,* September 27, 1865; "Trial of Capt. Wirz," *New York Times,* September 28, 1865; "Washington News," *New York Times,* October 15, 1865; "The Wirz Trial," *Harper's Weekly,* October 21, 1865; "The Trial of Captain Wirz," *Harper's Weekly,* September 16, 1865.

9. Chipman, *Tragedy of Andersonville,* 28, 32–35.

10. *Ibid.*, 32–35.

11. *Ibid.*, 35.

12. "The Rebel Assassins," *New York Times,* August 22, 1865.

13. Chipman, *Tragedy of Andersonville,* 28–30.

14. *Ibid.*

15. *Ibid.*, 32, 36–37.

16. *Ibid.*, 38–39.

17. *Ibid.*, 37–39.

18. *Ibid.*, 37.

19. *Ibid.*, 42.

20. *Ibid.*, 388; John Stibbs, "Andersonville and the Trial of Henry Wirz."

21. Chipman, *Tragedy of Andersonville,* 354.

22. *Ibid.*, 51–52, 84, 355.

23. *Ibid.*, 355.

24. *Ibid.*, 106, 202, 279.

25. *Ibid.*, 226.

26. *Ibid.*, 54, 128, 147.

27. *Ibid.*, 85, 88.

28. *Ibid.*, 86 [report of Dr. Joseph Jones].

29. *Ibid.*

30. *Ibid.*, 87.

31. *Ibid.*, 87, 90–91.

32. *Ibid.*, 359.

33. *Ibid.*, 243–244.

34. *Ibid.*, 248–249, 258, 277–278.

35. *Ibid.*, 124, 244, 250–251, 260, 275.

36. *Ibid.*, 94, 134–135.

37. *Ibid.*, 360, 406, 408.

38. *Ibid.*, 364.

39. *Ibid.*, 243–244, 254.

40. *Ibid.*, 244, 246, 248.

41. *Ibid.*, 249–250, 252, 340.

42. *Ibid.*, 260, 270, 320–321, 334.

43. *Ibid.*, 247, 258, 335, 338–339, 342, 347, 351–352.

44. *Ibid.*, 407–408.

45. *Ibid.*, 386.

46. *Ibid.*, 428–429.

47. *Ibid.*, 429–436.

48. *Ibid.*, 436.

49. Whitelaw Reid, *After the War: A Southern Tour,* 308–309; for revisionist accounts of trial, see, e.g., William Marvel, *Andersonville: The Last Depot,* 172–173, 243–246; Carolyn Kleiner, "The Demon of Andersonville," *Legal Affairs,* September/October 2002.

50. Chipman, *Tragedy of Andersonville,* 399.

51. *Ibid.*, 387–388.

52. *Ibid.*, 19.

53. Jefferson Davis, "Andersonville and Other War-Prisons," *Belford's Magazine,* January 1890 and February 1890.

54. Davis, "Andersonville and Other War-Prisons," January 1890.

55. Davis, "Andersonville and Other War-Prisons," January 1890 and February 1890.

56. Davis, "Andersonville and Other War-Prisons," January 1890.

57. *Ibid.*

58. Chipman, *Tragedy of Andersonville,* preface, 11–18, 24.

59. *Ibid.*, 21, 448.

60. *Ibid.*, 20.

61. Davis, Andersonville and Other War-Prisons, January 1890.

62. Chipman, *Tragedy of Andersonville,* 22–23.

63. *Ibid.*, 24.

64. Alan Dershowitz, "Introduction," in Chipman, *The Andersonville Prison Trial: The Trial of Captain Henry Wirz.*

Chapter 8

1. "Washington," *The New York Times,* November 21, 1870.

2. Mark Twain and Charles Dudley Warner, *The Gilded Age: A Tale of To-day,* 2:14–15.

3. *Ibid.*, 2:35.

4. Also descended from John and Hope Chipman, along with Nathaniel and Norton Parker Chipman, are U.S. presidents George H.W. Bush and George W. Bush, as well as the poet Ralph Waldo Emerson. Other descendants of John Howland and Elizabeth Tilley, the Mayflower immigrants, are U.S. president Franklin Delano Roosevelt, Mormon founder Joseph Smith, and actor Humphrey Bogart. If the Howland ancestral line is traced back to Henry Howland, born about 1576, the father of the original Mayflower Howland, descendants also include U.S. presidents Richard M. Nixon and Gerald R. Ford and British Prime Minister Winston Churchill.

5. Other descendants of John Lathrop included Ulysses S. Grant, Marjorie Merriweather

Post, founder of General Foods, and Jane Lathrop Stanford and Leland Stanford founders of Stanford University, as well as poet Henry Wadsworth Longfellow and inventor Eli Whitney.

6. Military service records of Chipman, National Archives.

7. Philip H. Sheridan, *Personal Memoirs of P.H. Sheridan,* 2:279–280.

8. "Washington News," *New York Times,* September 24, 1867.

9. *Ibid.*

10. Chipman to Elijah Hart, California Court of Appeal, Third Appellate District.

11. Stuart McConnell, *Glorious Contentment: The Grand Army of the Republic, 1865–1900,* 28.

12. *Congressional Record,* 67th Cong., 2d sess., 1922, 8997.

13. *Ibid.*

14. *Ibid.,* 8998.

15. Committee on Arrangements, Invitation and Order of Exercises for May 30, 1868, Library of Congress.

16. *Ibid.*

17. *Ibid.*

18. *Congressional Record,* 67th Cong., 2d sess., 1922, 8997–8998.

19. See U.S. House of Representatives, "Investigation into Indian Affairs, before the Committee on Appropriations of the House of Representatives. Argument of N.P. Chipman, on behalf of Hon. E.S. Parker, Commissioner of Indian Affairs," Washington, 1871.

20. James Huntington Whyte, *The Uncivil War: Washington During the Reconstruction 1865–1878,* 13–14.

21. *Ibid.,* 107; Charles Sumner, *The Works of Charles Sumner,* 15:206.

22. Whyte, *Uncivil War,* 107–109.

23. *Ibid.,* 133.

24. Andrew Lang, *Life, Letters, and Diaries of Sir Stafford Northcote, First Earl of Iddesleigh,* 2:32:33.

25. *Ibid.,* 2:33; Whyte, *Uncivil War,* 109–110.

26. Arthur Shepherd, "The District Government: Why General Chipman Should be Reelected to Congress," pamphlet of speech delivered July 29, 1872, Library of Congress.

27. Whyte, *Uncivil War,* 124, 129.

28. *Ibid.*

29. Chipman, speech, 1872, St. Joseph, Mo., U.S. Grant Assoc., Southern Illinois Univ.; tribute to Grant after his death, Chipman Collection.

30. Albert Bigelow Paine, *Th. Nast: His Period and His Pictures,* 222.

31. *Ibid.*

32. *Ibid.,* 224–225.

33. "Personals," *Harper's Weekly,* March 16, 1872.

34. Paine, *Th. Nast,* 224–225.

35. *Ibid.,* 226–227.

36. *Ibid.,* 231.

37. *Ibid.,* 233–234.

38. William Gillette, "Election of 1872," in *History of American Presidential Elections,* Arthur M. Schlesinger, Jr., ed., 2:1322.

39. "Washington Notes," *New York Times,* August 2, 1872.

40. Whyte, *Uncivil War,* 149–150.

41. *Ibid.,* 150, 156.

42. Chipman, *Annual Report to the California State Board of Trade,* title page.

Chapter 9

1. House Select Committee on the Washington National Monument, *Washington National Monument,* 43d Cong., 1st sess., 1874, H. Rep. 485, 1–4.

2. Twain and Warner, *Gilded Age,* 1:265.

3. *Ibid.,* 1:265–266.

4. Louis Torres, "*To the Immortal Name and Memory of George Washington,*" The United States Army Corps of Engineers and the Construction of the Washington Monument, 31.

5. *Journal of the House of Representatives of the United States,* vol. 74, p. 252, January 19, 1874; Francis Miller, *Argument before the Judiciary Committee of the House of Representatives.*

6. James Hugh Keeley, Sr., *Democracy or Despotism in the American Capital,* 174–179, 199.

7. *Ibid.,* 204, quoting Senator George E. Spencer.

8. Chipman, speech to House of Representatives, February 28, 1874, 26.

9. Keeley, *Democracy or Despotism,* 194.

10. Chipman, speech to House, February 28, 1874, 1.

11. *Ibid.,* 3–5.

12. *Ibid.,* 5.

13. *Ibid.,* 8.

14. *Ibid.*

15. *Ibid.,* 13.

16. *Ibid.,* 14–17.

17. *Ibid.,* 17.

18. *Ibid.,* 17–18.

19. *Ibid.,* 19–25.

20. *Ibid.,* 28–30.

21. *Ibid.,* 30–31.

22. House Select Committee, *Washington National Monument,* 1–3.

23. *Ibid.,* 3–4.

24. *Congressional Globe,* 42d Cong., 3d sess., 1873, appendix 97.

25. House Select Committee on the Washington Monument, *Washington Monument,* 42d Cong., 3d sess., 1873, H. Rep. 79, 1.

26. *Ibid.,* 8–9.

27. *Ibid.*, 2–3.
28. *Ibid.*, 3.
29. *Ibid.*, 7.
30. *Congressional Globe*, 42d Cong., 3d sess., 1873, appendix, 97; Grace Greenwood, "Washington Notes," *New York Times*, February 22, 1873.
31. *Congressional Globe*, 42d Cong., 3d sess., 1873, appendix 97–98.
32. *Congressional Record*, 43d Cong., 1st sess., 1874, vol. 2, 4577.
33. *Ibid.*, 4577–4578.
34. *Ibid.*, 4579.
35. *Ibid.*, 4579–4580.
36. *Ibid.*, 4580.
37. *Ibid.*, 4580–4581.
38. *Ibid.*, 4584–4586.
39. *Ibid.*, 4586–4587.
40. Keeley, *Democracy or Despotism*, 196–198.
41. *Ibid.*, 198.

Chapter 10

1. *Tehama County, California*, 78. Although Chipman was not listed as the author of the article (no author was listed) in the cited work, the introduction acknowledged he was one of many authors and this article on the Sierra Flume and Lumber Company is logically the part he would have contributed. (*Ibid.*, vii.) He refers to himself modestly as "a gentleman from the East" (*Ibid.*, 78), instead of using his own name.
2. *Ibid.*, 78, 107, 122; Eugene Serr, "General Chipman and the Flume Through the Canyon," *Tehama County Memories*.
3. Serr, "General Chipman."
4. *The Grass Valley Union*, December 17, 1891.
5. *Tehama County, California*, 78; Serr, "General Chipman"; W.H. Hutchinson, *California Heritage: A History of Northern California Lumbering*, 15; Jessica B. Tiesch, "Great Western Power, 'White Coal,' and Industrial Capitalism in the West," *Pacific Historical Review* 70 (2001) 232.
6. Hutchinson, *California Heritage*, 15.
7. *Ibid.*, 6.
8. *Ibid.*, 7.
9. *Ibid.*, 13.
10. *Ibid.*, 8.
11. *Ibid.*, 9–12.
12. *Tehama County, California*, 78, 81; Serr, "General Chipman."
13. *Tehama County, California*, 79; Hutchinson, *California Heritage*, 16.
14. *Tehama County, California*, 79; Hutchinson, *California Heritage*, 16.
15. Hutchinson, *California Heritage*, 16, referring to the *Northern Enterprise* publication.
16. *Tehama County, California*, 79; Hutchinson, *California Heritage*, 18.

17. *Tehama County, California*, 79.
18. *Ibid.*, 80; Hutchinson, *California Heritage*, 18; Serr, *Tehama County Memories*.
19. *Tehama County, California*, 80.
20. Hutchinson, *California Heritage*, 16.
21. *Tehama County, California*, 80–81.
22. *Ibid.*, 81–82.
23. Tiesch, "Great Western Power," 232; Hutchinson, *California Heritage*, 18; *Tehama County, California*, 82.
24. Serr, *Tehama County Memories*.
25. *Ibid.*
26. Hutchinson, *California Heritage*, 18–19; *Tehama County, California*, 83, 107.
27. *Tehama County, California*, 83.
28. *Ibid.*, 107.

Chapter 11

1. *Tehama County, California*, 107.
2. *Ibid.*, 97.
3. "Personal," *Harper's Weekly*, April 30, 1887.
4. "Chipman Sells Part of His Tehama Ranch," *San Francisco Chronicle*, November 20, 1916.
5. Frank C. Jordan, comp., *California Blue Book or State Roster 1913–1915*, 479; Chipman, *Annual Report to the California State Board of Trade*, title page.
6. Chipman, *Annual Report of Gen. N.P. Chipman, President, California State Board of Trade*, 1–2.
7. Chipman, "Greater California and the Trade of the Orient," *Overland Monthly*, vol. 34, no. 201, p. 196 (September 1899).
8. "Fruit or Wheat? Relative Importance of Two Great Industries," *The Morning Call*, May 28, 1893; Chipman, *Annual Report*, 1896, 1, 7.
9. "The Convention Meets," *Los Angeles Times*, July 26, 1894.
10. *State Fair of 1886: Opening address delivered by Hon. Thomas H. Laine, of San Jose, Santa Clara County, and Annual address delivered by General N.P. Chipman, of Red Bluff, Tehama County*, 187–218.
11. "Norton Parker Chipman," *Memorial and Biographical History of Northern California*; "Among the Politicians," *The Los Angeles Times*, May 14, 1890; "Colusa for Chipman," *The Los Angeles Times*, July 27, 1890.
12. C.F. Curry, comp., *California Blue Book*, 28, 651–653; Chipman, "The Judicial Department of California," in same compiled work, 657–658.
13. Curry, *California Blue Book*, 653–657; Chipman, "The Judicial Department of California," 658–660.
14. *Osgood v. Los Angeles Traction Co.*, 137 Cal.

280 (Cal. 1902); *People v. Hoagland*, 138 Cal. 338 (Cal. 1903); *Southern Pacific Co. v. Pomona*, 144 Cal. 339 (Cal. 1904); *Tingley v. Times-Mirror Co.*, 144 Cal. 205 (Cal. 1904).

15. Chipman, "The Judicial Department of California," 658–659. In 2007, a total of 112 Supreme Court and Court of Appeal justices served a population of more than 3.5 million in California, for a residents-per-justice ratio of 31,250, not far from the 33,333 ratio of 1850. Despite the apparent parity with respect to the population, justices of the Supreme Court and Court of Appeal today produce more than twice as many written opinions per justice (more than 130 per year) than were written in the period just before the creation of the Court of Appeal.

16. Curry, *California Blue Book*, 657.

17. Chipman, "The Judicial Department of California," 659–660.

18. "Judge Chipman Left an Estate Worth $30,000," *Sacramento Bee*, March 5, 1924; Chipman, Cherry Tree speech.

19. "Sacramento Voters Give Hard Jolt to Bosses," *Sacramento Bee*, November 7, 1906.

20. *Ibid.*

21. "Hart Gets Heavy Vote," *Sacramento Bee*, November 8, 1906.

22. "Republican Managers Say Chipman Has Met With Defeat," *Sacramento Bee*, November 9, 1906.

23. "Hughes is a Cheerful Loser," *Sacramento Bee*, November 10, 1906.

24. *Ibid.*

25. *A Volume of Memoirs And Genealogy of Representative Citizens of Northern California including biographies of many of those who have passed away*, 235–237.

26. Curry, *California Blue Book*, 448–449, 657.

27. "Judge Hart Knew Judge Chipman as a Fine Character," *Sacramento Bee*, February 2, 1924; "Judge Chipman Left an Estate Worth $30,000," *Sacramento Bee*, March 5, 1924.

28. "Judges Ready to Answer Charges," *Sacramento Bee*, December 12, 1911.

29. *Ibid.*

30. "Judge Chipman Denies Charges," *San Francisco Chronicle*, December 15, 1911; "Attorney's Charges Held Unfounded," *San Francisco Chronicle*, December 19, 1911.

31. "Wear Your Masks and Bring Your Little Pencils," *Sacramento Bee*, November 4, 1918.

Chapter 12

1. Military service records of Chipman, National Archives.

2. William D. Stephens to Chipman, April 8, 1921, Chipman Collection.

3. Military service records of Chipman, National Archives.

4. "A Notable Birthday," *The Recorder*, March 7, 1923.

5. Military service records of Chipman, National Archives; "Judge Hart Knew Judge Chipman as a Fine Character," *Sacramento Bee*, February 2, 1924. In his will, Chipman left the bulk of his estate, worth $30,000 to his daughters, Isabel Finnell and Alice Smith, as well as his devise to the Episcopal Church in memory of Belle. He also gave small sums to his nurse, Elise Anderson, and his grandsons by Alice, Chester C. Smith and Norton P. Smith. He left his papers, several scrapbook volumes, to his daughter, Isabel, to give either to a public library in Red Bluff or to the California State Library. "Judge Chipman Left An Estate Worth $30,000," *Sacramento Bee*, March 5, 1924. Those papers are preserved at the California State Library.

6. Military service records of Chipman, National Archives; *San Francisco Examiner*, February 2, 1924; "Judge Hart Knew Judge Chipman as a Fine Character," *Sacramento Bee*, February 2, 1924; "Judge Chipman Left an Estate Worth $30,000," *Sacramento Bee*, March 5, 1924.

7. "Judge Hart Knew Judge Chipman as a Fine Character," *Sacramento Bee*, February 2, 1924.

Epilogue

1. David McCullough, "The Glorious Cause of America," *BYU Magazine* (Winter 2006).

2. William T. Sherman, *Memoirs of General William T. Sherman*, 1:399.

3. Chipman, 1863 Political Speech.

4. The presiding justices of the California Court of Appeal, Third Appellate District, have been Norton Parker Chipman (1905–1921), William M. Finch (1921–1931), Hugh Lawson Preston (1931–1932), John Francis Pullen (1932–1941), Annette Abbott Adams, the first woman to serve as a California appellate court justice and presiding justice, (1942–1952), Benjamin Franklin Van Dyke (1952–1961), Paul Peek (1961–1962), Fred R. Pierce (1962–1971), Frank K. Richardson (1971–1974), Robert K. Puglia (1974–1998), and Arthur G. Scotland (1998 to present). The current members of the court are Presiding Justice Arthur G. Scotland and Associate Justices Coleman A. Blease, Richard M. Sims, III, Rodney Davis, George W. Nicholson, Vance W. Raye, Fred K. Morrison, Harry Hull, Ronald B. Robie, M. Kathleen Butz, and Tani G. Cantil-Sakauye.

Bibliography

Ambrose, Stephen E. *Halleck: Lincoln's Chief of Staff.* Baton Rogue: Louisiana State University Press, 1962.

Anderson, Galusha. *The Story of a Border City During the Civil War.* Boston: Little, Brown, 1908.

Basler, Roy P., ed. *The Collected Works of Abraham Lincoln.* New Brunswick, NJ: Rutgers University Press, 1953. 8 vols. Also available online at http://quod.lib.umich.edu/l/lincoln/.

Bates, J.C. *History of the Bench and Bar of California.* San Francisco: Bench and Bar, 1912.

Brockett, L.P., and Mary C. Vaughan. *Woman's Work in the Civil War: A Record of Heroism, Patriotism and Patience.* Philadelphia: Zeigler, McCurdy & Co., 1867.

California Supreme Court. *Osgood v. Los Angeles Traction Co.*, 137 Cal. 280 (Cal. 1902).

_____. *People v. Hoagland*, 138 Cal. 338 (Cal. 1903).

_____. *Southern Pacific Co. v. Pomona*, 144 Cal. 339 (Cal. 1904).

_____. *Tingley v. Times-Mirror Co.*, 144 Cal. 205 (Cal. 1904).

Chipman, N.P. "Abraham Lincoln." Speech, Cherry Tree Club, Sacramento, CA, February 22, 1906 (cited in notes as Cherry Tree speech). See the appendix for the full text.

_____. *Annual Report of Gen. N.P. Chipman, President, California State Board of Trade.* San Francisco: State Board of Trade, 1896.

_____. *Annual Report to the California State Board of Trade.* San Francisco: Pacific Rural Press, 1896.

_____. "Fruit or Wheat? Relative Importance of Two Great Industries." *The Morning Call.* May 28, 1893.

_____. "Greater California and the Trade of the Orient." *Overland Monthly*, vol. 34, no. 201, p. 196 (September 1899).

_____. "The Judicial Department of California," in Curry, *California Blue Book.*

_____. "Some Personal Recollections." *Sacramento Bee.* February 12, 1909.

_____. Speech, 1872, St. Joseph, MO. U.S. Grant Assoc., Southern Illinois University.

_____. Speech to House of Representatives, February 28, 1874. Washington, DC: Government Printing Office, 1874.

_____. *The Tragedy of Andersonville.* Sacramento: by the author, 1911.

Chipman Collection. California State Library, Sacramento, CA. 16 vols.

Clous, J.W., Judge Advocate General's Department. *The Army of the United States, Historical Sketches of Staff and Line with Portraits of Generals-in-Chief.* New York: Maynard, Merrill, 1896.

Conard, Howard L., ed. *Encyclopedia of the History of Missouri.* New York: Southern History, 1901. 6 vols.

Cox, Jacob Dolson. *Military Reminiscences of the Civil War.* New York: Charles Scribner's Sons, 1900.

Curry, C.F., comp. *California Blue Book.* Sacramento: State Printing Office, 1907.

Davis, Jefferson. "Andersonville and Other War-Prisons." *Belford's Magazine*, January 1890 and February 1890.

Dershowitz, Alan. "Introduction," in Chipman, *The Andersonville Prison Trial: The*

Trial of Captain Henry Wirz. Birmingham, AL: Notable Trials Library, 1990.

Dickens, Charles. *American Notes for General Circulation*. Paris: Baudry's European Library, 1842.

Eichelberger, Frank W. "Governor Kirkwood and the Skunk River War," in *Annals of Iowa*, vol. 19, 3d ser., 627.

Frassanito, William A. *Early Photography at Gettysburg*. Gettysburg, PA: Thomas Publications, 1995.

_____. *Gettysburg: A Journey in Time*. New York: Charles Scribner's Sons, 1975.

Futch, Ovid L. *History of Andersonville Prison*. Gainesville: University Press of Florida, 1999.

Garretson, O.A. "Traveling on the Underground Railroad in Iowa." *Iowa Journal of History and Politics*, no. 22 (July 1924).

Genoways, Ted, and Hugh H. Genoways. *A Perfect Picture of Hell*. Iowa City: University of Iowa Press, 2001.

Gienapp, William E. "Abraham Lincoln and the Border States." *Journal of the Abraham Lincoln Association,* vol. 13 (1992): 29.

Gillette, William. "Election of 1872," in Arthur M. Schlesinger, Jr., ed. *History of American Presidential Elections*. New York: Chelsea House, 1971.

Grand Army of the Republic. Committee on Arrangements. Invitation and Order of Exercises for May 30, 1868. Library of Congress.

Grant, Ulysses S. *Personal Memoirs of U.S. Grant*. 2 vols. New York: Charles S. Webster, 1885.

Greenwood, Grace. "Washington Notes." *New York Times*, February 22, 1873.

Gue, Benjamin. *History of Iowa: From the Earliest Times to the Beginning of the Twentieth Century*. 4 vols. New York: Century History, 1903.

Hansen, Marcus L. "Official Encouragement of Immigration to Iowa." *Iowa Journal of History and Politics* 14, no. 2 (April 1921).

Harper's Weekly. "Personal." April 30, 1887.

_____. "Personals." March 16, 1872.

_____. "The Trial of Captain Wirz." September 16, 1865.

_____. "The Wirz Trial." October 21, 1865.

Hill, N.N., Jr., comp. *History of Licking County, Ohio: Its Past and Present*. Newark, OH: A.A. Graham, 1881.

History of Henry County, Iowa. Western Historical, 1879.

The History of Union County. Chicago: W.H. Beers, 1883.

The History of Washington County, Iowa. Des Moines: Union Historical, 1880.

Holzer, Harold. "The Gettysburg Myth Revisited," in John Y. Simon, Harold Holzer, William D. Pederson, eds. *The Lincoln Forum: Abraham Lincoln, Gettysburg and the Civil War*. Mason City, IA: Savas, 1999.

_____, Edna Greene Medford, and Frank J. Williams. *The Emancipation Proclamation: Three Views*. Baton Rouge: Louisiana State University Press, 2006.

Hutchinson, W.H. *California Heritage: A History of Northern California Lumbering*. Santa Cruz, CA: Forest History Society, rev. 1974.

Ingersoll, Lurton Dunham. *Iowa and the Rebellion*. Philadelphia: J.B. Lippincott, 1866.

Iowa State Historical Society. "The Army of the South-West, and the First Campaign in Arkansas." *Annals of Iowa* (April 1868).

Irvine, Leigh H., ed. *History of the New California Its Resources and People*. 2 vols. Chicago: Lewis, 1905.

Jordan, Frank C., comp. *California Blue Book or State Roster 1913–1915*. Sacramento: State Printing Office, 1915.

Keeley, James Hugh, Sr. *Democracy or Despotism in the American Capital*. Riverdale, MD: Jessie Lane Keeley, 1939.

Kirkwood, Samuel J. "Organizing and Arming Volunteer Companies" in *Annals of Iowa*, vol. 19, 3d ser., 625.

Kleiner, Carolyn. "The Demon of Andersonville." *Legal Affairs*, September/October 2002.

Lamon, Ward Hill. *Recollections of Abraham Lincoln, 1847–1865*. Dorothy Lamon Teillard, ed. 2nd ed. Washington, DC, 1911.

Lang, Andrew. *Life, Letters, and Diaries of Sir Stafford Northcote, First Earl of Iddesleigh*. 2 vols. Edinburgh: Blackwood & Sons, 1890.

Leech, Margaret. *Reveille in Washington*. New York: Time, 1962.

Lincoln, Abraham. "Address before the Wisconsin State Agricultural Society, Milwaukee, Wisconsin," in Basler, *Collected Works of Abraham Lincoln*, 3:471.

_____. "First Inaugural Address," in Basler, *Collected Works of Abraham Lincoln*, 4:262.

Lincoln, Abraham, Papers. Library of Congress, Washington, DC. Also available online at http://memory.loc.gov/ammem/alhtml/malhome.html.

Los Angeles Times. "Among the Politicians." May 14, 1890.

_____. "Colusa for Chipman." July 27, 1890.

_____. "The Convention Meets." July 26, 1894.

Mahan, Bruce E., and Ruth A. Gallaher. *Stories of Iowa for Boys and Girls.* New York: Macmillan, 1931.

Marvel, William. *Andersonville: The Last Depot.* Chapel Hill: University of North Carolina Press, 1994.

McCausland, John. "The Burning of Chambersburg, Penn." *New Orleans Picayune,* August 2, 1906.

McConnell, Stuart. *Glorious Contentment: The Grand Army of the Republic, 1865–1900.* Chapel Hill: University of North Carolina Press, 1992.

McCullough, David. "The Glorious Cause of America." *BYU Magazine* (Winter 2006).

McFeely, William S. *Frederick Douglass.* New York: W.W. Norton, 1991.

_____. *Grant: A Biography.* New York: W.W. Norton, 1982.

McPherson, James M. *Battle Cry of Freedom.* Oxford: Oxford University Press, 1988.

Miller, Francis. *Argument Before the Judiciary Committee of the House of Representatives.* Washington, DC: Gibson Bros., 1874.

Moeller, Hubert L., and Hugh C. Mueller. *Our Iowa Its Beginning and Growth.* New York: Newsom, 1938.

Monaghan, Jay. *Civil War on the Western Border.* Boston: Little, Brown, 1955.

Mt. Pleasant News. "Story of the 'Old Mill.'" November 11, 1972.

National Archives. Military pension records of N.P. Chipman.

_____. Military service records of N.P. Chipman.

New York Times. "From Washington." August 21, 1865.

_____. "The Rebel Assassins." August 22, 1865.

_____. "Trial of Capt. Wirz." September 23, 1865.

_____. "Trial of Capt. Wirz." September 27, 1865.

_____. "Trial of Capt. Wirz." September 28, 1865.

_____. "Trial of Capt. Wirz." August 29, 1865.

_____. "Washington." November 21, 1870.

_____. "Washington News." October 15, 1865.

_____. "Washington News." September 24, 1867.

_____. "Washington Notes." August 2, 1872.

Newhall, John B. *A Glimpse of Iowa in 1846.* Iowa History Project.

Nicolay, John G. *A Short Life of Abraham Lincoln.* New York: Century, 1902.

"Norton Parker Chipman." *Memorial and Biographical History of Northern California.* University City, MO: Lewis Pub., 1891.

Paine, Albert Bigelow. *Th. Nast: His Period and His Pictures.* Princeton, NJ: Pyne, 1974.

Peckham, James. *General Nathaniel Lyon and Missouri in 1861.* New York: American News, 1866.

Porter, Horace. *Campaigning with Grant.* Collector's Library of the Civil War. New York: Century, 1897.

Portrait and Biographical Album—Washington County, Iowa. 1887.

Ransom, John L. *John Ransom's Andersonville Diary.* New York: Berkeley, 1986.

The Recorder. "A Notable Birthday." March 7, 1923.

Reid, Whitelaw. *After the War: A Southern Tour.* London: Sampson Low, Son, & Marston, 1866.

Roster and Record of Iowa Soldiers in the War of the Rebellion Together with Historical Sketches of Volunteer Organizations 1861–1866. Des Moines, IA: State Printer, 1908.

Sabin, Henry, and Edwin L. Sabin. *The Making of Iowa.* Chicago: A. Flanagan, 1900.

Sacramento Bee. "Hart Gets Heavy Vote." November 8, 1906.

_____. "Hughes is a Cheerful Loser." November 10, 1906.

_____. "Judge Chipman Left an Estate Worth $30,000." March 5, 1924.

_____. "Judge Hart Knew Judge Chipman as a Fine Character." February 2, 1924.

_____. "Judges Ready to Answer Charges." December 12, 1911.

_____. "Republican Managers Say Chipman Has Met with Defeat." November 9, 1906.

_____. "Sacramento Voters Give Hard Jolt to Bosses." November 7, 1906.

_____. "Wear Your Masks and Bring Your Little Pencils." November 4, 1918.

San Francisco Chronicle. "Attorney's Charges Held Unfounded." December 19, 1911.

_____. "Chipman Sells Part of His Tehama Ranch." November 20, 1916.

_____. "Judge Chipman Denies Charges." December 15, 1911.

Sandburg, Carl. *Abraham Lincoln: The Prairie*

Years and the War Years. Pleasantville, NY: Reader's Digest, 1970.

Serr, Eugene. "General Chipman and the Flume Through the Canyon," in *Tehama County Memories.* Red Bluff: Tehama County Genealogical and Historical Society, 1996.

Shepherd, Arthur. "The District Government: Why General Chipman Should be Reelected to Congress." Pamphlet of speech delivered July 29, 1872. Library of Congress.

Sheridan, Philip H. *Personal Memoirs of P.H. Sheridan.* 2 vols. New York: Webster, 1888.

Sherman, William T. *Memoirs of General William T. Sherman.* 2 vols. New York: D. Appleton, 1875.

Simon, John Y., ed. *The Papers of Ulysses S. Grant.* 30 vols. Carbondale: Southern Illinois University Press, 1982.

State Fair of 1886: Opening Address Delivered by Hon. Thomas H. Laine, of San Jose, Santa Clara County, and Annual Address Delivered by General N.P. Chipman, of Red Bluff, Tehama County. California State Agricultural Society, 1886.

Staudenraus, P.J., ed. *Mr. Lincoln's Washington; Selections from the Writings of Noah Brooks, Civil War Correspondent.* New York: Thomas Yoseloff, 1967.

Stibbs, John. "Andersonville and the Trial of Henry Wirz." *Iowa Journal of History and Politics.* Chicago: Iowa State Historical Society, January 1911.

Stuart, A.A. *Iowa Colonels and Regiments: Being a History of Iowa Regiments in the War of the Rebellion.* Des Moines, IA: Mills, 1865.

Sumner, Charles. *The Works of Charles Sumner.* Boston: Lee and Shepard, 1883.

Surdam, David G. "Traders or Traitors: Northern Cotton Trading During the Civil War." *Business and Economic History* (Winter 1999) 301.

Switzler, William F., ed. *History of Boone County, Missouri.* St. Louis: Western Historical Society, 1882.

Tehama County, California. San Francisco: Elliott & Moore, 1880.

Thomas, Benjamin P., and Harold M. Hyman. *Stanton: The Life and Times of Lincoln's Secretary of War.* New York: Alfred A. Knopf, 1962.

Tiesch, Jessica B. "Great Western Power, 'White Coal,' and Industrial Capitalism in the West." *Pacific Historical Review* 70 (2001) 232.

Torres, Louis. "*To the Immortal Name and Memory of George Washington,*" The United States Army Corps of Engineers and the Construction of the Washington Monument. Washington, DC: Office of the Chief of Engineers, 1984.

Trefousse, Hans L. *Andrew Johnson.* New York: W.W. Norton, 1989.

Trollope, Anthony. *North America.* New York: Harper & Bros., 1862.

Twain, Mark, and Charles Dudley Warner. *The Gilded Age: A Tale of To-day.* 2 vols. New York: Harper & Bros., 1903.

United States. House of Representatives. *Congressional Globe.* 42d Cong., 3d sess., 1873.

_____. _____. *Congressional Record.* 43d Cong., 1st sess., 1874, vol. 2, 4577.

_____. _____. *Congressional Record.* 67th Cong., 2d sess., 1922.

_____. _____. House Select Committee on the Washington National Monument. *Washington National Monument.* 43d Cong., 1st sess., 1874, H. Rep. 485, 1.

_____. _____. Committee on Appropriations. "Investigation into Indian Affairs, before the Committee on Appropriations of the House of Representatives. Argument of N.P. Chipman, on behalf of Hon. E.S. Parker, Commissioner of Indian Affairs." Washington, DC, 1871.

_____. _____. *Journal of the House of Representatives of the United States,* vol. 74, p. 252. Jan. 19, 1874.

_____. Supreme Court. *Dred Scott v. Sanford,* 60 U.S. 393 (1857).

The Vinton Eagle (Vinton, IA). "The Second Iowa at Fort Donelson." December 19, 1884.

A Volume of Memoirs and Genealogy of Representative Citizens of Northern California Including Biographies of Many of Those Who Have Passed Away. Chicago: Standard Genealogical, 1901.

Wallace, Lew. "The Capture of Fort Donelson." *The Century* (December 1884) vol. 29.

War of the Rebellion. Official Records of the Union and Confederate Armies (O.R.). Also available online at http://library5.library.cornell.edu/moa/.

Wert, Jeffry D. *From Winchester to Cedar Creek.* Mechanicsburg, PA: Stackpole, 1997.

Whitman, Walt. "Memoranda," in *Two Rivulets Including Democratic Vistas, Centennial Songs, and Passage to India.* Camden, NJ: author's edition, 1876.

Whyte, James Huntington. *The Uncivil War: Washington During the Reconstruction 1865–1878*. New York: Twayne, 1958.

Williams, Frank J. *Judging Lincoln*. Carbondale: Southern Illinois University Press, 2002.

Williams, Robert C. *Horace Greeley: Champion of American Freedom*. New York: New York University Press, 2006.

Williamson, James J. *History of Mosby's Command*. New York: Ralph B. Kenyon, 1896.

Wills, Garry. *Lincoln at Gettysburg*. London: Simon & Schuster, 1992.

Woods, Alice. "S.F. Man, Lincoln Escort, Tells of Martyr: Gen. Chipman, at 89, Gives 'Close Up' of Liberator." *The San Francisco Call*. Chipman Collection.

Index

Numbers in *bold italics* indicate pages with illustrations.